THE SHORT-STORY

SPECIMENS ILLUSTRATING
ITS DEVELOPMENT

EDITED

WITH INTRODUCTION AND NOTES

BY

BRANDER MATTHEWS, LL.D.

PROFESSOR OF DRAMATIC LITERATURE
IN COLUMBIA UNIVERSITY

NEW YORK ·:· CINCINNATI ·:· CHICAGO
AMERICAN BOOK COMPANY

COPYRIGHT, 1907, BY
BRANDER MATTHEWS

ENTERED AT STATIONERS' HALL, LONDON.

SHORT-STORY.

W. P. 1

PREFATORY NOTE

It was only in the later years of the nineteenth century that critics of literature came to recognize in the short-story a definite species, having possibilities of its own and also rigorous limitations. Although the short-story still lacks a satisfactory name, it is now seen to be clearly differentiated from the longer novel and also from the tale which merely chances to be not prolonged. From both of these it separates itself sharply — from the novel by its brevity and from the more brief tale by its unity, its totality, its concentration upon a single effect or a single sequence of effects.

In the following pages a number of specimen stories have been selected to show the development of the form, — the slow evolution of this literary species through the long centuries of advancing civilization. The earlier tales here presented are not true short-stories; each of them lacks one or another of the essential characteristics of the type. The more modern examples are true short-stories; and they have been chosen to exhibit the many varieties possible within the species. They have been selected from the chief modern literatures; and they present many contrasting shades of local color.

PREFATORY NOTE

The introduction traces the growth of the form through the history of literature and seeks to set forth its slow attainment of the essential type. The notes prefixed to the several specimens discuss succinctly the literary position of the authors. The notes appended to each of the specimens are intended to call the attention of the student to the merits and the defects of that particular story, considered as an example of the form.

B. M.

CONTENTS

		PAGE
INTRODUCTION		7
I.	THE HUSBAND OF AGLAES	41
	From *Gesta Romanorum*.	
II.	THE STORY OF GRISELDA	48
	By *Boccaccio*.	
III.	CONSTANTIA AND THEODOSIUS	67
	By *Joseph Addison*.	
IV.	RIP VAN WINKLE	76
	By *Washington Irving*.	
V.	DREAM-CHILDREN. A Revery	103
	By *Charles Lamb*.	
VI.	WANDERING WILLIE'S TALE	109
	By *Walter Scott*.	
VII.	MATEO FALCONE	137
	By *Prosper Mérimée*.	
VIII.	THE SHOT	156
	By *Alexander Pushkin*.	
IX.	THE STEADFAST TIN SOLDIER	175
	By *Hans Christian Andersen*.	
X.	THE FALL OF THE HOUSE OF USHER	182
	By *Edgar Allan Poe*.	
XI.	THE AMBITIOUS GUEST	210
	By *Nathaniel Hawthorne*.	
XII.	A CHILD'S DREAM OF A STAR	223
	By *Charles Dickens*.	

CONTENTS

		PAGE
XIII.	WHAT WAS IT? A Mystery	229
	By *Fitz-James O'Brien.*	
XIV.	THE FATHER	247
	By *Björnstjerne Björnson.*	
XV.	TENNESSEE'S PARTNER	253
	By *Bret Harte.*	
XVI.	THE SIEGE OF BERLIN	267
	By *Alphonse Daudet.*	
XVII.	THE INSURGENT	276
	By *Ludovic Halévy.*	
XVIII.	THE SUBSTITUTE	283
	By *François Coppée.*	
XIX.	MRS. KNOLLYS	298
	By *Frederic J. Stimson.*	
XX.	THE NECKLACE	318
	By *Guy de Maupassant.*	
XXI.	MARKHEIM	331
	By *Robert Louis Stevenson.*	
XXII.	THE MAN WHO WAS	355
	By *Rudyard Kipling.*	
XXIII.	A SISTERLY SCHEME	376
	By *H. C. Bunner.*	
APPENDIX	. . . .	391

INTRODUCTION

ONLY within the past few years have we come to see that there is an essential difference between the true short-story and the more carelessly composed tale which happens to be brief. Even now we have no distinctive name for the new form; and perhaps for the present, at least, we cannot do better than to make an arbitrary compound word and to write it "short-story," thereby distinguishing it, as far as may be, from the story which merely chances to be short, although it might very well have been long.

I

Brief tales there have been since the world began, since the art of the story-teller was first attempted, since the Cave-men filled the long evenings around the smoking fire with narratives of the mysterious deeds of the strange creatures of their own primitive fancy, since the earliest travelers who ventured abroad brought back episodic accounts of one or another of their misadventures, commingled of fact and of fiction. Strange stories were told about animals who talked and who had many of the characteristics of mankind; and by word of mouth these marvelous tales were passed down from generation to generation, growing in detail and gaining in precision, until there came to be the immense mass of beast-fable, surviving in oral tradition chiefly, but getting itself lifted up into literature now and again. It was from this fund of accumulated and transmitted lore of legend that Bidpai and Æsop made their selections, to be followed, after many a century, by that more accomplished artist in narrative, La Fontaine, the great master of the fable, which instructs and yet satirizes our common humanity.

Every fable has its moral, even though this is not always tagged to the tail of it; and the ethical intent of the story-teller who sets down what the animals say to one another is as obvious in the record of the doings of Reynard the Fox as it is in the sayings of B'rer Rabbit preserved for us by Uncle Remus. A moral there is also — and the sturdiest and wisest of morals — in the "Jungle Book" of Mr. Kipling, wherein we learn how Mowgli grew to manhood among the wild creatures of the field and of the forest. But the beast-fable, delightful as it may be when it is dealt with artistically, by the writers who have genuine sympathy with the lowly and clear insight into the conditions of life, — the beast-fable is only one of the many forms of the brief tale; and it has only a casual likeness to the true short-story.

INTRODUCTION

Brief tales of another kind were known to the ancients, Oriental in their origin, for the most part, and abounding in that liking for the supernatural, which characterizes the majority of the stories that have come to us from the East. There are the rambling Egyptian narratives, — the tale, for example, of the "Two Brothers" and the "Story of the Shipwrecked Sailors," which scholars have only recently replevined from the buried papyrus. There are the cleverly narrated anecdotes which we find here and there in the pages of Herodotus,[1] who was a historian with a full share of the gift of story-telling, and who was also a traveler with a natural desire ever to hear and to tell something new and something striking. There are the so-called "Lost Tales of Miletus," widely popular in the days of Greek decadence, when the enervating Orient had corrupted the sterner artistic sense of Athens and of its rival cities. But whether Grecian or Egyptian, the best of these straggling narratives is likely to reveal three characteristic defects, — to quote the opinion of a competent critic, Professor Peck[2] (of Columbia), —"a lack of

---

[1] See, for example, the tale of Polycrates and his ring, III, 39–43, and the longer narrative dealing with "Rhampsinitus and the Robber," II, 121.

[2] "Trimalchio's Dinner," by Petronius Arbiter, translated from the original Latin with an introduction and bibliographical appendix. By Harry Thurston Peck, New York.

variety in its themes, a lack of interest in its treatment, and a lack of originality in its form."

II

So far as the Greeks are concerned, this need not surprise us, since it was only in their decline that they took to prose. In the splendid period of their richest accomplishment they had found fit expression for their imaginings only in poetry; and there is significance in the fact that no one of the nine muses had been assigned to foster prose-fiction. The demoralizing and disintegrating influence of the Orient is visible also in Latin literature; and in prose-fiction, as in other fields of artistic endeavor, the Romans followed faithfully in the paths first trodden by the Athenians. The writers of their rambling narratives were also tempted to introduce the abnormal and the supernatural; and apparitions especially are frequent in the literature of the Latins. For example, there can be found in one of the younger Pliny's letters[1] a ghost-story, skillfully yet simply told, which is not without a certain likeness to one of the earliest of American tales, — Irving's "Dolph Heyliger."

Much the most famous of all the brief stories that survive in Latin is the tale of the "Matron of Ephesus," with its satiric ingenuity, which has

[1] "Epistles," VII, 27.

tempted the poets of every modern language to tell it anew, each in his own fashion. It is first to be found as an anecdote related by one of the characters in that early masterpiece of humorous realism, the "Satira" of Petronius.[1] And here occasion serves to note that it is only since the novel has succeeded in establishing itself as an artistic rival of the drama, and only since the scope of the true short-story has come to be recognized, that writers of fiction have given up the practice of padding their longer stories by the insertion of briefer tales, wholly unrelated to the main theme. Cervantes put into "Don Quixote" at least one minor narrative that merely distended his novel without benefiting it; and his example was followed by Scarron in the "Roman Comique," by Fielding in "Tom Jones," and by Dickens in the "Pickwick Papers." And it is in "Redgauntlet" that we find "Wandering Willie's Tale," a delightful example of Scott's commingled humor and fancy; it is properly in place in the longer romance in which it is embedded; and it is also one of the most interesting of those accidental anticipations of the true short-story, of which there are not a few to be discovered at irregular intervals in the history of fiction.

The "Matron of Ephesus" itself might also be

[1] Professor Peck has translated it into nervous English in the introduction to his "Trimalchio's Dinner," pp. 25–30.

accepted as one of these accidental anticipations, if it was not a little lacking in simplicity and in concision. But it is the sole specimen of the brief tale to be selected out of all Latin literature as prefiguring our latter-day type. From all Greek literature the one example to be chosen would be the lovely vignette of "Daphnis and Chloe," if this miniature idyl did not happen also to be a little too complicated in its episodes; in fact, it is a forerunner rather of the modern novelette, which stands midway between the brief tale and the ampler novel.

In the novelette we can often discover many of the special characteristics of the true short-story, more especially originality of theme and ingenuity of invention; but it always lacks the one essential of brevity. The late Locker-Lampson declared that Pope's "Rape of the Lock" would be the best possible example of *vers de société* in its perfection, if only it had not been quite so long-drawn as it is; and for the same reason even the most exquisite of novelettes, "Daphnis and Chloe," for instance, must be distinguished from the more compact short-story.

It may be well to note here, however, that the novelette is an interesting species of fiction, which has failed to receive the full critical consideration it deserves. Its history is highly honorable, illumined at the beginning by the gentle charm of

"Daphnis and Chloe," and lighted up later by the pathetic grace of "Aucassin and Nicolette." In the last two centuries we find in the literature of the several modern languages novelettes of the utmost variety of theme, — "Paul and Virginia" in French, "Undine" and "Peter Schlemihl" in German, and "Lear of the Steppe" in Russian, while in English we have a humorous fantasy like the "Case of Mr. Lucraft" of Besant and Rice, a searching apologue like the "Strange Case of Dr. Jekyll and Mr. Hyde" of Stevenson, and a veracious character-study like the "Daisy Miller" of Henry James. All of these were in spirit closely akin to the true short-story; but all of them are too ample in extent.

III

But even if the more careless prose-fictions of the Greeks and of the Latins are far inferior artistically to the larger Attic poems and to the lighter Roman lyrics, still they are immensely superior to the chaotic narratives which are all we can discover in the dark ages that followed the downfall of Imperial rule. Medieval fiction is not unfairly represented by the "Gesta Romanorum," that storehouse of tales of all sorts and of all lengths, gathered from the ends of the earth and heaped up at haphazard. There are a few good stories to be found in this bric-a-brac collection of anecdotes, repartees, narratives of one kind and another, — stories deserving of a better treatment than could be imparted by the monkish scribe who set them down in casual confusion; and more than one later poet and playwright has been able to pick a pearl of price out of this medieval medley.

The "Gesta Romanorum" represents the story-telling of the Middle Ages as it was in the hands of the half educated, who had only confused memories of the past. The story-telling of those who were frankly uneducated is represented by the beast-fable, which had then a renowned popularity throughout Europe, and also by a more engaging form, the *fabliau*. The word is French; and the thing itself was French also, with a full savor of Gallic salt. A *fabliau* is a brief tale, often little more than an anecdote, with a sharp sting at the end of it; frequently it was in rime; generally satiric in intent, it was full of frank gayety and of playful humor. It may be defined as a realistic folk tale, not bookish in its flavor, but with the simple shrewdness of the plain people. On occasion it is free to the extreme of coarseness; but on occasion also it can be brisk and bright, fresh and felicitous, with a verve and a vivacity all its own.[1]

[1] The fullest discussion of this interesting species is to be found in "Les Fabliaux," par Joseph Bedier, 2d ed., Paris, 1895.

IV

From the *fabliau*, and from the "Gesta Romanorum" also, the story-tellers of the Renascence borrowed many a hint; what they contributed themselves was a finer art of narrative. Their brief tales in prose or in verse were not only richer in substance, they were, above all, more shapely and more seemly, better proportioned and better balanced, more cleverly thought out and more skillfully wrought out. Chaucer, writing in rime in England, and Boccaccio, writing in prose in Italy, might now and again pick out a plot from the "Gesta Romanorum"; but the English poet and the Italian teller of tales in prose took over from the *fabliau* more than the bare suggestion of a situation, — they caught from it not a little of the grace, the lightness, and the ease that often characterizes the unpretending work of the unknown French narrators.

Boccaccio himself,[1] and the host of other Italians who trod the trail first blazed by the author of the "Decameron," dealt not only with the traditional material heaped up for the hand of the story-teller, but also with the somber and bloody incidents of contemporary life. Their swift tales, limned in

[1] In an inexpensive volume of his "Universal Library" the late Henry Morley printed forty tales, chosen out of the hundred which make up the "Decameron." He carefully excluded all those offensive to modern taste.

outline only, with scarcely a hint of the background, with only the most summary indication of individual characteristics, were comic or tragic as it might chance. Sometimes they present us with the amusing complexities of amorous intrigue; and sometimes they give us glimpses of sudden and deadly revenge. In this commingling of the grave and the gay they were imitated by the French and by the English. In the "Cent Nouvelles Nouvelles," and in the other collections of other authors using the same language, we observe that the French very naturally felt the influence of the *fabliau* and that they seem to prefer the comic. In Painter's "Palace of Pleasure," and in its rival adaptations into our own tongue, we perceive that the English liking was rather for the tragic. The Italian tales, translated or in the original, served as a treasury of grisly plots open before the Elizabethan playwrights, wherein they might make their choice of strange situations to set before their unlettered audiences, reveling in dark deeds and relishing Machiavellian motives.

Boccaccio was a born story-teller; and born story-tellers were also not a few of his followers. The *novella* of the Italian Renascence has often a unity of its own, and sometimes it even achieves what must be termed a fairly well-balanced construction, presenting us with the beginning, the middle, and the end of its action. And yet these

INTRODUCTION 17

fertile and accomplished narrators failed to see the manifold advantages of the compact simplicity which is the controlling characteristic of the modern short-story. Sometimes they proffer to us bare anecdotes deftly sketched; sometimes they present us with longer plots in outline only, lacking compression, lacking color, and lacking adequate solution of the central situation. Only on rare occasions, and, as it were, by chance, do they happen upon a form anticipating the real short-story as we know it now, with its direct unity and with its deliberate centering of interest in a single point.

Professor Baldwin (of Yale) has analyzed the century of tales contained in the "Decameron"; and the result of his investigation [1] is that more than a half of the hundred are little more than anecdotes, sometimes baldly narrated and sometimes more artistically elaborated, while nearly all of the remaining twoscore are but naked plots for stories, ingeniously set forth, but existing only in scenario, so to speak. He is able to indicate three which reveal an approximation to the true type of short-story as we recognize it to-day, and only two which actually attain to it. This cautious classification seems to show that Boccaccio had no definite stand-

---

[1] "American Short Stories," selected and edited with an introductory essay on the short-story, by Charles Sears Baldwin (The Wampum Library), New York and London: Longmans, Green & Co., 1904.

ard in mind, and that if he twice achieved the modern form it was all unwittingly and quite casually. And Bandello, the foremost of Boccaccio's followers, was — as the same astute critic declares — even looser in his structure and even more reckless in his disregard for the restraints of time and space.

V

The influence of the Italians was widespread throughout Europe; and it was more powerful than that of the Spaniards who were next to blossom forth as luxuriant inventors of adventure. It must be noted that the fertility of the Spaniards was revealed rather in their multitudinous drama than in their prose-fiction; and also that even in their prose-fiction their grandiloquence led them to display their fancy rather in long-drawn romances than in tales cut short. To Spain we seem to owe the interminable Romances of Chivalry, series within series; and to Spain also are we indebted for the humorous narratives of knavery, which are known as the Picaresque Romances.[1]

It was Spain also which bestowed on us the earliest indisputable masterpiece of prose-friction,

[1] An appreciative account of the Romances of Chivalry will be found in Sir Walter Scott's essay on "Amadis of Gaul." The best study of the Picaresque Tales is " Romances of Roguery, an episode in the history of the novel," by Frank Wadleigh Chandler. New York: Columbia University Press, 1899.

INTRODUCTION

— "Don Quixote." But Cervantes did not take himself too seriously; and even in his great work there are undeniable evidences of his artistic carelessness. Expressing himself freely in the fashion of his time and in the manner of his race, Cervantes could not be expected to have any prevision of the rigid limitations and of the compensating advantages of the short-story. In the minor narratives arbitrarily intercalated into "Don Quixote," and in the separate collection of his "Exemplary Novels," he has written neither true short-stories nor true novelettes, but specimens of the tale which chances to be fairly brief, although there is no intrinsic reason why it might not have been long.

This same disregard of formal beauty, this same sprawling looseness of structure is what we observe also in the two novelists of France, who reflect most openly the influence of Spain. Both Scarron and Le Sage borrowed abundantly from the plays and from the prose-fiction of their predecessors and contemporaries south of the Pyrenees; and they took over more than episodes and plots — they took over all the Spanish laxity of texture. The shorter narratives injected into the "Roman Comique" and the autobiographic digressions discoverable in "Gil Blas" do not differ in any way from the larger stories in which they are included. In fact, the more closely we consider the prose-fiction of France as it was when Scarron and Le

Sage were writing, the more clearly can we perceive that it had not then become conscious of its latent possibilities, realized only in a later century. All we can discover, then, is a certain skill in narration and in character-drawing. No anticipation can be detected either of the short-story or of the artfully built novel, as we were to receive it later from the hands of Balzac, of Hawthorne, and of Turgenieff. Neither form had then begun to differentiate itself from the more confused narrative which might be of any length. A carefully proportioned tale like the "Princess of Cleves" of Madame de La Fayette remains a rare exception amid the mass of French fiction of two centuries ago, most of which is invertebrate and conglomerate.

VI

Nor is there a marked advance in the art of fiction to be observed in the eighteenth century, so far, at least, as mere form is concerned. In France, Voltaire was the author of a series of *contes*, of philosophic tales, delightful in their wit and disintegrating in their irony. But "Candide" and its fellows were not called into being for their own sake, but to serve an ulterior purpose. They were missiles of assault, and not stories told for the sheer pleasure of telling. They were weapons in the warfare which Voltaire was waging against the conditions he detested and against the beliefs he wished to destroy. They were allegories or apologues, rather than sketches of life and character; and however interesting they may be in themselves, they are the intense expression of Voltaire himself, and therefore they bring us no further on the way to the modern short-story.

In England there is the Eighteenth Century Essay, as Steele devised it and as Addison enlarged it;[1] and in the *Tatler* and in the *Spectator* we have what we may salute as an early suggestion of the monthly magazine of our own time, with the same hospitality to many literary forms, — to the obituary article, for instance, to the book review, and to the theatrical criticism. There is the succession of papers devoted to Sir Roger de Coverley, which we can accept, if we choose, as a first attempt at the serial-story. There are the occasional Oriental tales and the more frequent sketches of character, which we may hail, if we will, as remote ancestors of the latter-day short-story. Half a century later this Oriental tale, as Addison had outlined it simply, was expanded by Johnson in his "Rasselas"; and in like manner the character-sketch, as Steele had attempted it, was enriched and elaborated by Goldsmith in the "Vicar of Wakefield."

[1] For an account of the origin and development of this delightful literary species, see "Eighteenth Century Essays," selected and annotated by Austin Dobson, London and New York, 1882.

At the end of the eighteenth century and at the beginning of the nineteenth we can catch the echo in English of a new note, — the note of German Romanticism. There was a reaction against the realities of life as Fielding and Maria Edgeworth and Jane Austen represented them. The ballads and the brief tales in prose which the English imported from Germany, or which they made for themselves on the German model, had a flavor of mysticism as well as an aroma of mystery. Scott translated Bürger; and Matthew Lewis compiled his "Tales of Horror." Specters became fashionable again, and ghosts walked the earth once more. The eerie imaginings and the morbid hallucinations of Zschokke and of Hoffmann found a warm welcome in the native land of the authors of the "Castle of Otranto" and of the "Mysteries of Udolpho." Although these German tales tended to be vague and formless, and although there was much that was freakish in their exuberance of fantasy, there was much also that was to prove profitable to the future masters of the short-story, — Hawthorne and Poe in the United States, Gautier and Mérimée in France.

VII

It is in France and in the United States, rather than in Great Britain, that we first find the true short-story; and we do not find it until the second quarter of the nineteenth century. In France, Gautier and Mérimée were preceded by Nodier, who had a feeling of the future form, but who failed finally to achieve it. In the United States, Hawthorne and Poe had a predecessor in Irving, whose delightful tales lack only a more vigorous restraint to be accepted as the earliest models of the short-story. In fact, it is only when we draw up a narrowly rigid definition of the form that we are forced to exclude Irving from the list of its originators. What Irving did not seek to bestow on his charming fantasies was the essential compression, the swift and straightforward movement, the unwillingness to linger by the way.

In fact, to linger by the way was exactly what Irving proposed to himself as a principle. "For my part," he wrote to a friend, "I consider a story merely as a frame on which to stretch the materials; it is the play of thought, and sentiment, and language, the weaving in of characters, lightly, yet expressively delineated; the familiar and faithful exhibition of scenes in common life; and the half-concealed vein of humor that is often playing through the whole, — these are among what I aim at, and upon which I felicitate myself in proportion as I think I succeed."[1] In this declaration Irving reveals the reason why he is to be considered as a

[1] "Life and Letters of Washington Irving," New York: G. P. Putnam's Sons, 1869. II, p. 227.

true heir of the eighteenth-century essayists. The "Sketch-Book" is the direct descendant of the *Spectator;* and in "Rip Van Winkle" and in the "Specter Bridegroom" and in the "Legend of Sleepy Hollow" we must see the connecting link between the brief tale as it had been generally essayed in the eighteenth century and the short-story as it was to be perfected in the nineteenth. While Irving's manner is the discursive manner of the essayist, his material is very much what the later writers of the short-story were glad to deal with.

Beyond all question, Irving had freshness, inventiveness, fantasy — all invaluable gifts for the short-story; but he did not strive for the implacable unity and the swift compactness which we now demand and which we find frequently in Hawthorne and always in Poe. And these are the essential qualities which we perceive also in the "Morte Amoureuse" of Gautier and in the "Vénus d'Ille" of Mérimée, which were published in France only a year or two after Poe had put forth "Berenice." If we may judge by their other efforts in fiction, Mérimée and Gautier, like Hawthorne, were led to attain the true short-story rather by artistic impulse than by deliberate effort acting in accord with a theory firmly held. But Poe was conscious; he knew what he was doing; he had a theory firmly held; and his principles were widely different from those laid down by Irving. His artistic aim, his conception of what a short-story ought to be, was clear before him, as it was not clear before Hawthorne, who was far less of a theorizer about his art, even if he was ethically a more richly endowed artist.

And it was in a review of Hawthorne's tales [1] that Poe first laid down the principles which governed his own construction and which have been quoted very often of late, because they have been accepted by the masters of the short-story in every modern language. In the paper on the "Philosophy of Composition" Poe had asserted that a poem ought not greatly to exceed a hundred lines in length, since this is as much as can be read with unbroken interest; and in this review of Hawthorne he applies the same principle to prose-fiction: —

"The ordinary story is objectionable from its length, for reasons already stated in substance. As it cannot be read at one sitting, it deprives itself, of course, of the immense force derivable from *totality*. Worldly interests intervening during the pauses of perusal modify, annul, or contract, in a greater or less degree, the impressions of the book. But simply cessation in reading would, of itself, be sufficient to destroy the true unity. In

---

[1] This criticism was contributed originally to *Graham's Magazine*, in 1842; it is now included in all editions of Poe's writings.

the brief tale, however, the author is enabled to carry out the fullness of his intention, be it what it may. During the hour of perusal the soul of the reader is at the writer's control. There are no external or extrinsic influences — resulting from weariness or interruption.

"A skillful literary artist has constructed a tale. If wise, he has not fashioned his thoughts to accommodate his incidents; but having conceived, with deliberate care, a certain unique or single *effect* to be wrought out, he then invents such incidents — then combines such events as may best aid him in establishing this preconceived effect. If his very initial sentence tend not to the outbringing of this effect, then he has failed in his first step. In the whole composition there should be no word written of which the tendency, direct or indirect, is not to the one preëstablished design. As by such means, with such care and skill, a picture is at length painted which leaves in the mind of him who contemplates it with a kindred art a sense of the fullest satisfaction. The idea of the tale has been presented unblemished, because undisturbed; and this is an end unattainable by the novel. Undue brevity is just as exceptionable here as in the poem; but undue length is yet more to be avoided."

This is definite and precise beyond all misunderstanding, — the short-story must do one thing only, and it must do this completely and perfectly; it must not loiter or digress; it must have unity of action, unity of temper, unity of tone, unity of color, unity of effect; and it must vigilantly exclude everything that might interfere with its singleness of intention.

The same essential principles were laid down again, almost half a century later, by another accomplished artist in fiction who also took an intelligent interest in the code of his craft. In one of his "Vailima Letters,"[1] Stevenson wrote to a friend, who had rashly ventured to suggest a different termination for one of his stories, that any alteration of that kind was absolutely impossible, since it would violate the law of the short-story: —

"Make another end to it? Ah, yes, but that's not the way I write; the whole tale is implied; I never use an effect when I can help it, unless it prepares the effects that are to follow; that's what a story consists in. To make another end, that is to make the beginning all wrong. The *dénouement* of a long story is nothing, it is just 'a full close,' which you may approach and accompany as you please — it is a coda, not an essential number in the rhythm; but the body and end of a short-story is bone of the bone and blood of the blood of the beginning."

---

[1] Written September 5, 1891, to Mr. Sidney Colvin, "Vailima Letters," I, p. 147.

VIII

After Poe, by his precept and by his practice, had revealed the possibilities of the short-story and had shown what it ought to be, it became conscious of itself. It felt itself to be differentiated as sharply from the novel as the lyric is differentiated from the epic. It was no longer to be accomplished by a lucky accident only; it could be achieved solely by deliberate and resolute effort. The restrictions were rigid, like those of the sonnet, and success was not easy; but the very difficulty of the undertaking was tempting to the true artist, ever eager for a grapple with technic. Of course, the easier brief tale, with its careless digressions, was still satisfactory to writers who lacked muscle and nerve to wrestle with the severer form, — just as the weaklings among the rimesters still content themselves with one of the looser arrangements of the sonnet.

In every modern literature there arose in time writers who mastered the short-story, made it supple, gave it scope, bent it to their own purpose, and dowered the readers of their own language with little masterpieces of narration, wholly free from the three defects which had characterized the brief tales of the Greeks, — "a lack of variety in its themes, a lack of interest in its treatment, and a lack of originality in its form." So we find

Verga in Italy, Kjelland in Norway, Turgenieff in Russia, taking over the perfected form, profiting by its enforced obligations of unity, simplicity, and harmony, and handling it with variety, with interest, and with originality. They dealt, each of them, with the life immediately around them, with the life of their own people, with the life they knew best; and they gave to the short-story a richness of human flavor that Poe had never sought, since his ultimate aim was rather construction than character-drawing.

Yet it was not in Italy, in Norway, or in Russia, that the short-story flourished first or most luxuriantly; it was in France and in the United States, the two countries in which it had been earliest achieved, almost simultaneously and quite independently. In Great Britain it was slow to establish itself; and not for many years did any one of the British masters of narrative art put forth his utmost endeavor in this minor form. They long preferred the leisurely amplitude of the full-grown novel, with its larger liberty and its looser facility; and in this they found a more certain reward. In London neither the monthly magazines nor the weeklies were eager to extend an encouraging hospitality to the short-story, relying rather on a single serial tale which might assure their circulation for a year. — Charles Reade once boasted that a certain novel of his "floated the *Argosy*.'

Brief tales there were, and in profusion, in these British magazines; but they were, for the most part, the unimportant productions of the less gifted writers. Indeed, the British were the last of the great peoples of the world to appreciate the finer possibilities of the short-story as a definite species of fiction; and therefore they were the slowest to take advantage of the new form. And as a result of this conservatism they lagged far behind France and the United States, in this department of literature, until its possibilities were suddenly made manifest to them by Stevenson and by Kipling, both of whom had come directly under the influence of Poe and of other American short-story writers. Stevenson had a certain spiritual kinship with Hawthorne also, disclosed most clearly in "Markheim," — which could not be excluded from any list of the world's most powerful short-stories. And to any list of the world's most beautiful short-stories Kipling could contribute "Without Benefit of Clergy," the "Brushwood Boy," and "They," even if a larger selection from his incomparably varied store did not impose itself. The British were sluggish in adventuring themselves in the new form, but when at last two of their most striking writers did undertake it, they won immediate acclaim as masters of this minor art.

IX

Perhaps the reason why the short-story established itself earlier in France was twofold, — first of all, the finer artistic appreciation of a gifted race which had inherited the Latin liking for logic, and which had long accepted the classicist code of unity and proportion; and, secondly, the inviting hospitality of Parisian journalism, which had always prided itself on a close connection with literature. The French are not rich in magazines, partly perhaps because their newspapers are ready to give them much that we who speak English expect to find only in our weeklies and our monthlies. It is in the daily journals of the city on the Seine that there were first published the most of the short-stories of Richepin, of Coppée and of Halévy, of Daudet and of Maupassant. And whenever the list of the world's most admirable short-stories is drawn up, it cannot fail to contain the title of more than one of Daudet's deliciously humorous fantasies, full of the flavor of the South; and it will be enriched also with the name of more than one of Maupassant's sturdily veracious portrayals of character, executed with a Northern fidelity to fact.

For the extraordinary expansion of the short-story here in the United States, in the American branch of English literature, in the mid-century when it was being neglected by the chief authors of the British branch of our literature, three reasons may be suggested. First of all, there is the important fact that the perfected form had been exemplified and proclaimed here by Poe, earlier than by any other writer elsewhere. Secondly, we need to note that our struggling magazines from the beginning had been forced to rely for their attractiveness largely on the short-story, if only because of the dearth at first of native novelists capable of carrying the burden of the lengthened serial. And, thirdly, we must recall certain of the special conditions of our civilization, — a vast country, a heterogeneous population, a wide variety of interests, all of which combined to make it almost an impossibility that we should ever bring forth a work of fiction which might be recognized as the Great American Novel.

What it was possible for our writers of fiction to do, and what it was most immediately profitable for them to do, was to forego the long novel and to avail themselves of the short-story in which they might begin modestly to deal directly with that special part of an immense country with which any one of them chanced to be most familiar, to limn its characters with absolute honesty, and to fix its characteristics before these were modified. In the middle of the nineteenth century the time was not yet ripe for the broader studies of Ameri-

INTRODUCTION

can life, like the "Rise of Silas Lapham" and "Huckleberry Finn," which could not arrive until later; but there was a tempting opening for those who might choose to cultivate what may be called the short-story of local color. In one sense Irving had set the example; and in "Rip Van Winkle" and its fellows he had peopled the banks of the Hudson with legendary figures. But more potent yet was the influence of Hawthorne with his searching analysis of the very soul of New England.

After Irving and Hawthorne there came forward a host of American writers of the short-story of local color, men and women, humorists and sentimentalists, fantasists and realists, Northerners and Southerners, differing in sincerity and differing in skill. For more than threescore years now they have been exploring these United States; and they have been explaining the people of one state to the population of the others, increasing our acquaintance with our fellow-citizens and broadening our sympathy. In no other country has anything like this probing inquisition of contemporary humanity ever been attempted, — perhaps because there is no other country in which it could be as useful and as necessary.

Bret Harte cast the cloak of romance upon the shoulders of the Argonauts of '49; and what he sought to do for the early Californians other writers have striven to do for the inhabitants of other states. There is romance in abundance in Mr. Cable's loving delineation of "Old Creole Days," in which there is also a wiser regard for the actual facts of life and of human character. What Mr. Cable did for Louisiana, Mr. Page has done for Virginia, and Mr. Harris for Georgia. With a franker realism, Miss Jewett and Miss Wilkins have depicted the sterner folk of Massachusetts, and Mr. Garland has etched the plain people of Wisconsin. And only recently the same searching method has been applied to the several quarters of the single city of New York with its confused medley of inhabitants drawn from every part of the Old World and now in the process of making over into citizens of the New.

X

It was Poe who first pointed out that the short-story has a right to exist, and that it is essentially different in its aim from the tale which merely chances not to be prolonged. Admitting the claim of the short-story to be received as a clearly defined species, Professor Perry (of Harvard) has considered the advantages of the form and its rigorous limitations.[1] He holds that the authors of fiction, whether novelists or tellers of short-stories, seek

[1] "A Study of Prose Fiction," by Bliss Perry, Boston and New York: Houghton, Mifflin & Co., 1902. Chapter XII, The Short-Story, pp. 300–334.

always to arouse the interest of the reader by showing him "certain persons doing certain things in certain circumstances." In other words, they deal with three elements, the characters, the plot, and the setting. As the time at the command of the writers of the short-story is strictly limited, they cannot deal with colorless characters, and if the "theme is character-development, then that development must be hastened by striking experiences." In other words, the short-story of character is likely to present a central figure more or less unusual and unexpected.

On the other hand, if the emphasis is laid rather on what happens than on the person to whom it happens, then the restriction of brevity tends toward an extreme simplification of the chief character. The heroine of the "Lady or the Tiger," for example, is simply *a* woman — not any woman in particular; and the hero of the "Pit and the Pendulum" is simply *a* man — not any man in particular. The situation itself is all sufficient to hold our attention for a brief space. Thus, if the interest of the short-story is focused on character, that character is likely to be out of the common, whereas if the attention is fixed rather on plot, then the character is likely to be commonplace. If, however, the author prefers to spend his effort chiefly on the setting, then he can get along almost without character and without plot. The setting alone will suffice to interest us, and our attention is held mainly by the pressure of the atmosphere. "The modern feeling for landscape, the modern curiosity about social conditions, the modern esthetic sense for the characteristic rather than for the beautiful, all play into the short-story writer's hands;" and he can give us the fullest satisfaction "if he can discover to us a new corner of the world, or sketch the familiar scene to our heart's desire, or illumine one of the great human occupations, as war, or commerce, or industry."

Professor Perry makes it clear that in the short-story "the powers of the reader are not kept long upon the stretch," and that this gives its writers an opportunity of which the novelist can venture to avail himself only at his peril, — the opportunity "for innocent didacticism, for posing problems without answering them, for stating arbitrary premises, for omitting unlovely details, and, conversely, for making beauty out of the horrible, and finally, for poetic symbolism." Then the critic calls attention to the demands which the short-story makes on the writer if he is really to achieve a masterpiece in this form; and he asserts that the short-story at its best "calls for visual imagination of a high order: the power to see the object; to penetrate to the essential nature; to select the one characteristic trait by which it may be represented." But the short-story does not require the possession of a sustained power of imagination; nor does it demand of its author "essential sanity, breadth, and tolerance of view." Dealing only with a fleeting phase of existence, employing only a brief moment of time, the writer of the short-story "need not be consistent; he need not think things through." Herein we see where the short-story falls below the level of the larger novel, which must needs be sane and consistent, and which calls for a prolonged exercise of interpretive imagination.

XI

In these pages consideration has been paid only to the short-story in prose; but attention should be called to the existence of certain brief tales in verse, a few of which achieve the true short-story form in spite of their rimes, although the most of them are merely metrical narratives not unduly prolonged. Of course, the earliest stories of all must have been first told rhythmically, since prose comes ever after verse; and the lyric habit survived the later mastery of the other harmony. In Alexandria Theocritus shrank from the stately epic, — perhaps because he had taken to heart the warning of Callimachus that "a great book is a great evil." He wrote delicate and delightful idyls, little pictures of life in town and in country, closely akin in their temper to the vignettes etched by certain modern poets of society.

Sometimes the distinction between the tales in prose and those in verse is very slight indeed. Chaucer put into rime some of the same fictions which Boccaccio was narrating in more pedestrian fashion but with almost equal felicity; and this material, common to these two early masters of narrative, was derived sometimes from an earlier French *fabliau* in rime. In the technic of storytelling the English poet was the better craftsman; he had a unity and a harmony to which his Italian contemporary could not pretend. Chaucer had also a far richer humor and a far more searching insight into human nature.

The employment of rhythm and of rime tends always to endow a tale with a lyrical elevation not quite what we expect in a short-story, not quite in keeping with its dominant tone. In other words, verse is likely to bestow on a story a certain ballad note; and much as a rimed tale may suggest a ballad, there is, after all, a distinction between them. Just as the novel differs from the epic, so the tale in verse differs from the ballad, even if this difference is not easy to declare precisely. The epic may be a reworking of older ballads; but it is an inferior epic which strikes us as being no more than a stringing together of ballad after ballad.

From out of the mass of tales in verse, from La Fontaine's lively *contes*, from Hugo's splendid

"Legend of the Ages," from Crabbe's homely "Tales of the Hall," and from Longfellow's graceful "Tales of a Wayside Inn," it would not be difficult to single out more than one tale in rime which approaches closely to the short-story form.[1] To be cited also are certain of Scott's narratives in rime, as well as Wordsworth's "Michael" and Tennyson's "Dora." The "Hermann and Dorothea" of Goethe is rather a novelette in verse than a short story; and its analogue in English is the "Courtship of Miles Standish." In French the *conte en vers* flourished intermittently all through the nineteenth century; and Coppée's vigorous and pathetic "Strike of the Iron Workers" is a true short-story, in verse, — to be compared with his own prose "Substitute" and with Halévy's "Insurgent."

XII

At the beginning of the seventeenth century the drama was the dominating literary form. In the eighteenth century the essay in its turn attracted the attention of almost every man of letters. In the nineteenth century the essay lost its popularity, just as the drama had lost its supremacy a hundred years earlier; and prose-fiction, borrow-

---

[1] For a fuller consideration of the rimed story, see "English Tales in Verse," with an introduction. By C. H. Herford, London: Blackie & Son. (The Warwick Library.)

ing much from both of these predecessors, attained a universal vogue and insisted on recognition as the equal of the drama which had formerly claimed an indisputable precedence. At the end of the nineteenth century no competent critic could deny that it had been the era of the novel; but even more indisputably had it been the era of the short-story. Now, at the beginning of the twentieth century, there are signs that the drama is again alive in our literature and that it is winning back adherents from the ranks of the novelists. But this rivalry of the drama, whatever effect it may have upon the novel, is not likely to interfere with the short-story, which stands apart by itself. Probably there is no rashness in a prophecy that the short-story will flourish even more luxuriantly in the immediate future than it has flourished in the immediate past. Of a certainty we can assert that a literary form as popular as the short-story, as well established in every modern literature, is deserving of serious consideration and is worthy of careful study.

I. THE HUSBAND OF AGLAES

From the "Gesta Romanorum"

In the Middle Ages many collections were made containing the floating tales of oral tradition. Most of them seem to have been intended to record good stories which might be introduced effectively into sermons. Of these medieval collections of fragmentary fiction the most famous is that called "Gesta Romanorum," compiled apparently toward the end of the thirteenth century and most probably in England. Written in monkish Latin, these tales reveal a complete ignorance of the past. The compiler was without a glimmering of what we now term "the historic sense," and to him all past periods are as one. He had also no great share of the gift of story-telling. But if his art was feeble, he had a quick eye for a good story. His book has served as a storehouse of suggestion for the more adroit narrators who came after him.

THE HUSBAND OF AGLAES

In Rome some time dwelt a mighty emperor named Philominus, who had one only daughter, who was fair and gracious in the sight of every man, who had to name

Aglaes. There was also in the emperor's palace a gentle knight that loved dearly this lady. It befell after on a day that this knight talked with this lady, and secretly uttered his desire to her. Then she said courteously, "Seeing you have uttered to me the secrets of your heart, I will likewise for your love utter to you the secrets of my heart: and truly I say, that above all other I love you best." Then said the knight, "I purpose to visit the Holy Land, and therefore give me your troth, that this seven years you shall take no other man, but only for my love to tarry for me so long, and if I come not again by this day seven years, then take what man you like best. And likewise I promise you that within this seven years I will take no wife." Then said she, "This covenant pleaseth me well." When this was said, each of them was betrothed to other, and then this knight took his leave of the lady, and went to the Holy Land.

Shortly after, the emperor treated with the king of Hungary for the marriage of his daughter. Then came the king of Hungary to the emperor's palace, and when he had seen his daughter, he liked marvelous well her beauty and her behavior, so that the emperor and the king were accorded in all things as touching the marriage, upon the condition that the damsel would consent. Then called the emperor the young lady to him, and said, "O, my fair daughter, I have provided for thee, that a king shall be thy husband, if thou list consent; therefore tell me what answer thou wilt give to this." Then said she to her father, "It pleaseth me well; but one thing, dear father, I entreat of you, if it might please you to grant me: I have vowed to keep my virginity,

THE HUSBAND OF AGLAES 43

and not to marry these seven years; therefore, dear father, I beseech you for all the love that is between your gracious fatherhood and me, that you name no man to be my husband till these seven years be ended, and then I shall be ready in all things to fulfill your will." Then said the emperor, "Sith it is so that thou hast thus vowed, I will not break thy vow; but when these seven years be expired, thou shalt have the king of Hungary to thy husband."

Then the emperor sent forth his letters to the king of Hungary, praying him if it might please him to stay seven years for the love of his daughter, and then he should speed without fail. Herewith the king was pleased and content to stay the prefixed day.

And when the seven years were ended, save a day, the young lady stood in her chamber window, and wept sore, saying, "Woe and alas, as to-morrow my love promised to be with me again from the Holy Land; and also the king of Hungary to-morrow will be here to marry me, according to my father's promise; and if my love comes not at a certain hour, then am I utterly deceived of the inward love I bear to him."

When the day came, the king hasted toward the emperor, to marry his daughter, and was royally arrayed in purple. And while the king was riding on his way, there came a knight riding on his way, who said, "I am of the empire of Rome, and now am lately come from the Holy Land, and am ready to do you the best service I can." And as they rode talking by the way, it began to rain so fast that all the king's apparel was sore wet. Then said the knight, "My lord, ye have done foolishly, for as much as ye brought not with you your house." Then said the king: "Why speakest thou so? My house is large and broad, and made of stones and mortar; how should I bring then with me my house? Thou speakest like a fool." When this was said, they rode on till they came to a great deep water, and the king smote his horse with his spurs, and leapt into the water, so that he was almost drowned. When the knight saw this, and was over on the other side of the water without peril, he said to the king, "Ye were in peril, and therefore ye did foolishly, because ye brought not with you your bridge." Then said the king, "Thou speakest strangely: my bridge is made of lime and stone, and containeth in quality more than half a mile; how should I then bear with me my bridge? therefore thou speakest foolishly." "Well," said the knight, "my foolishness may turn you to wisdom." When the king had ridden a little farther, he asked the knight what time of day it was. Then said the knight, "If any man hath list to eat, it is time of the day to eat. Wherefore, my lord, pray take a *modicum* with me, for that is no dishonor to you, but great honor to me before the states of this empire." Then said the king, "I will gladly eat with thee." They sat both down in a fair vine garden, and there dined together, both the king and the knight. And when dinner was done, and that the king had washed, the knight said unto the king, "My lord, ye have done foolishly, for that ye brought not with you your father and mother." Then said the king: "What sayest thou? My father is dead, and my mother is old, and may not travel; how should I then bring them with me? Therefore, to say the truth, a foolisher man than thou art did I never hear." Then said the knight, "Every work is praised at the end."

When the knight had ridden a little further, and nigh to the emperor's palace, he asked leave to go from him; for he knew a nearer way to the palace, to the young lady, that he might come first, and carry her away with him. Then said the king, "I pray thee tell me by what place thou purposest to ride?" Then said the knight: "I shall tell you the truth. This day seven years I left a net in a place, and now I purpose to visit it, and draw it to me, and if it be whole, then will I take it to me, and keep it as a precious jewel; if it be broken, then will I leave it." And when he had thus said, he took his leave of the king, and rode forth; but the king kept the broad highway.

When the emperor heard of the king's coming, he went toward him with a great company, and royally received him, causing him to shift his wet clothes, and to put on fresh apparel. And when the emperor and the king were set at meat, the emperor welcomed him with all the cheer and solace that he could. And when he had eaten, the emperor asked tidings of the king. "My lord," said he, "I shall tell you what I have heard this day by the way: there came a knight to me, and reverently saluted me; and anon after there fell a great rain, and greatly spoiled my apparel. And anon the knight said, 'Sir, ye have done foolishly, for that ye brought not with you your house.'" Then said the emperor, "What clothing had the knight on?" "A cloak," quoth the king. Then said the emperor, "Sure that was a wise man, for the house

whereof he spake was a cloak, and therefore he said to
you that you did foolishly, because had you come with
your cloak, then your clothes had not been spoiled with
rain." Then said the king: "When he had ridden a
little farther, we came to a deep water, and I smote my
horse with my spurs, and I was almost drowned, but he
rid through the water without any peril. Then said he
to me, 'You did foolishly, for that you brought not with
you your bridge.'" "Verily," said the emperor, "he
said truth, for he called the squires the bridge, that
should have ridden before you, and assayed the deepness
of the water." Then said the king: "We rode further,
and at the last he prayed me to dine with him. And
when he had dined, he said, I did unwisely, because I
brought not with me my father and mother." "Truly,"
said the emperor, "he was a wise man, and saith wisely:
for he called your father and mother, bread and wine,
and other victual." Then said the king: "We rode farther, and anon after he asked me leave to go from me,
and I asked earnestly whither he went; and he answered
again, and said, 'This day seven years I left a net in a
private place, and now I will ride to see it; and if it be
broken and torn, then will I leave it, but if it be as I left
it, then shall it be unto me right precious.'"

When the emperor heard this, he cried with a loud
voice, and said, "O ye my knights and servants, come
ye with me speedily unto my daughter's chamber, for
surely that is the net of which he spake." And forthwith his knights and servants went unto his daughter's
chamber, and found her not, for the aforesaid knight
had taken her with him. And thus the king was deceived

THE HUSBAND OF AGLAES

of the damsel, and he went home again to his own country ashamed.

NOTE.—This tale is ingenious enough in its invention, and it might have been made interesting if the writer had known how. But as presented here, it is merely the bald plot of a story, told with no appreciation of its possibilities, with no feeling for dramatic effect, and with no realization of individual character.

II. THE STORY OF GRISELDA

By Boccaccio — [1313–1375]

Boccaccio was one of the masters of the brief tale which the Italians call the *novella* and which might vary in length from a mere repartee, a simple anecdote, to a more elaborate narrative, having almost plot enough for a full-blown romance. It was in 1353 that he published the "Decameron," in which there are one hundred specimens of the *novella*, supposed to be told on ten days by ten friends gathered in a country house to escape the plague in Florence.

The contrast between the "Gesta Romanorum" and the "Decameron" is striking. Although the several stories are sometimes identical, the advance in the art of narrative is obvious. The earlier book is a miscellany of ill-told tales, and the later is a formal work of literary art containing brief models of narration. Boccaccio was a born story-teller; and he seems to have had a favorite formula. Generally he begins by the introduction of his chief characters, then he proceeds to develop the plot, and finally he gives us the solution of the situation.

THE STORY OF GRISELDA

It is a great while since, when among those that were Lord Marquesses of Saluzzo, the very greatest and worthiest man of them all was a young noble lord, named Gualtieri, who, having neither wife nor child, spent his time in nothing else but hawking and hunting. Nor had he any mind of marriage, or to enjoy the benefit of children, wherein many did repute him the wiser. But this being distasteful to his subjects, they very often solicited him to match himself with a wife, to the end that he might not decease without an heir, nor they be left destitute of a succeeding lord, offering themselves to provide him of such a one, so well descended by father and mother as not only should confirm their hope, but also yield him high contentment, whereto the Marquess thus answered: —

"Worthy friends, you would constrain me to the thing wherewith I never had any intent to meddle, considering how difficult a case it is to meet with such a woman, who can agree with a man in all his conditions. And how great the number is of them who daily happen on the contrary! but most, and worst of all the rest, how wretched and miserable proves the life of that man who is bound to live with a wife not fit for him! And in saying you can learn to understand the custom and qualities of children by behavior of the fathers and mothers, and so to provide me of a wife, it is a mere argument of folly; for neither shall I comprehend, or you either, the secret inclinations of parents — I mean of the father, and much less the complexion of the mother. But admit it were within compass of power to know them, yet it is a frequent sight, and observed every day, that daughters do resemble neither father nor mother, but that they are naturally governed by their own instinct.

"But because you are so desirous to have me fettered in the chains of wedlock, I am content to grant what you request. And because I would have no complaint made of any but myself, if matters should not happen answerable to expectation, I will make mine own eyes my electors, and not see by any other sight. Giving you this assurance before, that if she whom I shall make choice of be not of you honored and respected as your lady and mistress, it will ensue to your detriment, how much you have displeased me, to take a wife at your request and against mine own will."

The noblemen answered that they were well satisfied, provided that he took a wife.

Some indifferent space of time before the beauty, manners, and well-seeming virtues of a poor countryman's daughter, dwelling in no far distant village, had appeared very pleasing to the Lord Marquess, and gave him full persuasion that with her he should lead a comfortable life. And therefore without any farther search or inquisition he absolutely resolved to marry her, and having conferred with her father, agreed that his daughter should be his wife. Whereupon the Marquess made a general convocation of all his lords, barons, and other of his special friends, from all parts of his dominion, and when they were assembled together he then spake to them in manner as followeth: —

"Honorable friends, it appeared pleasing to you all,

THE STORY OF GRISELDA 51

and yet, I think, you are of the same mind, that I should dispose myself to take a wife, and I thereto condescended, more to yield you contentment than for any particular desire in myself. Let me now remember you of your solemn made promise, with full consent to honor and obey her whomsoever as your sovereign lady and mistress, that I shall elect to make my wife; and now the time is come for my exacting the performance of that promise, and which I look you must constantly keep. I have made choice of a young virgin, answerable to mine own heart and liking, dwelling not far off hence, whom I intend to make my wife, and within few days to have her brought home to my palace. Let your care and diligence then extend so far as to see that the feast may be sumptuous and her entertainment to be most honorable, to the end that I may receive as much contentment in your promise performed as you shall perceive I do in my choice."

The lords and all the rest were wonderfully joyful to hear him so well inclined, expressing no less by their shouts and jocund suffrages, protesting cordially that she should be welcomed with pomp and majesty, and honored of them all as their liege lady and sovereign. Afterward they made preparation for a princely and magnificent feast, as the Marquess did the like, for a marriage of extraordinary state and quality, inviting all his kindred, friends, and acquaintances in all parts and provinces about him. He made also ready most rich and costly garments, shaped by the body of a comely young gentlewoman, whom he knew to be equal in proportion and stature to her of whom he had made his election.

When the appointed nuptial day was come, the Lord

Marquess, about nine of the clock in the morning, mounted on horseback, as all the rest did, who came to attend him honorably, and having all things in due readiness with them, he said, "Lords, it is time for us to fetch the bride." So on he rode with his train to the same poor village whereat she dwelt, and when he was come to her father's house, he saw the maiden returning very hastily from a well, where she had been to fetch a pail of water, which she set down, and stood, accompanied with other maidens, to see the passage of the Lord Marquess and his train. Gualtieri called her by her name, which was Griselda, and asked her where her father was, who bashfully answered him, and with an humble courtesy, saying, "My gracious lord, he is in the house."

Then the Marquess dismounted from his horse, commanding every one to attend him, then all alone he entered into the poor cottage, where he found the maid's father, being named Giannuculo, and said unto him: "God speed, good father, I am come to espouse thy daughter Griselda, but first I have a few demands to make, which I will utter to her in thy presence." Then he turned to the maid and said: —

"Fair Griselda, if I make you my wife, will you do your best endeavor to please me in all things which I shall do or say? will you be also gentle, humble and patient?" with divers other the like questions, whereto she still answered that she would, so near as Heaven with grace should enable her.

Presently he took her by the hand, so led her forth of the poor man's homely house, and in the presence of all his company, with his own hands he took off her

THE STORY OF GRISELDA

mean wearing garments, smock and all, and clothed her with those robes of state which he had purposely brought thither for her, and plaiting her hair over her shoulders, he placed a crown of gold on her head. Whereat every one standing as amazed, and wondering not a little, he said, "Griselda, wilt thou have me to thy husband?" Modestly blushing and kneeling on the ground, she answered, "Yes, my gracious lord, if you will accept so poor a maiden to be your wife." "Yes, Griselda," quoth he, "with this holy kiss I confirm thee for my wife;" and so espoused her before them all. Then mounting her on a milk-white palfrey, brought thither for her, she was thus honorably conducted to her palace.

Now concerning the marriage feast and triumphs, they were performed with no less pomp than if she had been daughter to the King of France. And the young bride apparently declared that, with her garments, her mind and behavior were quite changed. For indeed she was, as it were shame to speak otherwise, a rare creature, both of person and perfections, and not only was she absolute for beauty, and so sweetly amiable, gracious, and goodly, as if she were not the daughter of poor Giannuculo, and a country shepherdess, but rather of some noble lord, whereat every one wondered that formerly had known her. Besides all this, she was so obedient to her husband, so fervent in all dutiful offices, and patient, without the very least provoking, as he held himself much more than contented, and the only happy man that lived in the world.

In like manner, toward the subjects of her lord and husband she showed herself always so benign and gracious, as there was not any one but the more they looked on her the better they loved her, honoring her voluntarily and praying to the Heavens for her health, dignity, and welfare's long continuance, speaking now quite contrary to their former opinion of the Marquess, honorably and worthily, that he had shown himself a singular wise man in the election of his wife, which few else but he in the world would ever have done, because their judgment might fall far short of discerning those great and precious virtues, veiled under a homely habit, and obscured in a poor country cottage. To be brief, in very short time not only the Marquisate itself, but all neighboring provinces about, had no other common talk but of her rare course of life, devotion, charity, and all good actions else whatsoever, quite quailing all sinister constructions of her husband, before he had received her in matrimony.

About four or five years after the birth of her daughter she conceived with child again, and at the limited hour of deliverance had a goodly son, to the no little liking of the Marquess. Afterward a strange humor entered into his brain; namely, that by a long-continued experience, and courses of an intolerable quality, he would needs make proof of his fair wife's patience. First he began to provoke her by injurious speeches, showing fierce and frowning looks to her, intimating that his people grew displeased with him, in regard of his wife's base birth and education, and so much the rather because she was likely to bring children who, by her blood, were no better than beggars, and murmured at the daughter already born. Which words, when Griselda heard, without any alteration of countenance, or the least distemperature in any appearing action, she said: —

"My honorable and gracious lord, dispose of me as you think best for your own dignity and contentment, for I shall therewith be well pleased, as she that knows herself far inferior to the meanest of your people, much less worthy of the honor whereto you liked to advance me."

This answer was very welcome to the Marquess, as apparently perceiving hereby that the dignity whereto he had exalted her, or any particular favors besides, could not infect her with any pride, coyness, or disdain. Not long after having told her in plain and open speeches that her subjects could not endure the daughter born of her, he instructed and despatched to her one of his servants, who, sorry, sad, and much perplexed in mind, said: "Madam, except I intend to lose my own life, I must accomplish what my lord hath strictly enjoined me, which is, to take this your young daughter, and then —" He said no more. The lady hearing these words, and noting his frowning looks, remembering also what the Marquess himself had formerly said, imagined that he had commanded his servant to kill the child. Suddenly, therefore, she took it out of the cradle, and having sweetly kissed, and bestowed her blessing on it, albeit her heart throbbed with the inward affection of a mother, without any alteration of countenance, she tenderly laid it in the servant's arms and said: "Here, friend, take it, and do with it as thy lord and mine hath commanded thee; but leave it in no rude place where birds or savage beasts may devour it, except it be his will."

The servant departing from her with the child, and reporting to the Marquess what his lady had said, he wondered at her incomparable constancy. Then he sent it by the same servant to Bologna, to an honorable lady his kinswoman, requesting her, without revealing whose child it was, to see it both nobly and carefully educated.

At time convenient afterward, being with child again, and delivered of a princely son, than which nothing could be more joyful to the Marquess, yet all this was not sufficient for him, but with far ruder language than before, and looks expressing harsh intentions, he said unto her: "Griselda, though thou pleasest me wonderfully by the birth of this princely boy, yet my subjects are not therewith contented, but blunder abroad maliciously that the grandchild of Giannuculo, a poor country peasant, when I am dead and gone, must be their sovereign lord and master. Which makes me stand in fear of their expulsion, and to prevent that, I must be rid of this child, as well as the other, and then send thee away from hence, that I may take another wife more pleasing to them."

Griselda, with a patient, suffering soul, hearing what he had said, returned no other answer but this: "Most gracious and honorable lord, satisfy and please your own royal mind, and never use any respect of me, for nothing is precious or pleasing to me, but what may agree with your good liking." Within a while after, the noble Marquess in the like manner as he did before for his daughter, so he sent the same servant for his son, and seeming as if he had sent it to have been slain, conveyed it to be nursed at Bologna, in company of his sweet sister. Whereat the lady showed no other discontentment in any kind than formerly she had done for her daughter, to the no mean marvel of the Marquess, who protested in his soul that the like woman was not in all the world beside. And were it not for his heedful observation, how loving and careful she was of her children, prizing them as dearly as her own life, rash opinion might have persuaded him that she had no more in her than a carnal affection, not caring how many she had so she might thus easily be rid of them; but he knew her to be a truly virtuous mother, and wisely liable to endure his severest impositions.

His subjects believing that he had caused his children to be slain, blamed him greatly, thought him to be a most cruel man, and did highly compassionate the lady's case, who when she came in company of other gentlewomen, which mourned for their deceased children, would answer nothing else but that they could not be more pleasing to her than they were to the father that begot them.

Within certain years after the birth of these children, the Marquess purposed with himself to make his last and final proof of fair Griselda's patience, and said to some near about him that he could no longer endure to keep Griselda as his wife, confessing he had done foolishly, and according to a young, giddy brain when he was so rash in the marriage of her. Wherefore he would send to the Pope and purchase a dispensation from him to repudiate Griselda and take another wife. Wherein, although they greatly reproved him, yet he told them plainly it must needs be so.

The lady hearing this news, and thinking she must return again to her poor father's house and estate, and perhaps to her old occupation of keeping of sheep, as in her younger days she had done; understanding withal that another must enjoy him whom she dearly loved and honored, you may well think, worthy ladies, that her patience was now put to the main proof indeed. Nevertheless, as with an invincible, true, virtuous courage, she had overstood all the other injuries of fortune, so did she constantly settle her soul to bear this with an undaunted countenance and behavior.

At such time as was prefixed for the purpose, counterfeit letters came to the Marquess, as sent from Rome, which he caused to be publicly read in the hearing of his subjects, that the Pope had dispensed with him to leave Griselda, and marry with another wife; wherefore, sending for her immediately, in presence and before them all, thus he spake to her: "Woman, by concession sent me from the Pope, he hath dispensed me to make choice of another wife, and to free myself from thee. And because my predecessors have been noblemen and great lords in this country, thou being the daughter of a poor country clown, and their blood and mine notoriously imbased by my marriage with thee, I intend to have thee no longer for my wife, but will return thee home to thy father's house with all the rich dowry thou broughtest me; and then I will take another wife, with whom I am already contracted, better beseeming my birth, and far more contenting and pleasing to my people."

The lady hearing these words, not without much pain and difficulty, restrained her tears, quite contrary to the natural inclination of women, and thus answered: "Great Marquess, I never was so empty of discretion, but did always acknowledge that my base and humble condition could not in any manner suit with your high blood and nobility, and my being with you, I ever acknowledged to

THE STORY OF GRISELDA 59

proceed from Heaven and you, not any merit of mine, but only as a favor lent me, which you being now pleased to recall back again, I ought to be pleased, and so am, that it be restored. Here is the ring wherewith you espoused me: here, in all humility, I deliver it to you. You command me to carry home the marriage dowry which I brought with me; there is no need of a treasurer to repay it me, neither any new purse to carry it in, much less any sumpter to be laden with it. For, noble lord, it was never out of my memory that you took me stark naked, and if it shall seem sightly to you that this body that hath borne two children, begotten by you, must again be seen naked, willingly must I depart hence naked. But I humbly beg of your excellency, in recompense of my virginity which I brought you blameless, so much as in thought, that I might have but one of my wedding smocks, only to conceal the shame of nakedness, and then I shall depart rich enough."

The Marquess, whose heart wept bloody tears, as his eyes would likewise gladly have yielded their natural tribute, covered all with a dissembling angry countenance, and starting up, said: "Go, give her a smock only, and so send her gadding." All there present then entreated him to let her have a petticoat, because it might not be said that she who had been his wife thirteen years and more was sent away so poorly in her smock; but all their persuasions prevailed not with him. Naked in her smock, without hose or shoes, bareheaded, and not so much as a cloth or rag about her neck, to the great grief and mourning of all that saw her, she went home to her own father's house.

And he, good man, never believing that the Marquess would long keep his daughter as his wife, but rather expecting daily what now happened, had safely laid up the garments whereof the Marquess despoiled her the same morning when he espoused her. Wherefore he delivered them to her, and she fell to her father's household business, according as formerly she had done, sustaining with a great and unconquerable spirit all the cruel assaults of her enemy, Fortune.

About such time also, as suited with his own disposition, the Marquess made publicly known to his subjects that he meant to join in marriage again with the daughter to one of the Counts of Panago, and causing preparation to be made for a sumptuous wedding, he sent for Griselda, and she being come, thus he spake to her: "The wife that I have made new election of is to arrive here within very few days, and at her first coming I would have her to be most honorably entertained. Thou knowest I have no woman in my house that can deck up the chambers and set all requisite things in due order befitting so solemn a feast, and therefore I sent for thee, who, knowing better than any other all the parts, provision, and goods in the house, mayest set everything in such order as thou shalt think necessary.

"Invite such ladies and gentlewomen as thou wilt, and give them welcome as if thou wert the lady of the house, and when the marriage is ended, return then home to thy father again."

Although these words pierced like wounding daggers the heart of the poor but noble, patient Griselda, as being unable to forget the unequaled love she bare the Marquess, though the dignity of her former fortune more easily slipped out of her remembrance, yet nevertheless thus she answered: —

"My gracious lord, I am glad that I can do you any service wherein you shall find me both willing and ready." In the same poor garments as she came from her father's house, although she was turned out in her smock, she began to sweep and make clean the chambers, rub the stools and benches in the hall, and ordered everything in the kitchen, as if she were the worst maid in all the house, never ceasing or giving over, till all things were in due and decent order, as best beseemed in such a case. After all which was done, the Marquess having invited all the ladies of the country to be present at so great a feast, when the marriage day was come, Griselda in her gown of country gray, gave them welcome in honorable manner, and graced them all with very cheerful countenance.

Gualtieri the Marquess, who had caused his two children to be nobly nourished at Bologna with a near kinswoman of his, who had married with one of the Counts of Panago, his daughter being now aged twelve years old and somewhat more, as also his son about six or seven, he sent a gentleman expressly to his kindred to have them come and visit him at Saluzzo, bringing his daughter and son with them, attended in very honorable manner, and publishing everywhere as they came along that the young virgin, known to none but himself and them, should be the wife to the Marquess, and that only was the cause of her coming. The gentleman was not slack in the execution of trust reposed in him, but having made convenient preparation, with the kindred, son, daughter, and a worthy company attending on them, arrived at Saluzzo about dinner time, where wanted no resort, from all neighboring parts round about, to see the coming of the Lord Marquess's new spouse.

By the lords and ladies she was joyfully entertained, and coming into the great hall, where the tables were ready covered, Griselda, in her homely country habit, humbled herself before her, saying, "Gracious welcome to the new-elected spouse of the Lord Marquess."

All the ladies there present, who had very earnestly importuned Gualtieri, but in vain, that Griselda might better be shut up in some chamber, or else to lend her the wearing of any other garment which formerly had been her own, because she should not so poorly be seen among strangers; being seated at the tables, she waited on them very serviceably. The young virgin was observed by every one, who spared not to say that the Marquess had made an excellent change; but, above them all, Griselda did most commend her, and so did her brother likewise, as young as he was, yet not knowing her to be his sister.

Now was the Marquess sufficiently satisfied in his soul that he had seen so much as he desired concerning the patience of his wife, who in so many heart-grieving trials was never noted so much as to alter her countenance; and being absolutely persuaded that this proceeded not from any want of understanding in her, because he knew her to be singularly wise, he thought it high time now to free her from all these afflicting oppressions, and give her such assurance as she ought to have. Wherefore, commanding her into his presence, openly before all his assembled friends, smiling on her, he said: "What thinkest thou, Griselda, of our new-chosen spouse?" "My lord," quoth she, "I like her exceedingly well; and if she be so wise as she is fair, which verily I think she is, I make no doubt but you shall live with her as the only happy man of the world. But I humbly entreat your honor, if I have any power in me to prevail by, that you would not give her such cutting and unkind language as you did to your other wife, for I cannot think her armed with such patience as should indeed support them; as well in regard she is much younger, as also her more delicate breeding and education, whereas she whom you had before was brought up in continual toil and travail."

When the Marquess perceived that Griselda believed verily this young daughter of hers should be his wife, and answered him in so honest and modest manner, he commanded her to sit down by him, and said: "Griselda, it is now more than fit time that thou shouldest taste the fruit of thy long admired patience, and that they who have thought me cruel, harsh, and uncivil-natured, should at length observe that I have done nothing at all basely or unadvisedly. For this was a work premeditated before for instructing thee what it is to be a married wife, and to let them know, whosoever they be, how to take and to keep a wife; which hath begotten to me perpetual joy and happiness so long as I have a day to live with thee, a matter whereof I stood before greatly in fear, and which in marriage I thought would never happen to me.

"It is not unknown to thee, in how many kinds, for my first proof, I gave thee harsh and unpleasant speeches, which drew no discontentment from thee, either in looks, words, or behavior, but rather such comfort as my soul desired, and so in my other succeeding afterward. In one minute now I purpose to give thee that consolation which I bereft thee of in my tempestuous storms, and make a sweet restoration for all thy former sour sufferings. My fair and dear affected Griselda, she whom thou supposest for my new-elected spouse, with a glad and cheerful heart embrace for thine own daughter, and this also her brother, being both of them thy children and mine, in common opinion of the whole vulgar multitude imagined to be, by my command, long since slain. I am thy honorable lord and husband, who doth and will love thee far above all women else in the world, giving thee justly this deserved praise and commendation, that no man living hath the like wife as I have."

So, sweetly kissing her infinitely, and hugging her joyfully in his arms, the tears now streaming like new-let loose rivers down her fair face, which no disaster before could force from her, he brought her and seated her by her daughter, who was not a little amazed at so rare an alteration. She having, in zeal of affection, kissed and embraced them both, all else present being clearly resolved from the former doubt, which too long deluded them, the ladies arose jocundly from the tables, and attending on Griselda to her chamber, in sign of a more successful augury to follow, took off her poor contemptible rags, and put on such costly robes which, as Lady Marchioness, she used to wear before.

Afterward they waited on her into the hall again, being their sovereign lady and mistress, as she was no less in her poorest garments; where, all rejoicing for the new-restored mother and happy recovery of so noble a son and daughter, the festival continued many months after. Now, every one thought the Marquess to be a noble and a wise prince, though somewhat sharp and unsufferable in the severe experience made of his wife; but above all they reputed Griselda to be a most wise, patient, and virtuous lady. The Count of Panago, within a few days after, returned back to Bologna; and the Lord Marquess, fetching home old Giannuculo from his country drudgery, to live with him as his father-in-law in his princely palace, gave him honorable maintenance, wherein he long continued and ended his days. Afterward he matched his daughter in a noble marriage, he and Griselda living long time together in the highest honor that possibly could be.

What can now be said to the contrary, but that poor country cottages may yield as divine and excellent spirits as the most stately and royal mansions, which breed and bring up some more worthy to be hog-rubbers than hold any sovereignty over men? Where is any other besides Griselda who, not only without a wet eye, but emboldened by a valiant and invincible courage, could suffer the sharp rigors, and never the like heard-of proofs, made by the Marquess? Perhaps he might have met with another who would have quitted him in a contrary kind, and for thrusting her forth of doors in her smock, could have found better succor somewhere else, rather than walk so nakedly in the cold streets.

NOTE. — Griselda is one of the favorite figures of the Middle Ages; and that the tale of her sufferings was acceptable, sheds a strange light on those distant days. Boccaccio tells it anew with no suggestion of revolt against the intolerable brutality of the husband. He tells it adroitly, as was his custom; but his interest is wholly in his narrative. His characters are but outlined; and they exist for the sake of the story itself. The analysis of the feelings of the suffering heroine does not tempt him. He is satisfied to set forth the sequence of events, without entering into any explanation or discussion.

III. CONSTANTIA AND THEODOSIUS

By Joseph Addison (1672–1719)

In the *Spectator* of Steele and Addison there are a few stories, apologues most of them, and told in the leisurely fashion of the true essayist. The story here selected is as good as any; and it may be accepted as a specimen of the art of narrative in England at the beginning of the eighteenth century. It first appeared as No. 164 in the *Spectator*, published on September 7, 1711.

CONSTANTIA AND THEODOSIUS

Constantia was a woman of extraordinary wit and beauty, but very unhappy in a father who, having arrived at great riches by his own industry, took delight in nothing but his money. Theodosius was the younger son of a decayed family, of great parts and learning, improved by a genteel and virtuous education. When he was in the twentieth year of his age he became acquainted with Constantia, who had not then passed her fifteenth. As he lived but a few miles distant from her father's house, he had frequent opportunities of seeing her; and by the advantages of a good person, and a pleasing conversation, made such an impression on her heart as it was impossible for time to efface. He was himself no less smitten with Constantia. A long acquaintance made them still discover new beauties in each other, and by degrees raised in them that mutual passion which had an influence on their following lives. It unfortunately happened that in the midst of this intercourse of love and friendship between Theodosius and Constantia, there broke out an irreparable quarrel between their parents, the one valuing himself too much upon his birth, the other upon his possessions. The father of Constantia was so incensed at the father of Theodosius, that he contracted an unreasonable aversion toward his son, insomuch that he forbade him his house, and charged his daughter upon her duty never to see him more. In the meantime, to break off all communication between the two lovers, who he knew entertained secret hopes of some favorable opportunity that should bring them together, he found out a young gentleman of a good fortune and an agreeable person, whom he pitched upon as a husband for his daughter. He soon concerted this affair so well, that he told Constantia it was his design to marry her to such a gentleman, and that her wedding should be celebrated on such a day. Constantia, who was overawed with the authority of her father, and unable to object anything against so advantageous a match, received the proposal with a profound silence, which her father commended in her, as the most decent manner of a virgin's giving her consent to an overture of that kind. The noise of this intended marriage soon reached Theodosius, who, after a long tumult of passions, which naturally rise in a lover's heart on such an occasion, writ the following letter to Constantia : —

"The thought of my Constantia, which for some years has been my only happiness, is now become a greater torment to me than I am able to bear. Must I then live to see you another's? The streams, the fields, and meadows, where we have so often talked together, grow painful to me; life itself is become a burden. May you long be happy in the world, but forget that there was ever such a man in it as

"THEODOSIUS."

This letter was conveyed to Constantia that very evening, who fainted at the reading of it; and the next morning she was much more alarmed by two or three messengers, that came to her father's house, one after another, to inquire if they had heard anything of Theodosius, who it seems had left his chamber about midnight, and could nowhere be found. The deep melancholy which had hung upon his mind some time before, made them apprehend the worst that could befall him. Constantia, who knew that nothing but the report of her marriage could have driven him to such extremities, was not to be comforted. She now accused herself of having so tamely given an ear to the proposal of a husband, and looked upon the new lover as the murderer of Theodosius. In short she resolved to suffer the utmost effects of her father's displeasure, rather than comply with a marriage which appeared to her so full of guilt and horror. The father, seeing himself entirely rid of Theodosius, and likely to keep a considerable portion in his family, was not very much concerned at the obstinate refusal of his daughter; and did not find it very difficult to excuse himself upon that account to his intended son-in-law, who had all along regarded this alliance rather as a marriage of convenience than of love. Constantia had now no relief but in her devotions and exercises of religion, to which her afflictions had so entirely subjected her mind, that after some years had abated the violence of her sorrows, and settled her thoughts in a kind of tranquillity, she resolved to pass the remainder of her days in a convent. Her father was not displeased with a resolution which would save money in his family, and readily complied with his daughter's intentions. Accordingly, in the twenty-fifth year of her age, while her beauty was yet in all its height and bloom, he carried her to a neighboring city, in order to look out a sisterhood of nuns among whom to place his daughter. There was in this place a father of a convent who was very much renowned for his piety and exemplary life; and as it is usual in the Romish church for those who are under any great affliction, or trouble of mind, to apply themselves to the most eminent confessors for pardon and consolation, our beautiful votary took the opportunity of confessing herself to this celebrated father.

We must now return to Theodosius, who, the very morning that the above-mentioned inquiries had been made after him, arrived at a religious house in the city, where now Constantia resided; and desiring that secrecy and concealment of the fathers of the convent which is very usual upon any extraordinary occasion, he made himself one of the order, with a private vow never to inquire after Constantia; whom he looked upon as given away to his rival upon the day on which, according to common fame, their marriage was to have been solemnized.

Having in his youth made a good progress in learning, that he might dedicate himself more entirely to religion, he entered into holy orders, and in a few years became renowned for his sanctity of life and those pious sentiments which he inspired into all who conversed with him. It was this holy man to whom Constantia had determined to apply herself in confession, though neither she nor any other, besides the prior of the convent, knew anything of his name or family. The gay, the amiable Theodosius had now taken upon him the name of Father Francis, and was so far concealed in a long beard, a shaven head, and a religious habit, that it was impossible to discover the man of the world in the venerable conventual.

As he was one morning shut up in his confessional, Constantia, kneeling by him, opened the state of her soul to him; and after having given him the history of a life full of innocence, she burst out into tears, and entered upon that part of her story in which he himself had so great a share. "My behavior," says she, "has, I fear, been the death of a man who had no fault but that of loving me too much. Heaven only knows how dear he was to me whilst he lived, and how bitter the remembrance of him has been to me since his death." She here paused, and lifted up her eyes that streamed with tears toward the father; who was so moved with the sense of her sorrows that he could only command his voice, which was broke with sighs and sobbings, so far as to bid her proceed. She followed his directions, and in a flood of tears poured out her heart before him. The father could not forbear weeping aloud, insomuch that in the agonies of his grief the seat shook under him. Constantia, who thought the good man was thus moved by his compassion toward her, and by the horror of her guilt, proceeded with the utmost contrition to acquaint him with that vow of virginity in which she was going to engage herself, as the proper atonement for her sins, and the only sacrifice she could make to the memory of Theodosius. The father, who by this time had pretty well composed himself, burst out again into tears upon hearing that name to which he had been so long disused, and upon receiving this instance of an unparalleled fidelity from one who he thought had several years since given herself up to the possession of another. Amidst the interruptions of his sorrow, seeing his pentitent overwhelmed with grief, he was only able to bid her from time to time be comforted — to tell her that her sins were forgiven her — that her guilt was not so great as she apprehended — that she should not suffer herself to be afflicted above measure. After which he recovered himself enough to give her the absolution in form; directing her at the same time to repair to him the next day that he might encourage her in the pious resolutions she had taken, and give her suitable exhortations for her behavior in it. Constantia retired, and the next morning renewed her applications. Theodosius, having manned his soul with proper thoughts and reflections, exerted himself on this occasion in the best manner he could to animate his penitent in the course of life she was entering upon, and wear out of her mind those groundless fears and apprehensions which had taken possession of it; concluding with a promise to her, that he would from time to time continue his admonitions when she should have taken upon her the holy veil. " The rules of our respective orders," says he, " will not permit that I should see you, but you may assure yourself not only of having a place in my prayers, but of receiving such frequent instructions as I can convey to you by letters. Go on cheerfully in the glorious course you have undertaken, and you will quickly find such a peace and satisfaction in your mind, which is not in the power of the world to give."

Constantia's heart was so elevated with the discourse of Father Francis, that the very next day she entered upon her vow. As soon as the solemnities of her reception were over, she retired, as it is usual, with the abbess into her own apartment.

The abbess had been informed the night before of all that had passed between her novitiate and Father Francis, from whom she now delivered to her the following letter: —

"As the first fruits of those joys and consolations which you may expect from the life you are now engaged in, I must acquaint you that Theodosius, whose death sits so heavily upon your thoughts, is still alive; and that the father to whom you have confessed yourself, was once that Theodosius whom you so much lament. The love which we have had for one another will make us more happy in its disappointment than it could have done in its success. Providence has disposed of us for our advantage, though not according to our wishes. Consider your Theodosius still as dead, but assure yourself of one who will not cease to pray for you in father

"FRANCIS."

Constantia saw that the handwriting agreed with the contents of the letter; and upon reflecting upon the voice of the person, the behavior, and above all the extreme sorrow of the father during her confession, she discovered Theodosius in every particular. After having wept with tears of joy, "It is enough," says she; "Theodosius is still in being; I shall live with comfort and die in peace."

The letters which the father sent her afterward are yet extant in the nunnery where she resided, and are often read to the young religious, in order to inspire them with good resolutions and sentiments of virtue. It so happened that, after Constantia had lived about ten years in the cloister, a violent fever broke out in the place, which swept away great multitudes, and among others, Theodosius. Upon his deathbed he sent his benediction in a very moving manner to Constantia, who at that time was so far gone in the same fatal distemper that she lay delirious. Upon the interval which generally precedes death in sickness of this nature, the abbess, finding that the physicians had given her over, told her that Theodosius was just gone before her, and that he had sent her his benediction in his last moments. Constantia received it with pleasure. "And now," says she, "if I do not ask anything improper, let me be buried by Theodosius. My vow reaches no farther than the grave: what I ask is, I hope, no violation of it." — She died soon after, and was interred according to her request.

Their tombs are still to be seen, with a short Latin inscription over them to the following purpose: —

"Here lie the bodies of Father Francis and Sister Constance. They were lovely in their lives, and in their deaths they were not divided."

NOTE. — This story has several situations which are dramatic in themselves, but which the writer does not present dramatically. One or another of these might have been taken as the center of a true short-story. Modern readers are likely to dismiss the tale as dull, simply because the writer did not know how to get the full effect of his material. He failed to select a central situation or a central character and to focus the interest of the reader on this. In fact this tale is an excellent example of the story which is short but which is not a short-story.

IV. RIP VAN WINKLE

By Washington Irving (1783-1859)

Irving was the earliest American writer to win fame outside of his own country; and it was fit that he should be liked in England, because he was heir of the British essayists, — Steele and Addison and Goldsmith. His "Sketch-Book," published in 1819-1820, was a miscellany of essays, sketches, and stories, including "Rip Van Winkle," which is Irving's masterpiece in fiction. Although it seems to have been suggested by a German folk-tale, Irving made the legend his own by a fuller appreciation of its possibilities. He told it with a characteristic blending of quaint pathos and of lambent humor. He placed his lovable vagabond in the Catskills, and by so doing he gave us what is perhaps the first American short-story of local color.

RIP VAN WINKLE

A POSTHUMOUS WRITING OF DIEDRICH KNICKERBOCKER

(The following tale was found among the papers of the late Diedrich Knickerbocker, an old gentleman of New

York, who was very curious in the Dutch history of the province, and the manners of the descendants from its primitive settlers. His historical researches, however, did not lie so much among books as among men; for the former are lamentably scanty on his favorite topics; whereas he found the old burghers, and still more their wives, rich in that legendary lore so invaluable to true history. Whenever, therefore, he happened upon a genuine Dutch family, snugly shut up in its low-roofed farmhouse, under a spreading sycamore, he looked upon it as a little clasped volume of black-letter, and studied it with the zeal of a bookworm.

The result of all these researches was a history of the province during the reign of the Dutch governors, which he published some years since. There have been various opinions as to the literary character of his work, and, to tell the truth, it is not a whit better than it should be. Its chief merit is its scrupulous accuracy, which indeed was a little questioned on its first appearance, but has since been completely established; and it is now admitted into all historical collections as a book of unquestionable authority.

The old gentleman died shortly after the publication of his work, and now that he is dead and gone it cannot do much harm to his memory to say that his time might have been much better employed in weightier labors. He, however, was apt to ride his hobby in his own way; and though it did now and then kick up the dust a little in the eyes of his neighbors and grieve the spirit of some friends, for whom he felt the truest deference and affection, yet his errors and follies are remembered "more in sorrow than in anger"; and it begins to be suspected that he never intended to injure or offend. But however his memory may be appreciated by critics, it is still held dear among many folk whose good opinion is well worth having; particularly by certain biscuit bakers, who have gone so far as to imprint his likeness on their New Year cakes, and have thus given him a chance for immortality, almost equal to the being stamped on a Waterloo medal or a Queen Anne's farthing.)

By Woden, God of Saxons,
From whence comes Wensday, that is Wodensday,
Truth is a thing that ever I will keep
Unto thylke day in which I creep into
My sepulchre —   CARTWRIGHT.

Whoever has made a voyage up the Hudson must remember the Catskill Mountains. They are a dismembered branch of the great Appalachian family, and are seen away to the west of the river, swelling up to a noble height, and lording it over the surrounding country. Every change of season, every change of weather, indeed, every hour of the day, produces some change in the magical hues and shapes of these mountains, and they are regarded by all the good wives, far and near, as perfect barometers. When the weather is fair and settled, they are clothed in blue and purple, and print their bold outlines on the clear evening sky; but sometimes, when the rest of the landscape is cloudless, they will gather a hood of gray vapors about their summits, which, in the last rays of the setting sun, will glow and light up like a crown of glory.

At the foot of these fairy mountains the voyager may have descried the light smoke curling up from a village whose shingle roofs gleam among the trees, just where the blue tints of the upland melt away into the fresh green of the nearer landscape. It is a little village of great antiquity, having been founded by some of the Dutch colonists, in the early times of the province, just about the beginning of the government of the good Peter Stuyvesant (may he rest in peace!), and there were some of the houses of the original settlers standing within a few years, with lattice windows, gable fronts surmounted with weathercocks, and built of small yellow bricks brought from Holland.

In that same village, and in one of these very houses (which, to tell the precise truth, was sadly time-worn and weather-beaten), there lived many years since, while the country was yet a province of Great Britain, a simple, good-natured fellow, of the name of Rip Van Winkle. He was a descendant of the Van Winkles who figured so gallantly in the chivalrous days of Peter Stuyvesant, and accompanied him to the siege of Fort Christina. He inherited, however, but little of the martial character of his ancestors. I have observed that he was a simple, good-natured man; he was, moreover, a kind neighbor and an obedient, henpecked husband. Indeed, to the latter circumstance might be owing that meekness of spirit which gained him such universal popularity; for those men are most apt to be obsequious and conciliating abroad who are under the discipline of shrews at home. Their tempers, doubtless, are rendered pliant and malleable in the fiery furnace of domestic tribulation, and a curtain lecture is worth all the sermons in the world for teaching the virtues of patience and long-suffering. A termagant wife may, therefore, in some respects, be considered a tolerable blessing; and if so, Rip Van Winkle was thrice blessed.

Certain it is that he was a great favorite among all the good wives of the village, who, as usual with the amiable sex, took his part in all family squabbles, and never failed, whenever they talked those matters over in their evening gossipings, to lay all the blame on Dame Van Winkle. The children of the village, too, would shout with joy whenever he approached. He assisted at their sports, made their playthings, taught them to fly kites and shoot marbles, and told them long stories of ghosts, witches, and Indians. Whenever he went dodging about the village, he was surrounded by a troop of them, hanging on his skirts, clambering on his back, and playing a thousand tricks on him with impunity; and not a dog would bark at him throughout the neighborhood.

The great error in Rip's composition was an insuperable aversion to all kinds of profitable labor. It could not be from the want of assiduity or perseverance; for he would sit on a wet rock, with a rod as long and heavy as a Tartar's lance, and fish all day without a murmur, even though he should not be encouraged by a single nibble. He would carry a fowling piece on his shoulder, for hours together, trudging through woods and swamps, and up hill and down dale, to shoot a few squirrels or wild pigeons. He would never even refuse to assist a neighbor in the roughest toil, and was a foremost man at all country frolics for husking Indian corn, or building stone fences. The women of the village, too, used to employ him to run their errands, and to do such little odd jobs as their less obliging husbands would not do for them; in a word, Rip was ready to attend to anybody's business but his own; but as to doing family duty, and keeping his farm in order, it was impossible.

In fact, he declared it was of no use to work on his farm; it was the most pestilent little piece of ground in the whole country; everything about it went wrong, and would go wrong, in spite of him. His fences were continually falling to pieces; his cow would either go astray or get among the cabbages; weeds were sure to grow quicker in his fields than anywhere else; the rain always made a point of setting in just as he had some outdoor work to do; so that though his patrimonial estate had dwindled away under his management, acre by acre, until there was little more left than a mere patch of Indian corn and potatoes, yet it was the worst-conditioned farm in the neighborhood.

His children, too, were as ragged and wild as if they belonged to nobody. His son Rip, an urchin begotten in his own likeness, promised to inherit the habits, with the old clothes of his father. He was generally seen trooping like a colt at his mother's heels, equipped in a pair of his father's cast-off galligaskins, which he had much ado to hold up with one hand, as a fine lady does her train in bad weather.

Rip Van Winkle, however, was one of those happy mortals, of foolish, well-oiled dispositions, who take the world easy, eat white bread or brown, whichever can be got with least thought or trouble, and would rather starve on a penny than work for a pound. If left to himself, he would have whistled life away, in perfect contentment; but his wife kept continually dinning in his ears about his idleness, his carelessness, and the ruin he was bringing on his family. Morning, noon, and night, her tongue was incessantly going, and everything he said or did was sure to produce a torrent of household eloquence. Rip had but one way of replying to all lectures of the kind, and that, by frequent use, had grown into a habit. He shrugged his shoulders, shook his head, cast up his eyes, but said nothing. This, however, always provoked a fresh volley from his wife, so that he was fain to draw off his forces, and take to the outside of the house — the only side which, in truth, belongs to a henpecked husband.

Rip's sole domestic adherent was his dog Wolf, who was as much henpecked as his master; for Dame Van Winkle regarded them as companions in idleness, and even looked upon Wolf with an evil eye, as the cause of his master's so often going astray. True it is, in all points of spirit befitting an honorable dog, he was as courageous an animal as ever scoured the woods — but what courage can withstand the ever-during and all-besetting terrors of a woman's tongue? The moment Wolf entered the house his crest fell, his tail drooped to the ground, or curled between his legs; he sneaked about with a gallows air, casting many a sidelong glance at Dame Van Winkle, and at the least flourish of a broomstick or ladle would fly to the door with yelping precipitation.

Times grew worse and worse with Rip Van Winkle as

years of matrimony rolled on; a tart temper never mellows with age, and a sharp tongue is the only edged tool that grows keener by constant use. For a long while he used to console himself, when driven from home, by frequenting a kind of perpetual club of the sages, philosophers, and other idle personages of the village, which held its sessions on a bench before a small inn, designated by a rubicund portrait of his majesty George the Third. Here they used to sit in the shade, of a long lazy summer's day, talking listlessly over village gossip, or telling endless sleepy stories about nothing. But it would have been worth any statesman's money to have heard the profound discussions which sometimes took place, when by chance an old newspaper fell into their hands, from some passing traveler. How solemnly they would listen to the contents, as drawled out by Derrick Van Bummel, the schoolmaster, a dapper, learned little man, who was not to be daunted by the most gigantic word in the dictionary; and how sagely they would deliberate upon public events some months after they had taken place.

The opinions of this junto were completely controlled by Nicholas Vedder, a patriarch of the village, and landlord of the inn, at the door of which he took his seat from morning till night, just moving sufficiently to avoid the sun, and keep in the shade of a large tree; so that the neighbors could tell the hour by his movements as accurately as by a sun-dial. It is true, he was rarely heard to speak, but smoked his pipe incessantly. His adherents, however (for every great man has his adherents), perfectly understood him, and knew how to gather his opinions. When anything that was read or related displeased him, he was observed to smoke his pipe vehemently, and send forth short, frequent, and angry puffs; but when pleased, he would inhale the smoke slowly and tranquilly, and emit it in light and placid clouds, and sometimes taking the pipe from his mouth, and letting the fragrant vapor curl about his nose, would gravely nod his head in token of perfect approbation.

From even this stronghold the unlucky Rip was at length routed by his termagant wife, who would suddenly break in upon the tranquillity of the assemblage, and call the members all to nought; nor was that august personage, Nicholas Vedder himself, sacred from the daring tongue of this terrible virago, who charged him outright with encouraging her husband in habits of idleness.

Poor Rip was at last reduced almost to despair; and his only alternative, to escape from the labor of the farm and clamor of his wife, was to take gun in hand and stroll away into the woods. Here he would sometimes seat himself at the foot of a tree, and share the contents of his wallet with Wolf, with whom he sympathized as a fellow-sufferer in persecution. "Poor Wolf," he would say, "thy mistress leads thee a dog's life of it; but never mind, my lad, while I live thou shalt never want a friend to stand by thee!" Wolf would wag his tail, look wistfully in his master's face, and if dogs can feel pity, I verily believe he reciprocated the sentiment with all his heart.

In a long ramble of the kind on a fine autumnal day, Rip had unconsciously scrambled to one of the highest parts of the Catskill Mountains. He was after his favorite sport of squirrel shooting, and the still solitudes had echoed and reëchoed with the reports of his gun.

Panting and fatigued, he threw himself, late in the afternoon, on a green knoll, covered with mountain herbage, that crowned the brow of a precipice. From an opening between the trees he could overlook all the lower country for many a mile of rich woodland. He saw at a distance the lordly Hudson, far, far below him, moving on its silent but majestic course, the reflection of a purple cloud, or the sail of a lagging bark, here and there sleeping on its glassy bosom, and at last losing itself in the blue highlands.

On the other side he looked down into a deep mountain glen, wild, lonely, and shagged, the bottom filled with fragments from the impending cliffs, and scarcely lighted by the reflected rays of the setting sun. For some time Rip lay musing on this scene; evening was gradually advancing; the mountains began to throw their long blue shadows over the valleys; he saw that it would be dark long before he could reach the village, and he heaved a heavy sigh when he thought of encountering the terrors of Dame Van Winkle.

As he was about to descend, he heard a voice from a distance, hallooing, "Rip Van Winkle! Rip Van Winkle!" He looked around, but could see nothing but a crow winging its solitary flight across the mountain. He thought his fancy must have deceived him, and turned again to descend, when he heard the same cry ring through the still evening air: "Rip Van Winkle! Rip Van Winkle!" — at the same time Wolf bristled up his back, and giving a low growl, skulked to his master's side, looking fearfully down into the glen. Rip now felt a vague apprehension stealing over him; he looked anxiously in the same direction, and perceived a strange figure slowly toiling up the rocks, and bending under the weight of something he carried on his back. He was surprised to see any human being in this lonely and unfrequented place, but supposing it to be some one of the neighborhood in need of assistance, he hastened down to yield it.

On nearer approach, he was still more surprised at the singularity of the stranger's appearance. He was a short, square-built old fellow, with thick bushy hair, and a grizzled beard. His dress was of the antique Dutch fashion — a cloth jerkin strapped around the waist — several pair of breeches, the outer one of ample volume, decorated with rows of buttons down the sides, and bunches at the knees. He bore on his shoulders a stout keg, that seemed full of liquor, and made signs for Rip to approach and assist him with the load. Though rather shy and distrustful of this new acquaintance, Rip complied with his usual alacrity, and mutually relieving one another, they clambered up a narrow gully, apparently the dry bed of a mountain torrent. As they ascended, Rip every now and then heard long rolling peals, like distant thunder, that seemed to issue out of a deep ravine, or rather cleft between lofty rocks, toward which their rugged path conducted. He paused for an instant, but supposing it to be the muttering of one of those transient thunder showers which often take place in mountain heights, he proceeded. Passing through the ravine, they came to a hollow, like a small amphitheater, surrounded by perpendicular precipices, over the brinks of which impending trees shot their branches, so that you only caught glimpses of the azure sky and the bright evening cloud. During the whole time, Rip and his

RIP VAN WINKLE 87

companion had labored on in silence; for though the former marveled greatly what could be the object of carrying a keg of liquor up this wild mountain, yet there was something strange and incomprehensible about the unknown that inspired awe and checked familiarity.

On entering the amphitheater, new objects of wonder presented themselves. On a level spot in the center was a company of odd-looking personages playing at ninepins. They were dressed in a quaint, outlandish fashion: some wore short doublets, others jerkins, with long knives in their belts, and most had enormous breeches, of similar style with that of the guide's. Their visages, too, were peculiar: one had a large head, broad face, and small, piggish eyes; the face of another seemed to consist entirely of nose, and was surmounted by a white sugar-loaf hat set off with a little red cock's tail. They all had beards, of various shapes and colors. There was one who seemed to be the commander. He was a stout old gentleman, with a weather-beaten countenance; he wore a laced doublet, broad belt and hanger, high-crowned hat and feather, red stockings, and high-heeled shoes, with roses in them. The whole group reminded Rip of the figures in an old Flemish painting, in the parlor of Dominie Van Schaick, the village parson, and which had been brought over from Holland at the time of the settlement.

What seemed particularly odd to Rip, was that though these folks were evidently amusing themselves, yet they maintained the gravest faces, the most mysterious silence, and were, withal, the most melancholy party of pleasure he had ever witnessed. Nothing interrupted the stillness of the scene but the noise of the balls, which, whenever they were rolled, echoed along the mountains like rumbling peals of thunder.

As Rip and his companion approached them, they suddenly desisted from their play, and stared at him with such fixed statue-like gaze, and such strange, uncouth, lack-luster countenances, that his heart turned within him, and his knees smote together. His companion now emptied the contents of the keg into large flagons, and made signs to him to wait upon the company. He obeyed with fear and trembling; they quaffed the liquor in profound silence, and then returned to their game.

By degrees, Rip's awe and apprehension subsided. He even ventured, when no eye was fixed upon him, to taste the beverage, which he found had much of the flavor of excellent Hollands. He was naturally a thirsty soul, and was soon tempted to repeat the draught. One taste provoked another, and he reiterated his visits to the flagon so often, that at length his senses were overpowered, his eyes swam in his head, his head gradually declined, and he fell into a deep sleep.

On awaking, he found himself on the green knoll from whence he had first seen the old man of the glen. He rubbed his eyes — it was a bright sunny morning. The birds were hopping and twittering among the bushes, and the eagle was wheeling aloft and breasting the pure mountain breeze. "Surely," thought Rip, "I have not slept here all night." He recalled the occurrences before he fell asleep. The strange man with a keg of liquor — the mountain ravine — the wild retreat among the rocks — the woe-begone party at ninepins — the flagon —

"Oh! that flagon! that wicked flagon!" thought Rip — "what excuse shall I make to Dame Van Winkle?"

He looked round for his gun, but in place of the clean, well-oiled fowling piece, he found an old firelock lying by him, the barrel incrusted with rust, the lock falling off, and the stock worm-eaten. He now suspected that the grave roysters of the mountain had put a trick upon him, and having dosed him with liquor, had robbed him of his gun. Wolf, too, had disappeared, but he might have strayed away after a squirrel or partridge. He whistled after him, shouted his name, but all in vain; the echoes repeated his whistle and shout, but no dog was to be seen.

He determined to revisit the scene of the last evening's gambol, and if he met with any of the party, to demand his dog and gun. As he rose to walk, he found himself stiff in the joints, and wanting in his usual activity. "These mountain beds do not agree with me," thought Rip, "and if this frolic should lay me up with a fit of the rheumatism, I shall have a blessed time with Dame Van Winkle." With some difficulty he got down into the glen; he found the gully up which he and his companion had ascended the preceding evening; but to his astonishment a mountain stream was now foaming down it, leaping from rock to rock, and filling the glen with babbling murmurs. He, however, made shift to scramble up its sides, working his toilsome way through thickets of birch, sassafras, and witch-hazel, and sometimes tripped up or entangled by the wild grape vines that twisted their coils and tendrils from tree to tree, and spread a kind of network in his path.

At length he reached to where the ravine had opened through the cliffs to the amphitheater; but no traces of such opening remained. The rocks presented a high, impenetrable wall, over which the torrent came tumbling in a sheet of feathery foam, and fell into a broad, deep basin, black from the shadows of the surrounding forest. Here, then, poor Rip was brought to a stand. He again called and whistled after his dog; he was only answered by the cawing of a flock of idle crows, sporting high in air about a dry tree that overhung a sunny precipice; and who, secure in their elevation, seemed to look down and scoff at the poor man's perplexities. What was to be done? the morning was passing away, and Rip felt famished for want of his breakfast. He grieved to give up his dog and gun; he dreaded to meet his wife; but it would not do to starve among the mountains. He shook his head, shouldered the rusty firelock, and, with a heart full of trouble and anxiety, turned his steps homeward.

As he approached the village, he met a number of people, but none whom he knew, which somewhat surprised him, for he had thought himself acquainted with every one in the country round. Their dress, too, was of a different fashion from that to which he was accustomed. They all stared at him with equal marks of surprise, and whenever they cast their eyes upon him, invariably stroked their chins. The constant recurrence of this gesture induced Rip, involuntarily, to do the same, when, to his astonishment, he found his beard had grown a foot long!

He had now entered the skirts of the village. A troop of strange children ran at his heels, hooting after him, and pointing at his gray beard. The dogs, too, none of which he recognized for his old acquaintances, barked at him as he passed. The very village was altered: it was larger and more populous. There were rows of houses which he had never seen before, and those which had been his familiar haunts had disappeared. Strange names were over the doors — strange faces at the windows — everything was strange. His mind now began to misgive him; he doubted whether both he and the world around him were not bewitched. Surely this was his native village, which he had left but the day before. There stood the Catskill Mountains — there ran the silver Hudson at a distance — there was every hill and dale precisely as it had always been — Rip was sorely perplexed — "That flagon last night," thought he, "has addled my poor head sadly!"

It was with some difficulty he found the way to his own house, which he approached with silent awe, expecting every moment to hear the shrill voice of Dame Van Winkle. He found the house gone to decay — the roof fallen in, the windows shattered, and the doors off the hinges. A half-starved dog, that looked like Wolf, was skulking about it. Rip called him by name, but the cur snarled, showed his teeth, and passed on. This was an unkind cut indeed — "My very dog," sighed poor Rip, "has forgotten me!"

He entered the house, which, to tell the truth, Dame Van Winkle had always kept in neat order. It was empty, forlorn, and apparently abandoned. This desolateness overcame all his connubial fears — he called loudly for his wife and children — the lonely chambers rung for a moment with his voice, and then all again was silence.

He now hurried forth, and hastened to his old resort, the little village inn — but it too was gone. A large rickety wooden building stood in its place, with great gaping windows, some of them broken, and mended with old hats and petticoats, and over the door was painted, "The Union Hotel, by Jonathan Doolittle." Instead of the great tree which used to shelter the quiet little Dutch inn of yore, there now was reared a tall naked pole, with something on the top that looked like a red nightcap, and from it was fluttering a flag, on which was a singular assemblage of stars and stripes — all this was strange and incomprehensible. He recognized on the sign, however, the ruby face of King George, under which he had smoked so many a peaceful pipe, but even this was singularly metamorphosed. The red coat was changed for one of blue and buff, a sword was stuck in the hand instead of a scepter, the head was decorated with a cocked hat, and underneath was painted in large characters, GENERAL WASHINGTON.

There was, as usual, a crowd of folk about the door, but none whom Rip recollected. The very character of the people seemed changed. There was a busy, bustling, disputatious tone about it, instead of the accustomed phlegm and drowsy tranquillity. He looked in vain for the sage Nicholas Vedder, with his broad face, double chin, and fair long pipe, uttering clouds of tobacco smoke instead of idle speeches; or Van Bummel, the schoolmaster, doling forth the contents of an ancient newspaper. In place of these, a lean, bilious-looking fellow, with his pockets full of handbills, was haranguing vehemently about rights of citizens — election — members of Congress — liberty — Bunker's Hill — heroes of '76 — and other words, that were a perfect Babylonish jargon to the bewildered Van Winkle.

The appearance of Rip, with his long grizzled beard, his rusty fowling piece, his uncouth dress, and the army of women and children that had gathered at his heels, soon attracted the attention of the tavern politicians. They crowded around him, eying him from head to foot, with great curiosity. The orator bustled up to him, and drawing him partly aside, inquired " on which side he voted?" Rip stared in vacant stupidity. Another short but busy little fellow pulled him by the arm, and raising on tiptoe, inquired in his ear, " whether he was Federal or Democrat." Rip was equally at a loss to comprehend the question; when a knowing, self-important old gentleman, in a sharp cocked hat, made his way through the crowd, putting them to the right and left with his elbows as he passed, and planting himself before Van Winkle, with one arm akimbo, the other resting on his cane, his keen eyes and sharp hat penetrating, as it were, into his very soul, demanded, in an austere tone, " what brought him to the election with a gun on his shoulder, and a mob at his heels, and whether he meant to breed a riot in the village?" "Alas! gentlemen," cried Rip, somewhat dismayed, "I am a poor quiet man, a native of the place, and a loyal subject of the king, God bless him!"

Here a general shout burst from the bystanders — " A Tory! a Tory! a spy! a refugee! hustle him! away with him!" It was with great difficulty that the self-important man in the cocked hat restored order; and having assumed a tenfold austerity of brow, demanded again of the unknown culprit, what he came there for, and whom he was seeking. The poor man humbly assured him that he meant no harm; but merely came there in search of some of his neighbors, who used to keep about the tavern.

"Well — who are they? — name them."

Rip bethought himself a moment, and then inquired, "Where's Nicholas Vedder?"

There was silence for a little while, when an old man replied in a thin, piping voice, "Nicholas Vedder? why, he is dead and gone these eighteen years! There was a wooden tombstone in the churchyard that used to tell all about him, but that's rotted and gone, too."

"Where's Brom Dutcher?"

"Oh, he went off to the army in the beginning of the war; some say he was killed at the battle of Stony Point — others say he was drowned in a squall, at the foot of Antony's Nose. I don't know — he never came back again."

"Where's Van Bummel, the schoolmaster?"

"He went off to the wars, too, was a great militia general, and is now in Congress."

Rip's heart died away, at hearing of these sad changes in his home and friends, and finding himself thus alone in the world. Every answer puzzled him, too, by treating of such enormous lapses of time, and of matters which he could not understand: war — Congress — Stony Point! — he had no courage to ask after any more friends, but cried out in despair, "Does nobody here know Rip Van Winkle?"

"Oh, Rip Van Winkle!" exclaimed two or three, "Oh, to be sure! that's Rip Van Winkle yonder, leaning against the tree."

Rip looked, and beheld a precise counterpart of himself, as he went up the mountain: apparently as lazy, and certainly as ragged. The poor fellow was now completely confounded. He doubted his own identity, and whether he was himself or another man. In the midst of his bewilderment, the man in the cocked hat demanded who he was, and what was his name?

"God knows," exclaimed he, at his wit's end; "I'm not myself — I'm somebody else — that's me yonder — no — that's somebody else, got into my shoes — I was myself last night, but I fell asleep on the mountain, and they've changed my gun, and everything's changed, and I'm changed, and I can't tell what's my name, or who I am!"

The bystanders began now to look at each other, nod, wink significantly, and tap their fingers against their foreheads. There was a whisper, also, about securing the gun, and keeping the old fellow from doing mischief; at the very suggestion of which, the self-important man in the cocked hat retired with some precipitation. At this critical moment a fresh, likely woman pressed through the throng to get a peep at the gray-bearded man. She had a chubby child in her arms, which, frightened at his looks, began to cry. "Hush, Rip," cried she, "hush, you little fool, the old man won't hurt you." The name of the child, the air of the mother, the tone of her voice, all awakened a train of recollections in his mind. "What is your name, my good woman?" asked he.

"Judith Gardenier."

"And your father's name?"

"Ah, poor man, his name was Rip Van Winkle; it's twenty years since he went away from home with his gun, and never has been heard of since — his dog came home without him; but whether he shot himself, or was carried away by the Indians, nobody can tell. I was then but a little girl."

Rip had but one question more to ask; but he put it with a faltering voice: —

"Where's your mother?"

"Oh, she too had died but a short time since; she broke a blood vessel in a fit of passion at a New England peddler."

There was a drop of comfort, at least, in this intelligence. The honest man could contain himself no longer. — He caught his daughter and her child in his arms. — "I am your father!" cried he — "Young Rip Van Winkle once — old Rip Van Winkle now! — Does nobody know poor Rip Van Winkle!"

All stood amazed, until an old woman, tottering out from among the crowd, put her hand to her brow, and peering under it in his face for a moment, exclaimed, "Sure enough! it is Rip Van Winkle — it is himself. Welcome home again, old neighbor. — Why, where have you been these twenty long years?"

Rip's story was soon told, for the whole twenty years had been to him but as one night. The neighbors stared when they heard it; some were seen to wink at each other, and put their tongues in their cheeks; and the self-important man in the cocked hat, who, when the alarm was over, had returned to the field, screwed down the corners of his mouth, and shook his head — upon which there was a general shaking of the head throughout the assemblage.

It was determined, however, to take the opinion of old Peter Vanderdonk, who was seen slowly advancing up the road. He was a descendant of the historian of that name, who wrote one of the earliest accounts of the province. Peter was the most ancient inhabitant of the village, and well versed in all the wonderful events and traditions of the neighborhood. He recollected Rip at once, and corroborated his story in the most satisfactory manner. He assured the company that it was a fact, handed down from his ancestor the historian, that the Catskill Mountains had always been haunted by strange beings. That it was affirmed that the great Hendrick Hudson, the first discoverer of the river and country, kept a kind of vigil there every twenty years, with his crew of the *Half-Moon*, being permitted in this way to revisit the scenes of his enterprise, and keep a guardian eye upon the river, and the great city called by his name. That his father had once seen them in their old Dutch dresses playing at ninepins in a hollow of the mountain; and that he himself had heard, one summer afternoon, the sound of their balls, like long peals of thunder.

To make a long story short, the company broke up, and returned to the more important concerns of the election. Rip's daughter took him home to live with her; she had a snug, well-furnished house, and a stout cheery farmer for a husband, whom Rip recollected for one of the urchins that used to climb upon his back. As to Rip's son and heir, who was the ditto of himself, seen leaning against the tree, he was employed to work on the farm; but evinced an hereditary disposition to attend to anything else but his business.

Rip now resumed his old walks and habits; he soon found many of his former cronies, though all rather the worse for the wear and tear of time; and preferred making friends among the rising generation, with whom he soon grew into great favor.

Having nothing to do at home, and being arrived at that happy age when a man can do nothing with impunity, he took his place once more on the bench, at the inn door, and was reverenced as one of the patriarchs of the village, and a chronicle of the old times " before the war." It was some time before he could get into the regular track of gossip, or could be made to comprehend the strange events that had taken place during his torpor. How that there had been a revolutionary war — that the country had thrown off the yoke of old England — and that, instead of being a subject of his Majesty, George III., he was now a free citizen of the United States. Rip, in fact, was no politician; the changes of states and empires made but little impression on him; but there was one species of despotism under which he had long groaned, and that was — petticoat government; happily, that was at an end; he had got his neck out of the yoke of matrimony, and could go in and out whenever he pleased, without dreading the tyranny of Dame Van Winkle. Whenever her name was mentioned, however, he shook his head, shrugged his shoulders, and cast up his eyes ; which might pass either for an expression of resignation to his fate, or joy at his deliverance.

He used to tell his story to every stranger that arrived at Dr. Doolittle's hotel. He was observed, at first, to vary on some points every time he told it, which was, doubtless, owing to his having so recently awaked. It at last settled down precisely to the tale I have related, and not a man, woman, or child in the neighborhood but knew it by heart. Some always pretended to doubt the reality of it, and insisted that Rip had been out of his head, and this was one point on which he always remained flighty. The old Dutch inhabitants, however, almost universally gave it full credit. Even to this day they never hear a thunder-storm of a summer afternoon, about the Catskills, but they say Hendrick Hudson and his crew are at their game of ninepins ; and it is a common wish of all henpecked husbands in the neighborhood, when life hangs heavy on their hands, that they might have a quieting draught out of Rip Van Winkle's flagon.

NOTE. — The foregoing tale, one would suspect, had been suggested to Mr. Knickerbocker by a little German superstition about the Emperor Frederick and the Kypphauser Mountain ; the subjoined note, however, which he had appended to the tale, shows that it is an absolute fact, narrated with his usual fidelity.

"The story of Rip Van Winkle may seem incredible to many, but nevertheless I give it my full belief, for I know the vicinity of our old Dutch settlements to have been very subject to marvelous events and appearances. Indeed, I have heard many stranger stories than this, in the villages along the

Hudson; all of which were too well authenticated to admit of a doubt. I have even talked with Rip Van Winkle myself, who, when last I saw him, was a very venerable old man, and so perfectly rational and consistent on every other point, that I think no conscientious person could refuse to take this into the bargain; nay, I have seen a certificate on the subject taken before a country justice and signed with a cross, in the justice's own handwriting. The story, therefore, is beyond the possibility of a doubt.

"D. K."

POSTSCRIPT [1]. — The following are traveling notes from a memorandum book of Mr. Knickerbocker: —

The Kaatsberg, or Catskill Mountains, have always been a region full of fable. The Indians considered them the abode of spirits, who influenced the weather, spreading sunshine or clouds over the landscape, and sending good or bad hunting seasons. They were ruled by an old squaw spirit, said to be their mother. She dwelt on the highest peak of the Catskills, and had charge of the doors of day and night to open and shut them at the proper hour. She hung up the new moon in the skies, and cut up the old ones into stars. In times of drought, if properly propitiated, she would spin light summer clouds out of cobwebs and morning dew, and send them off from the crest of the mountain, flake after flake, like flakes of carded cotton, to float in the air; until, dissolved by the heat of the sun, they would fall in gentle showers, causing the grass to spring, the fruits to ripen, and the corn to grow an inch an hour. If displeased, however, she would brew up clouds black as ink, sitting in the midst of them like a bottle-bellied spider in the midst of its web; and when these clouds broke, woe betide the valleys!

In old times, say the Indian traditions, there was a kind of

---

[1] Not in the first edition.

Manitou or Spirit, who kept about the wildest recesses of the Catskill Mountains, and took a mischievous pleasure in wreaking all kinds of evils and vexations upon the red men. Sometimes he would assume the form of a bear, a panther, or a deer, lead the bewildered hunter a weary chase through tangled forests and among ragged rocks; and then spring off with a loud ho! ho! leaving him aghast on the brink of a beetling precipice or raging torrent.

The favorite abode of this Manitou is still shown. It is a great rock or cliff on the loneliest part of the mountains, and, from the flowering vines which clamber about it, and the wild flowers which abound in its neighborhood, is known by the name of the Garden Rock. Near the foot of it is a small lake, the haunt of the solitary bittern, with water snakes basking in the sun on the leaves of the pond lilies which lie on the surface. This place was held in great awe by the Indians, insomuch that the boldest hunter would not pursue his game within its precincts. Once upon a time, however, a hunter who had lost his way, penetrated to the Garden Rock, where he beheld a number of gourds placed in the crotches of trees. One of these he seized, and made off with it, but in the hurry of his retreat he let it fall among the rocks, when a great stream gushed forth, which washed him away and swept him down precipices, where he was dashed to pieces, and the stream made its way to the Hudson, and continues to flow to the present day; being the identical stream known by the name of Kaaterskill.

NOTE. — The telling of this tale is leisurely, as was Irving's habit. He was in no hurry, and he liked to linger by the wayside. He said that he considered "a story merely a frame on which to stretch the materials"; and he aimed at "the play of thought and sentiment and language" and "the familiar exhibition of scenes in common life." This is why his stories, delightful as they are, lack something of the swiftness, of the directness, and of the compactness which we find in the later masters of the short-story form. And yet Irving has here attained the fundamental unity of tone; and "Rip Van Winkle" marks a distinct step in the development of the short-story. Irving had pointed out the path; and those who followed in his footsteps were able to attain a more vigorous simplicity by avoiding the digressions in which he delighted.

V. DREAM–CHILDREN; A REVERY

By Charles Lamb (1775–1834)

Lamb is the heir of the eighteenth-century essayists, but with a richer imagination and a more delicate sensibility. He is an essayist rather than a story-teller, — an essayist of an intense individuality. But he could dream dreams as the other poets have done; and here is one of them, contained in the "Essays of Elia," published in 1822.

DREAM–CHILDREN; A REVERY

Children love to listen to stories about their elders, when *they* were children; to stretch their imagination to the conception of a traditionary great-uncle or grandame, whom they never saw. It was in this spirit that my little ones crept about me the other evening to hear about their great-grandmother Field, who lived in a great house in Norfolk (a hundred times bigger than that in which they and papa lived) which had been the scene — so at least it was generally believed in that part of the country — of the tragic incidents which they had lately become familiar with from the ballad of the Children in the Wood. Certain it is that the whole story of the children and their cruel uncle was to be seen fairly carved out in wood upon the chimney-piece of the great hall, the whole story down to the Robin Redbreasts, till a foolish rich person pulled it down to set up a marble one of modern invention in its stead, with no story upon it. Here Alice put out one of her dear mother's looks, too tender to be called upbraiding. Then I went on to say, how religious and how good their great-grandmother Field was, how beloved and respected by everybody, though she was not indeed the mistress of this great house, but had only the charge of it (and yet in some respects she might be said to be the mistress of it too) committed to her by the owner, who preferred living in a newer and more fashionable mansion which he had purchased somewhere in the adjoining county; but still she lived in it in a manner as if it had been her own, and kept up the dignity of the great house in a sort while she lived, which afterward came to decay, and was nearly pulled down, and all its old ornaments stripped and carried away to the owner's other house, where they were set up, and looked as awkward as if some one were to carry away the old tombs they had seen lately at the Abbey, and stick them up in Lady C.'s tawdry gilt drawing-room. Here John smiled, as much as to say, "that would be foolish indeed." And then I told how, when she came to die, her funeral was attended by a concourse of all the poor, and some of the gentry too, of the neighborhood for many miles round, to show their respect for her memory, because she had been such a good and religious woman; so good indeed that she knew all the Psaltery by heart, aye, and a great part of the Testament besides. Here little Alice spread her hands. Then I told what a tall, upright, graceful person their great-grandmother Field once was; and how in her youth she was esteemed the best dancer — here Alice's little right foot played an involuntary movement, till upon my looking grave, it desisted — the best dancer, I was saying, in the county, till a cruel disease, called a cancer, came, and bowed her down with pain; but it could never bend her good spirits, or make them stoop, but they were still upright, because she was so good and religious. Then I told how she was used to sleep by herself in a lone chamber of the great lone house; and how she believed that an apparition of two infants was to be seen at midnight gliding up and down the great staircase near where she slept, but she said " those innocents would do her no harm "; and how frightened I used to be, though in those days I had my maid to sleep with me, because I was never half so good or religious as she — and yet I never saw the infants. Here John expanded all his eyebrows and tried to look courageous. Then I told how good she was to all her grand-children, having us to the great house in the holidays, where I in particular used to spend many hours by myself, in gazing upon the old busts of the Twelve Cæsars, that had been Emperors of Rome, till the old marble heads would seem to live again, or I to be turned into marble with them; how I never could be tired with roaming about that huge mansion, with its vast empty rooms, with their worn-out hangings, fluttering tapestry, and carved oaken panels, with the gilding almost rubbed out — sometimes in the spacious old-fashioned gardens, which I had almost to myself, unless when now and then a solitary gardening man would cross me — and how the nectarines and peaches hung upon the walls, without my ever offering to pluck them, because they were forbidden fruit, unless now and then, — and because I had more pleasure in strolling about among the old melancholy-looking yew trees, or the firs, and picking up the red berries, and the fir apples, which were good for nothing but to look at — or in lying about upon the fresh grass, with all the fine garden smells around me — or basking in the orangery, till I could almost fancy myself ripening, too, along with the oranges and the limes in that grateful warmth — or in watching the dace that darted to and fro in the fish pond, at the bottom of the garden, with here and there a great sulky pike hanging midway down the water in silent state, as if it mocked at their impertinent friskings, — I had more pleasure in these busy-idle diversions than in all the sweet flavors of peaches, nectarines, oranges, and such like common baits of children. Here John slyly deposited back upon the plate a bunch of grapes, which, not unobserved by Alice, he had meditated dividing with her, and both seemed willing to relinquish them for the present as irrelevant. Then, in somewhat a more heightened tone, I told how, though their great-grandmother Field loved all her grandchildren, yet in an especial manner she might be said to love their uncle, John L——, because he was so handsome and spirited a youth, and a king to the rest of us; and, instead of moping about in solitary corners, like some of us, he would mount the most mettlesome horse he could get, when but an imp no bigger than themselves, and make it carry him half over the county in a morning, and join the hunters when there were any out — and yet he loved the old great house and gardens too, but had too much spirit to be always pent up within their boundaries

— and how their uncle grew up to man's estate as brave as he was handsome, to the admiration of everybody, but of their great-grandmother Field most especially; and how he used to carry me upon his back when I was a lame-footed boy — for he was a good bit older than me — many a mile when I could not walk for pain; — and how in after life he became lame-footed too, and I did not always (I fear) make allowances enough for him when he was impatient, and in pain, nor remember sufficiently how considerate he had been to me when I was lame-footed; and how when he died, though he had not been dead an hour, it seemed as if he had died a great while ago, such a distance there is betwixt life and death; and how I bore his death as I thought pretty well at first, but afterward it haunted and haunted me; and though I did not cry or take it to heart as some do, and as I think he would have done if I had died, yet I missed him all day long, and knew not till then how much I had loved him. I missed his kindness, and I missed his crossness, and wished him to be alive again, to be quarreling with him (for we quarreled sometimes), rather than not have him again, and was as uneasy without him, as he their poor uncle must have been when the doctor took off his limb. Here the children fell a crying, and asked if their little mourning which they had on was not for uncle John, and they looked up and prayed me not to go on about their uncle, but to tell them some stories about their pretty, dead mother. Then I told them how for seven long years, in hope sometimes, sometimes in despair, yet persisting ever, I courted the fair Alice W———n; and, as much as children could understand, I explained to them what coyness, and difficulty, and denial meant in maidens — when suddenly, turning to Alice, the soul of the first Alice looked out at her eyes with such a reality of re-presentment, that I became in doubt which of them stood there before me, or whose that bright hair was; and while I stood gazing, both the children gradually grew fainter to my view, receding, and still receding till nothing at last but two mournful features were seen in the uttermost distance, which, without speech, strangely impressed upon me the effects of speech: "We are not of Alice, nor of thee, nor are we children at all. The children of Alice call Bartrum father. We are nothing; less than nothing, and dreams. We are only what might have been, and must wait upon the tedious shores of Lethe millions of ages before we have existence, and a name" — and immediately awaking, I found myself quietly seated in my bachelor armchair, where I had fallen asleep, with the faithful Bridget unchanged by my side — but John L. (or James Elia) was gone forever.

NOTE. — This is hardly a story at all; it is so slight in substance and in texture; it is a revery only. Yet it has its movement and its climax; it makes only a single impression; and thus it is seen to have certain of the essential qualities of the true short-story.

VI. WANDERING WILLIE'S TALE

By WALTER SCOTT (1771–1832)

SCOTT relished rather the free amplitude of the novel than the compression of the short-story; and it is only by accident that he adventured himself in the briefer form. Strictly speaking, his one masterpiece is not exactly a short-story, since it is only a narrative placed in the mouth of one of the characters in "Redgauntlet." The novel was published in 1824; and perhaps "Wandering Willie's Tale" is what it is because Scott had read "Rip Van Winkle" four or five years earlier. Scott had a high regard for Irving's tales; and he praised one of them as a fantasy equal to the best German attempts at the eerie and uncanny. The Scotsman here achieves the same commingling of the humorous and the supernatural that the American had already essayed successfully.

WANDERING WILLIE'S TALE

"Honest folks like me! How do ye ken whether I am honest, or what I am? I may be the deevil himsell for what ye ken, for he has power to come disguised like an angel of light; and, besides, he is a prime fiddler. He played a sonata to Corelli, ye ken."

There was something odd in this speech, and the tone in which it was said. It seemed as if my companion was not always in his constant mind, or that he was willing to try if he could frighten me. I laughed at the extravagance of his language, however, and asked him in reply if he was fool enough to believe that the foul fiend would play so silly a masquerade.

"Ye ken little about it — little about it," said the old man, shaking his head and beard, and knitting his brows. "I could tell ye something about that."

What his wife mentioned of his being a tale-teller as well as a musician now occurred to me; and as, you know, I like tales of superstition, I begged to have a specimen of his talent as we went along.

"It is very true," said the blind man, "that when I am tired of scraping thairm or singing ballants I whiles make a tale serve the turn among the country bodies; and I have some fearsome anes, that make the auld carlines shake on the settle, and the bits o' bairns skirl on their minnies out frae their beds. But this that I am going to tell you was a thing that befell in our ain house in my father's time — that is, my father was then a hafflins callant; and I tell it to you, that it may be a lesson to you that are but a young thoughtless chap, wha ye draw up wi' on a lonely road; for muckle was the dool and care that came o' 't to my gudesire."

He commenced his tale accordingly, in a distinct narrative tone of voice, which he raised and depressed with considerable skill; at times sinking almost into a whisper, and turning his clear but sightless eyeballs upon my face, as if it had been possible for him to witness the impression which his narrative made upon my features. I will not spare a syllable of it, although it be of the longest; so I make a dash — and begin: —

Ye maun have heard of Sir Robert Redgauntlet of that ilk, who lived in these parts before the dear years. The country will lang mind him; and our fathers used to draw breath thick if ever they heard him named. He was out wi' the Hielandmen in Montrose's time; and again he was in the hills wi' Glencairn in the saxteen hundred and fifty-twa; and sae when King Charles the Second came in, wha was in sic favor as the laird of Redgauntlet? He was knighted at Lonon Court, wi' the king's ain sword; and being a red-hot prelatist, he came down here, rampauging like a lion, with commissions of lieutenancy (and of lunacy, for what I ken), to put down a' the Whigs and Covenanters in the country. Wild wark they made of it; for the Whigs were as dour as the Cavaliers were fierce, and it was which should first tire the other. Redgauntlet was aye for the strong hand; and his name is kend as wide in the country as Claverhouse's or Tam Dalyell's. Glen, nor dargle, nor mountain, nor cave could hide the puir hill-folk when Redgauntlet was out with bugle and bloodhound after them, as if they had been sae mony deer. And, troth, when they fand them, they didna make muckle mair ceremony than a Hielandman wi' a roebuck. It was just, "Will ye tak' the test?" If not — "Make ready — present — fire!" and there lay the recusant.

Far and wide was Sir Robert hated and feared. Men thought he had a direct compact with Satan; that he was proof against steel, and that bullets happed aff his buff-coat like hailstanes from a hearth; that he had a mear that would turn a hare on the side of Carrifra-gauns; and muckle to the same purpose, of whilk mair anon. The best blessing they wared on him was, "Deil scowp wi' Redgauntlet!" He wasna a bad master to his ain folk, though, and was weel aneugh liked by his tenants; and as for the lackeys and troopers that rade out wi' him to the persecutions, as the Whigs caa'd those killing-times, they wad hae drunken themsells blind to his health at ony time.

Now you are to ken that my gudesire lived on Redgauntlet's grund — they ca' the place Primrose Knowe. We had lived on the grund, and under the Redgauntlets, since the riding days, and lang before. It was a pleasant bit; and I think the air is calleror and fresher there than onywhere else in the country. It's a' deserted now; and I sat on the broken doorcheek three days since, and was glad I couldna see the plight the place was in — but that's a' wide o' the mark. There dwelt my gudesire, Steenie Steenson; a rambling, rattling chiel' he had been in his young days, and could play weel on the pipes; he was famous at "hoopers and girders," a' Cumberland couldna touch him at "Jockie Lattin," and he had the finest finger for the back-lilt between Berwick and Carlisle. The like o' Steenie wasna the sort that they made Whigs o'. And so he became a Tory, as they ca' it, which we now ca' Jacobites, just out of a kind of needcessity, that he might belang to some side or other.

He had nae ill-will to the Whig bodies, and liked little to see the blude rin, though, being obliged to follow Sir Robert in hunting and hoisting, watching and warding, he saw muckle mischief, and maybe did some that he couldna avoid.

Now Steenie was a kind of favorite with his master, and kend a' the folk about the castle, and was often sent for to play the pipes when they were at their merriment. Auld Dougal MacCallum, the butler, that had followed Sir Robert through gude and ill, thick and thin, pool and stream, was specially fond of the pipes, and aye gae my gudesire his gude word wi' the laird; for Dougal could turn his master round his finger.

Weel, round came the Revolution, and it had like to hae broken the hearts baith of Dougal and his master. But the change was not a'thegether sae great as they feared and other folk thought for. The Whigs made an unco crawing what they wad do with their auld enemies, and in special wi' Sir Robert Redgauntlet. But there were owermony great folks dipped in the same doings to make a spick-and-span new warld. So Parliament passed it a' ower easy; and Sir Robert, bating that he was held to hunting foxes instead of Covenanters, remained just the man he was. His revel was as loud, and his hall as weel lighted, as ever it had been, though maybe he lacked the fines of the nonconformists, that used to come to stock his larder and cellar; for it is certain he began to be keener about the rents than his tenants used to find him before, and they behooved to be prompt to the rent day, or else the laird wasna pleased. And he was sic an awsome body that naebody cared to anger him;

for the oaths he swore, and the rage that he used to get into, and the looks that he put on made men sometimes think him a devil incarnate.

Weel, my gudesire was nae manager — no that he was a very great misguider — but he hadna the saving gift, and he got twa terms' rent in arrear. He got the first brash at Whitsunday put ower wi' fair word and piping; but when Martinmas came there was a summons from the grund officer to come wi' the rent on a day preceese, or else Steenie behooved to flit. Sair wark he had to get the siller; but he was weel freended, and at last he got the haill scraped thegether — a thousand merks. The maist of it was from a neighbor they caa'd Laurie Lapraik — a sly tod. Laurie had wealth o' gear, could hunt wi' the hound and rin wi' the hare, and be Whig or Tory, saunt or sinner, as the wind stood. He was a professor in this Revolution warld, but he liked an orra sough of this warld, and a tune on the pipes, weel aneugh at a by-time; and, bune a', he thought he had gude security for the siller he len my gudesire ower the stocking at Primrose Knowe.

Away trots my gudesire to Redgauntlet Castle wi' a heavy purse and a light heart, glad to be out of the laird's danger. Weel, the first thing he learned at the castle was that Sir Robert had fretted himsell into a fit of the gout because he did no appear before twelve o'clock. It wasna a'thegether for sake of the money, Dougal thought, but because he didna like to part wi' my gudesire aff the grund. Dougal was glad to see Steenie, and brought him into the great oak parlor; and there sat the laird his leesome lane, excepting thar he had beside him a great, ill-favored jackanape that was a special pet of his. A cankered beast it was, and mony an ill-natured trick it played; ill to please it was, and easily angered — ran about the haill castle, chattering and rowling, and pinching and biting folk, specially before ill weather, or disturbance in the state. Sir Robert caa'd it Major Weir, after the warlock that was burnt; and few folk liked either the name or the conditions of the creature — they thought there was something in it by ordinar — and my gudesire was not just easy in mind when the door shut on him, and he saw himsell in the room wi' naebody but the laird, Dougal MacCullum, and the major — a thing that hadna chanced to him before.

Sir Robert sat, or, I should say, lay, in a great armchair, wi' his grand velvet gown, and his feet on a cradle; for he had baith gout and gravel, and his face looked as gash and ghastly as Satan's. Major Weir sat opposite to him, in a red-laced coat, and the laird's wig on his head; and aye as Sir Robert girned wi' pain, the jackanape girned too, like a sheep's head between a pair of tangs — an ill-faur'ed, fearsome couple they were. The laird's buff-coat was hung on a pin behind him, and his broadsword and his pistols within reach; for he keepit up the auld fashion of having the weapons ready, and a horse saddled day and night, just as he used to do when he was able to loup on horseback, and sway after ony of the hill-folk he could get speerings of. Some said it was for fear of the Whigs taking vengence, but I judge it was just his auld custom — he wasna gine not fear onything. The rental book, wi' its black cover and brass clasps, was lying beside him; and a book of sculduddery sangs was put betwixt the leaves, to keep it open at the place where it bore evidence against the goodman of Primrose Knowe, as behind the hand with his mails and duties. Sir Robert gave my gudesire a look, as if he would have withered his heart in his bosom. Ye maun ken he had a way of bending his brows that men saw the visible mark of a horseshoe in his forehead, deep-dinted, as if it had been stamped there.

"Are ye come light-handed, ye son of a toom whistle?" said Sir Robert. "Zounds! if you are —"

My gudesire, with as gude a countenance as he could put on, made a leg, and placed the bag of money on the table wi' a dash, like a man that does something clever. The laird drew it to him hastily. "Is all here, Steenie, man?"

"Your honor will find it right," said my gudesire.

"Here, Dougal," said the laird, "gie Steenie a tass of brandy, till I count the siller and write the receipt."

But they werena weel out of the room when Sir Robert gied a yelloch that garr'd the castle rock. Back ran Dougal; in flew the liverymen; yell on yell gied the laird, ilk ane mair awfu' than the ither. My gudesire knew not whether to stand or flee, but he ventured back into the parlor, where a' was gaun hirdie-girdie — naebody to say "come in" or "gae out." Terribly the laird roared for cauld water to his feet, and wine to cool his throat; and "Hell, hell, hell, and its flames," was aye the word in his mouth. They brought him water, and when they plunged his swoln feet into the tub, he cried out it was burning; and folks say that it *did* bubble and sparkle like a seething caldron. He flung the cup at Dougal's head and said he had given him blood instead of Burgundy; and, sure aneugh, the lass washed clotted blood aff the carpet the neist day. The jackanape they caa'd Major Weir, it jibbered and cried as if it was mocking its master. My gudesire's head was like to turn; he forgot baith siller and receipt, and downstairs he banged; but, as he ran, the shrieks came fainter and fainter; there was a deep-drawn shivering groan, and word gaed through the castle that the laird was dead.

Weel, away came my gudesire wi' his finger in his mouth, and his best hope was that Dougal had seen the money bag and heard the laird speak of writing the receipt. The young laird, now Sir John, came from Edinburgh to see things put to rights. Sir John and his father never 'greed weel. Sir John had been bred an advocate, and afterward sat in the last Scots Parliament and voted for the Union, having gotten, it was thought, a rug of the compensations — if his father could have come out of his grave he would have brained him for it on his awn hearthstane. Some thought it was easier counting with the auld rough knight than the fair-spoken young ane — but mair of that anon.

Dougal MacCallum, poor body, neither grat nor graned, but gaed about the house looking like a corpse, but directing, as was his duty, a' the order of the grand funeral. Now Dougal looked aye waur and waur when night was coming, and was aye the last to gang to his bed, whilk was in a little round just opposite the chamber of dais, whilk his master occupied while he was living, and where he now lay in state, as they caa'd it, weeladay! The night before the funeral Dougal could keep his awn counsel nae longer;

he came doun wi' his proud spirit, and fairly asked auld Hutcheon to sit in his room with him for an hour. When they were in the round, Dougal took a tass of brandy to himsell, and gave another to Hutcheon, and wished him all health and lang life, and said that, for himsell, he wasna lang for this world; for that every night since Sir Robert's death his silver call had sounded from the state chamber just as it used to do at nights in his lifetime to call Dougal to help to turn him in his bed. Dougal said that, being alone with the dead on that floor of the tower (for naebody cared to wake Sir Robert Redgauntlet like another corpse), he had never daured to answer the call, but that now his conscience checked him for neglecting his duty; for, "though death breaks service," said MacCallum, "it shall never weak my service to Sir Robert; and I will answer his next whistle, so be you will stand by me, Hutcheon."

Hutcheon had nae will to the wark, but he had stood by Dougal in battle and broil, and he wad not fail him at this pinch; so doun the carles sat ower a stoup of brandy, and Hutcheon, who was something of a clerk, would have read a chapter of the Bible; but Dougal would hear naething but a blaud of Davie Lindsay, whilk was the waur preparation.

When midnight came, and the house was quiet as the grave, sure enough the silver whistle sounded as sharp and shrill as if Sir Robert was blowing it; and up got the twa auld serving men, and tottered into the room where the dead man lay. Hutcheon saw aneugh at the first glance; for there were torches in the room, which showed him the foul fiend, in his ain shape, sitting on the laird's coffin!

Ower he couped as if he had been dead. He could not tell how lang he lay in a trance at the door, but when he gathered himself he cried on his neighbor, and getting nae answer raised the house, when Dougal was found lying dead within twa steps of the bed where his master's coffin was placed. As for the whistle, it was gane anes and aye; but mony a time was it heard at the top of the house on the bartizan, and amang the auld chimneys and turrets where the howlets have their nests. Sir John hushed the matter up, and the funeral passed over without mair bogie wark.

But when a' was ower, and the laird was beginning to settle his affairs, every tenant was called up for his arrears, and my gudesire for the full sum that stood against him in the rental book. Weel, away he trots to the castle to tell his story, and there he is introduced to Sir John, sitting in his father's chair, in deep mourning, with weepers and hanging cravat, and a small walking rapier by his side, instead of the auld broadsword that had a hunderweight of steel about it, what with blade, chape, and basket hilt. I have heard their communings so often tauld ower that I almost think I was there mysell, though I couldna be born at the time. (In fact, Alan, my companion, mimicked, with a good deal of humor, the flattering, conciliating tone of the tenant's address and the hypocritical melancholy of the laird's reply. His grandfather, he said, had, while he spoke, his eye fixed on the rental book, as if it were a mastiff dog that he was afraid would spring up and bite him.)

"I wuss ye joy, sir, of the head seat and the white loaf and the brid lairdship. Your father was a kind man to freends and followers; muckle grace to you, Sir John, to fill his shoon — his boots, I suld say, for he seldom wore shoon, unless it were muils when he had the gout.

"Aye, Steenie," quoth the laird, sighing deeply, and putting his napkin to his een, "his was a sudden call, and he will be missed in the country; no time to set his house in order — weel prepared Godward, no doubt, which is the root of the matter; but left us behind a tangled hesp to wind, Steenie. Hem! hem! We maun go to business, Steenie; much to do, and little time to do it in."

Here he opened the fatal volume. I have heard of a thing they call Doomsday-book — I am clear it has been a rental of back-ganging tenants.

"Stephen," said Sir John, still in the same soft, sleekit tone of voice — "Stephen Stephenson, or Steenson, ye are down here for a year's rent behind the hand — due at last term."

Stephen. Please your honor, Sir John, I paid it to your father.

Sir John. Ye took a receipt, then, doubtless, Stephen, and can produce it?

Stephen. Indeed, I hadna time, and it like your honor; for nae sooner had I set doun the siller, and just as his honor, Sir Robert, that's gaen, drew it till him to count it and write out the receipt, he was ta'en wi' the pains that removed him.

"That was unlucky," said Sir John, after a pause. "But ye maybe paid it in the presence of somebody. I want but a *talis qualis* evidence, Stephen. I would go ower-strictly to work with no poor man."

Stephen. Troth, Sir John, there was naebody in the

room but Dougal MacCallum, the butler. But, as your honor kens, he has e'en followed his auld master.

"Very unlucky again, Stephen," said Sir John, without altering his voice a single note. "The man to whom ye paid the money is dead, and the man who witnessed the payment is dead, too; and the siller, which should have been to the fore, is neither seen nor heard tell of in the repositories. How am I to believe a' this?"

Stephen. I dinna ken, your honor; but there is a bit memorandum note of the very coins, for, God help me! I had to borrow out of twenty purses; and I am sure that ilka man there set down will take his grit oath for what purpose I borrowed the money.

Sir John. I have little doubt ye *borrowed* the money, Steenie. It is the *payment* that I want to have proof of.

Stephen. The siller maun be about the house, Sir John. And since your honor never got it, and his honor that was canna have ta'en it wi' him, maybe some of the family may hae seen it.

Sir John. We will examine the servants, Stephen; that is but reasonable.

But lackey and lass, and page and groom, all denied stoutly that they had ever seen such a bag of money as my gudesire described. What saw waur, he had unluckily not mentioned to any living soul of them his purpose of paying his rent. Ae quean had noticed something under his arm, but she took it for the pipes.

Sir John Redgauntlet ordered the servants out of the room, and then said to my gudesire: "Now, Steenie, ye see ye have fair play; and, as I have little doubt ye ken better where to find the siller than ony other body, I beg in fair terms, and for your own sake, that you will end this fasherie; for, Stephen, ye maun pay or flit."

"The Lord forgie your opinion," said Stephen, driven almost to his wit's end — "I am an honest man."

"So am I, Stephen," said his honor; "and so are all the folks in this house, I hope. But if there be a knave among us, it must be he that tells the story he cannot prove." He paused, and then added, mair sternly: "If I understand your trick, sir, you want to take advantage of some malicious reports concerning things in this family, and particularly respecting my father's sudden death, thereby to cheat me out of the money, and perhaps take away my character by insinuating that I have received the rent I am demanding. Where do you suppose this money to be? I insist upon knowing."

My gudesire saw everything look so muckle against him that he grew nearly desperate. However, he shifted from one foot to another, looked to every corner of the room, and made no answer.

"Speak out, sirrah," said the laird, assuming a look of his father's, a very particular ane, which he had when he was angry — it seemed as if the wrinkles of his frown made that selfsame fearful shape of a horse's shoe in the middle of his brow; "speak out, sir! I *will* know your thoughts; do you suppose that I have this money?"

"Far be it frae me to say so," said Stephen.

"Do you charge any of my people with having taken it?"

"I wad be laith to charge them that may be innocent," said my gudesire; "and if there be any one that is guilty, I have nae proof."

"Somewhere the money must be, if there is a word of

WANDERING WILLIE'S TALE

truth in your story," said Sir John; "I ask where you think it is — and demand a correct answer!"

"In hell, if you *will* have my thoughts of it," said my gudesire, driven to extremity — "in hell! with your father, his jackanape, and his silver whistle."

Down the stairs he ran (for the parlor was nae place for him after such a word) and he heard the laird swearing blood and wounds behind him, as fast as ever did Sir Robert, and roaring for the bailie and the baron-officer.

Away rode my gudesire to his chief creditor (him they caa'd Laurie Lapraik), to try if he could make onything out of him; but when he tauld his story, he got but the worst word in his wame — thief, beggar, and dyvour were the saftest terms; and to the boot of these hard terms, Laurie brought up the auld story of dipping his hand in the blood of God's saunts, just as if a tenant could have helped riding with the laird, and that a laird like Sir Robert Redgauntlet. My gudesire was, by this time, far beyond the bounds of patience, and, while he and Laurie were at deil speed the liars, he was wanchancie aneugh to abuse Lapraik's doctrine as weel as the man, and said things that garr'd folks' flesh grue that heard them — he wasna just himsell, and he had lived wi' a wild set in his day.

At last they parted, and my gudesire was to ride hame through the wood of Pitmurkie, that is a' fou of black firs, as they say. I ken the wood, but the firs may be black or white for what I can tell. At the entry of the wood there is a wild common, and on the edge of the common a little lonely change house, that was keepit then by an hostler wife — they suld hae caa'd her Tibbie Faw — and there puir Steenie cried for a mutchkin of brandy, for he had had no refreshment the haill day. Tibbie was earnest wi' him to take a bite of meat, but he couldna think o' 't, nor would he take his foot out of the stirrup, and took off the brandy wholely at twa draughts, and named a toast at each. The first was, the memory of Sir Robert Redgauntlet, and may he never lie quiet in his grave till he had righted his poor bond tenant; and the second was, a health to Man's Enemy, if he would but get him back the pock of siller, or tell him what came o' 't, for he saw the haill world was like to regard him as a thief and a cheat, and he took that waur than even the ruin of his house and hauld.

On he rode, little caring where. It was a dark night turned, and the trees made it yet darker, and he let the beast take its ain road through the wood; when all of a sudden, from tired and wearied that it was before, the nag began to spring and flee and stend, that my gudesire could hardly keep the saddle. Upon the whilk, a horseman, suddenly riding up beside him, said, "That's a mettle beast of yours, freend; will you sell him?" So saying, he touched the horse's neck with his riding wand, and it fell into its auld heigh-ho of a stumbling trot. "But his spunk's soon out of him, I think," continued the stranger, "and that is like mony a man's courage, that thinks he wad do great things."

My gudesire scarce listened to this, but spurred his horse, with "Gude-e'en to you, freend."

But it's like the stranger was ane that doesna lightly yield his point; for, ride as Steenie liked, he was aye beside him at the selfsame pace. At last my gudesire,

Steenie Steenson, grew half angry, and, to say the truth, half feard.

"What is it that you want with me, freend?" he said. "If ye be a robber, I have nae money; if ye be a leal man, wanting company, I have nae heart to mirth or speaking; and if ye want to ken the road, I scarce ken it mysell."

"If you will tell me your grief," said the stranger, "I am one that, though I have been sair miscaa'd in the world, am the only hand for helping my freends."

So my gudesire, to ease his ain heart, mair than from any hope of help, told him the story from beginning to end.

"It's a hard pinch," said the stranger; "but I think I can help you."

"If you could lend the money, sir, and take a lang day — I ken nae other help on earth," said my gudesire.

"But there may be some under the earth," said the stranger. "Come, I'll be frank wi' you; I could lend you the money on bond, but you would maybe scruple my terms. Now I can tell you that your auld laird is disturbed in his grave by your curses and the wailing of your family, and if ye daur venture to go to see him, he will give you the receipt."

My gudesire's hair stood on end at this proposal, but he thought his companion might be some humorsome chield that was trying to frighten him, and might end with lending him the money. Besides, he was bauld wi' brandy, and desperate wi' distress; and he said he had courage to go to the gate of hell, and a step farther, for that receipt. The stranger laughed.

Weel, they rode on through the thickest of the wood, when, all of a sudden, the horse stopped at the door of a great house; and, but that he knew the place was ten miles off, my father would have thought he was at Redgauntlet Castle. They rode into the outer courtyard, through the muckle faulding yetts, and aneath the auld portcullis; and the whole front of the house was lighted, and there were pipes and fiddles, and as much dancing and deray within as used to be at Sir Robert's house at Pace and Yule, and such high seasons. They lap off, and my gudesire, as seemed to him, fastened his horse to the very ring he had tied him to that morning when he gaed to wait on the young Sir John.

"God!" said my gudesire, "if Sir Robert's death be but a dream!"

He knocked at the ha' door just as he was wont, and his auld acquaintance, Dougal MacCallum — just after his wont, too — came to open the door, and said, "Piper Steenie, are ye there, lad? Sir Robert has been crying for you."

My gudesire was like a man in a dream — he looked for the stranger, but he was gane for the time. At last he just tried to say: "Ha! Dougal Driveower, are you living? I thought ye had been dead."

"Never fash yoursell wi' me," said Dougal, "but look to yoursell; and see ye tak' naething frae onybody here, neither meat, drink, or siller, except the receipt that is your ain."

So saying, he led the way out through halls and trances that were weel kend to my gudesire, and into the auld oak parlor; and there was as much singing of profane sangs, and birling of red wine, and blasphemy sculduddery as had ever been in Redgauntlet Castle when it was at the blythest.

But Lord take us in keeping! what a set of ghastly revelers there were that sat around that table! My gudesire kend mony that had long before gane to their place, for often had he piped to the most part in the hall of Redgauntlet. There was the fierce Middleton, and the dissolute Rothes, and the crafty Lauderdale; and Dalyell, with his bald head and a beard to his girdle; and Earlshall, with Cameron's blude on his hand; and wild Bonshaw, that tied blessed Mr. Cargill's limbs till the blude sprung; and Dumbarton Douglas, the twice-turned traitor baith to country and king. There was the Bludy Advocate MacKenzie, who, for his worldly wit and wisdom, had been to the rest as a god. And there was Claverhouse, as beautiful as when he lived, with his long, dark, curled locks streaming down over his laced buff-coat, and with his left hand always on his right spule-blade, to hide the wound that the silver bullet had made. He sat apart from them all, and looked at them with a melancholy, haughty countenance; while the rest hallooed and sang and laughed, and the room rang. But their smiles were fearfully contorted from time to time; and their laughter passed into such wild sounds as made my gudesire's very nails grow blue, and chilled the marrow in his banes.

They that waited at the table were just the wicked serving men and troopers that had done their work and cruel bidding on earth. There was the Lang Lad of the Nethertown, that helped to take Argyle; and the bishop's summoner, that they called the Deil's Rattlebag; and the wicked guardsmen in their laced coats; and the savage Highland Amorites, that shed blood like water; and mony a proud serving man, haughty of heart and bloody of hand, cringing to the rich, and making them wickeder than they would be; grinding the poor to powder when the rich had broken them to fragments. And mony, mony mair were coming and ganging, a' as busy in their vocation as if they had been alive.

Sir Robert Redgauntlet, in the midst of a' this fearful riot, cried, wi' a voice like thunder, on Steenie Piper to come to the board-head where he was sitting, his legs stretched out before him, and swathed up with flannel, with his holster pistols aside him, while the great broadsword rested against his chair, just as my gudesire had seen him the last time upon earth; the very cushion for the jackanape was close to him; but the creature itsell was not there — it wasna its hour, it's likely; for he heard them say, as he came forward, "Is not the major come yet?" And another answered, "The jackanape will be here betimes the morn." And when my gudesire came forward, Sir Robert, or his ghaist, or the deevil in his likeness, said, "Weel, piper, hae ye settled wi' my son for the year's rent?"

With much ado my father gat breath to say that Sir John would not settle without his honor's receipt.

"Ye shall hae that for a tune of the pipes, Steenie," said the appearance of Sir Robert — "play us up Weel Hoddled, Luckie."

Now this was a tune my gudesire learned frae a warlock, that heard it when they were worshiping Satan at their meetings; and my gudesire had sometimes played it at the ranting suppers in Redgauntlet Castle, but never very willingly; and now he grew cauld at the very name of it, and said, for excuse, he hadna his pipes wi' him.

"MacCallum, ye limb of Beelzebub," said the fearfu' Sir Robert, "bring Steenie the pipes that I am keeping for him!"

MacCallum brought a pair of pipes might have served the piper of Donald of the Isles. But he gave my gudesire a nudge as he offered them; and looking secretly and closely, Steenie saw that the chanter was of steel, and heated to a white heat; so he had fair warning not to trust his fingers with it. So he excused himsell again, and said he was faint and frightened, and had not wind aneugh to fill the bag.

"Then ye maun eat and drink, Steenie," said the figure; "for we do little else here; and it's ill speaking between a fou man and a fasting." Now these were the very words that the bloody Earl of Douglas said to keep the king's messenger in hand while he cut the head off MacLellan of Bombie, at the Threave Castle; and that put Steenie mair and mair on his guard. So he spoke up like a man, and said he came neither to eat nor drink, nor make minstrelsy; but simply for his ain — to ken what was come o' the money he had paid, and to get a discharge for it; and he was so stout-hearted by this time that he charged Sir Robert for conscience' sake (he had no power to say the holy name), and as he hoped for peace and rest, to spread no snares for him, but just to give him his ain.

The appearance gnashed its teeth and laughed, but it took from a large pocket-book the receipt, and handed it to Steenie. "There is your receipt, ye pitiful cur; and for the money, my dog-whelp of a son may go look for it in the Cat's Cradle."

My gudesire uttered mony thanks, and was about to retire, when Sir Robert roared aloud: "Stop, though, thou sack-doudling son of a —! I am not done with thee. HERE we do nothing for nothing; and you must return on this very day twelvemonth to pay your master the homage that you owe me for my protection."

My father's tongue was loosed of a suddenty, and he said aloud, " I refer myself to God's pleasure, and not to yours."

He had no sooner uttered the word than all was dark around him; and he sank on the earth with such a sudden shock that he lost both breath and sense.

How lang Steenie lay there he could not tell; but when he came to himsell he was lying in the auld kirkyard of Redgauntlet parochine, just at the door of the family aisle, and the scutcheon of the auld knight, Sir Robert, hanging over his head. There was a deep morning fog on grass and gravestane around him, and his horse was feeding quietly beside the ministers twa cows. Steenie would have thought the whole was a dream, but he had the receipt in his hand fairly written and signed by the auld laird; only the last letters of his name were a little disorderly, written like one seized with sudden pain.

Sorely troubled in his mind, he left that dreary place, rode through the mist to Redgauntlet Castle, and with much ado he got speech of the laird.

"Well, you dyvour bankrupt," was the first word, "have you brought me my rent?"

"No," answered my gudesire, "I have not; but I have brought your honor Sir Robert's receipt for it."

"How, sirrah? Sir Robert's receipt! You told me he had not given you one."

"Will your honor please to see if that bit line is right?"

Sir John looked at every line, and at every letter, with much attention; and at last at the date, which my gudesire had not observed — "From my appointed place," he read, "this twenty-fifth of November."

"What! That is yesterday! Villain, thou must have gone to hell for this!"

"I got it from your honor's father; whether he be in heaven or hell, I know not," said Steenie.

"I will debate you for a warlock to the Privy Council!" said Sir John. "I will send you to your master, the devil, with the help of a tar barrel and a torch!"

"I intend to debate mysell to the Presbytery," said Steenie, "and tell them all I have seen last night, whilk are things fitter for them to judge of than a borrel man like me."

Sir John paused, composed himself, and desired to hear the full history; and my gudesire told it him from point to point, as I have told it you — neither more nor less.

Sir John was silent again for a long time, and at last he said, very composedly: "Steenie, this story of yours concerns the honor of many a noble family besides mine; and if it be a leasing-making, to keep yoursell out of my danger, the least you can expect is to have a red-hot iron driven through your tongue, and that will be as bad as scaulding your fingers wi' a red-hot chanter. But yet it may be true, Steenie; and if the money cast up, I shall not know what to think of it. But where shall we find the Cat's Cradle? There are cats enough about the old house, but I think they kitten without the ceremony of bed or cradle."

"We were best ask Hutcheon," said my gudesire; "he kens a' the odd corners about as weel as — another serving man that is now gane, and that I wad not like to name."

Aweel, Hutcheon, when he was asked, told them that a ruinous turret lang disused, next to the clock house, only accessible by a ladder, for the opening was on the outside, above the battlements, was called of old the Cat's Cradle.

"There will I go immediately," said Sir John; and he took — with what purpose Heaven kens — one of his father's pistols from the hall table, where they had lain since the night he died, and hastened to the battlements.

It was a dangerous place to climb, for the ladder was auld and frail, and wanted ane or twa rounds. However, up got Sir John, and entered at the turret door, where his body stopped the only little light that was in the bit turret. Something flees at him wi' a vengeance, maist dang him back ower — bang! gaed the knight's pistol, and Hutcheon, that held the ladder, and my gudesire, that stood beside him, hears a loud skelloch. A minute after, Sir John flings the body of the jackanape down to them, and cries that the siller is fund, and that they should come up and help him. And there was the bag of siller sure aneugh, and mony orra thing besides, that had been missing for mony a day. And Sir John, when he had riped the turret weel, led my gudesire into the dining-parlor, and took him by the hand, and spoke kindly to him, and said he was sorry he should have doubted his word, and that he would hereafter be a good master to him, to make amends.

"And now, Steenie," said Sir John, "although this vision of yours tends, on the whole, to my father's credit as an honest man, that he should, even after his death, desire to see justice done to a poor man like you, yet you are sensible that ill-dispositioned men might make bad constructions upon it concerning his soul's health. So, I think, we had better lay the haill dirdum on that ill-deedie creature, Major Weir, and say naething about your dream in the wood of Pitmurkie. You had taen ower-muckle brandy to be very certain about onything; and, Steenie, this receipt"—his hand shook while he held it out—"it's but a queer kind of document, and we will do best, I think, to put it quietly in the fire."

"Od, but for as queer as it is, it's a' the voucher I have for my rent," said my gudesire, who was afraid, it may be, of losing the benefit of Sir Robert's discharge.

"I will bear the contents to your credit in the rental book, and give you a discharge under my own hand," said Sir John, "and that on the spot. And, Steenie, if you can hold your tongue about this matter, you shall sit, from this time downward, at an easier rent."

"Mony thanks to your honor," said Steenie, who saw easily in what corner the wind was; "doubtless I will be conformable to all your honor's commands; only I would willingly speak wi' some powerful minister on the subject, for I do not like the sort of soumons of appointment whilk your honor's father—"

"Do not call the phantom my father!" said Sir John, interrupting him.

"Well, then, the thing that was so like him," said my gudesire; "he spoke of my coming back to see him this time twelvemonth, and it's a weight on my conscience."

"Aweel, then," said Sir John, "if you be so much distressed in mind, you may speak to our minister of the parish; he is a douce man, regards the honor of our family, and the mair that he may look for some patronage from me."

Wi' that, my father readily agreed that the receipt should be burned; and the laird threw it into the chimney with his ain hand. Burn it would not for them, though; but away it flew up the lum, wi' a lang train of sparks at its tail, and a hissing noise like a squib.

My gudesire gaed down to the manse, and the minister, when he had heard the story, said it was his real opinion that, though my gudesire had gane very far in tampering with dangerous matters, yet as he had refused the devil's arles (for such was the offer of meat and drink), and had refused to do homage by piping at his bidding, he hoped that, if he held a circumspect walk hereafter, Satan could take little advantage by what was come and gane. And, indeed, my gudesire, of his ain accord, lang forswore baith the pipes and the brandy— it was not even till the year was out, and the fatal day past, that he would so much as take the fiddle or drink usquebaugh or tippenny.

Sir John made up his story about the jackanape as he liked himsell; and some believe till this day there was no more in the matter than the filching nature of the brute. Indeed, ye'll no hinder some to thread that it was nane o' the auld Enemy that Dougal and Hutcheon saw in the laird's room, but only that wanchancie creature the major, capering on the coffin; and that, as to the blawing on the laird's whistle that was heard after he was dead, the filthy brute could do that as weel as the laird himsell, if not better. But Heaven kens the truth, whilk first came out by the minister's wife, after Sir John and her ain gudeman were baith in the molds. And then my gudesire, wha was failed in his limbs, but not in his judgment or memory — at least nothing to speak of — was obliged to tell the real narrative to his freends, for the credit of his good name. He might else have been charged for a warlock.

The shades of evening were growing thicker around us as my conductor finished his long narrative with this moral: "You see, birkie, it is nae chancy thing to tak' a stranger traveler for a guide when you are in an uncouth land."

"I should not have made that inference," said I. "Your grandfather's adventure was fortunate for himself, whom it saved from ruin and distress; and fortunate for his landlord."

"Aye, but they had baith to sup the sauce o' 't sooner or later," said Wandering Willie; "what was fristed wasna forgiven. Sir John died before he was much over threescore; and it was just like of a moment's illness. And for my gudesire, though he departed in fullness of life, yet there was my father, a yauld man of forty-five, fell down betwixt the stilts of his plow, and rase never again, and left nae bairn but me, a puir, sightless, fatherless, motherless creature, could neither work nor want. Things gaed weel aneugh at first; for Sir Regwald Redgauntlet, the only son of Sir John and the oye of auld Sir Robert, and, wae 's me! the last of the honorable house, took the farm aff our hands, and brought me into his household to have care of me. My head never settled since I lost him; and if I say another word about it, deil a bar will I have the heart to play the night. Look out, my gentle chap," he resumed, in a different tone; "ye should see the lights at Brokenburn Glen by this time."

NOTE.—Generally Scott is an improviser, affluent, easy, and careless in his story-telling. Here he is careful and swift. He was interested in the tale he had invented; and he evidently did his best to set it forth as artistically as he could. One of his biographers, who has examined his proof-sheets, records that Scott took far more pains over those pages than was his custom. Scott notes that he had heard some such wild tale in his youth; and it may be that he had retold it orally more than once, —which would help to account for its directness when he came to amplify it as an episode in his novel.

VII. MATEO FALCONE

By Prosper Mérimée (1803–1870)

Mérimée was a scholar and a traveler; and he liked to present what he had imagined as though it was the casual result of his voyaging. A man of deep feeling, he veiled his emotion behind a mask of irony; and he told his stories with stark directness as though he had no sympathy with the creatures of his imagination. He knew Russian, and he had translated more than one tale by Pushkin and by Turgenieff; but he had none of the pity which is characteristic of the Russian writers. He had abundant invention, with a leaning toward tragedy, seized in its intensest aspects. These qualities are visible in "Mateo Falcone," published in 1829, as well as in the longer "Carmen."

MATEO FALCONE[1]

Coming out of Porto-Vecchio, and turning northwest toward the center of the island, the ground is seen to rise very rapidly, and, after three hours' walk by tortuous

[1] Translation printed by permission of Frank S. Holby, the publisher of the writings of Prosper Mérimée in English.

paths, blocked by large bowlders of rocks, and sometimes cut by ravines, the traveler finds himself on the edge of a very broad *mâquis*, or open plateau. These plateaus are the home of the Corsican shepherds, and the resort of those who have come in conflict with the law. The Corsican peasant sets fire to a certain stretch of forest to spare himself the trouble of manuring his lands: so much the worse if the flames spread further than is needed. Whatever happens, he is sure to have a good harvest by sowing upon this ground, fertilized by the ashes of the trees which grew on it. When the corn is gathered, the straw is left because it is too much trouble to gather. The roots, which remain in the earth without being consumed, sprout, in the following spring, into very thick shoots, which, in a few years, reach to a height of seven or eight feet. It is this kind of underwood which is called *mâquis*. It is composed of different kinds of trees and shrubs mixed up and entangled as in a wild state of nature. Only with hatchet in hand can a man open a way through it, and there are *mâquis* so dense and so thick that not even the wild sheep can penetrate them.

If you have killed a man, go into the *mâquis* of Porto-Vecchio, with a good gun and powder and shot, and you will live there in safety. Do not forget to take a brown cloak, furnished with a hood, which will serve as a coverlet and mattress. The shepherds will give you milk, cheese, chestnuts, and you will have nothing to fear from the hand of the law, nor from the relatives of the dead, except when you go down into town to renew your stock of ammunition.

When I was in Corsica in 18—, Mateo Falcone's house was half a league from this *mâquis*. He was a comparatively rich man for that country, living handsomely, that is to say, without doing anything, from the produce of his herds, which the shepherds, a sort of nomadic people, led to pasture here and there over the mountains. When I saw him, two years after the event that I am about to tell, he seemed about fifty years of age at the most. Imagine a small, but robust man, with jet-black, curly hair, an aquiline nose, thin lips, large piercing eyes, and a deeply tanned complexion. His skill in shooting passed for extraordinary, even in his country, where there are so many crack shots. For example, Mateo would never fire on a sheep with swanshot, but, at one hundred and twenty paces, he would strike it with a bullet in its head or shoulders as he chose. He could use his gun at night as easily as by day, and I was told the following examples of his adroitness, which will seem almost incredible to those who have not traveled in Corsica. A lighted candle was placed behind a transparent piece of paper, as large as a plate, at eighty paces off. He put himself into position, then the candle was extinguished, and in a minute's time, in complete darkness, he shot and pierced the paper three times out of four.

With this conspicuous talent Mateo Falcone had earned a great reputation. He was said to be a loyal friend, but a dangerous enemy; in other respects he was obliging and gave alms, and he lived at peace with everybody in the district of Porto-Vecchio. But it is told of him that when at Corte, where he had found his wife, he had very quickly freed himself of a rival reputed to be equally formidable in love as in war; at any rate, people attributed to Mateo a certain gunshot which surprised his rival while in the act of shaving before a small mirror hung in his window. After the affair had been hushed up, Mateo married. His wife Giuseppa at first presented him with three daughters, which enraged him, but finally a son came whom he named Fortunato; he was the hope of the family, the inheritor of its name. The girls were well married; their father could reckon in case of need upon the poniards and rifles of his sons-in-law. The son was only ten years old, but he had already shown signs of a promising disposition.

One autumn day Mateo and his wife set out early to visit one of their flocks in a clearing of the *mâquis*. Little Fortunato wanted to go with them, but the clearing was too far off; besides, it was necessary that some one should stay and mind the house; so his father refused. We shall soon see that he had occasion to repent of this.

He had been gone several hours, and little Fortunato was quietly lying out in the sunshine, looking at the blue mountains, and thinking that on the following Sunday he would be going to town to have dinner at his uncle's, the corporal,[1] when his meditations were suddenly interrupted

[1] Corporals were formerly the chief officers of the Corsican communes after they had rebelled against the feudal lords. To-day the name is still given sometimes to a man who, by his property, his connections, and his clients, exercises influence, and a kind of effective magistracy over a *pieve*, or canton. By an ancient custom Corsicans divide themselves into five castes: gentlemen (of whom some are of higher, *magnifiques*, some of lower, *signori*, estate), corporals, citizens, plebeians, and foreigners.

by the firing of a gun. He got up and turned toward that side of the plain from which the sound had proceeded. Other shots followed, fired at irregular intervals, and each time they came nearer and nearer until he saw a man on the path which led from the plain to Mateo's house. He wore a pointed cap like a mountaineer, he was bearded, and clothed in rags, and he dragged himself along with difficulty, leaning on his gun. He had just received a gunshot in the thigh.

This man was a *bandit* (Corsican for one who is proscribed) who, having set out at night to get some powder from the town, had fallen on the way into an ambush of Corsican soldiers.[1] After a vigorous defense he had succeeded in escaping, but they gave chase hotly, firing at him from rock to rock. He was only a little in advance of the soldiers, and his wound made it out of the question to reach the *mâquis* before being overtaken.

He came up to Fortunato and said : —

"Are you the son of Mateo Falcone?"

"Yes."

"I am Gianetto Sanpiero. I am pursued by the yellow-collars.[2] Hide me, for I cannot go any further."

"But what will my father say if I hide you without his permission?"

"He will say that you did right."

"How do you know?"

"Hide me quickly ; they are coming."

---

[1] *Voltigeurs :* a body raised of late years by the Government, which acts in conjunction with the gendarmes in the maintenance of order.

[2] The uniform of the *voltigeurs* was brown, with a yellow collar.

"Wait till my father returns."

"Good Lord! how can I wait? They will be here in five minutes. Come, hide me, or I will kill you."

Fortunato answered with the utmost coolness: —

"Your gun is unloaded, and there are no more cartridges in your *carchera*."[1]

"I have my stiletto."

"But could you run as fast as I can?"

With a bound he put himself out of reach.

"You are no son of Mateo Falcone! Will you let me be taken in front of his house?"

The child seemed moved.

"What will you give me if I hide you?" he said, drawing nearer.

The bandit felt in the leather pocket that hung from his side and took out a five-franc piece, which he had put aside, no doubt, for powder. Fortunato smiled at the sight of the piece of silver, and, seizing hold of it, he said to Gianetto: —

"Don't be afraid."

He quickly made a large hole in a haystack which stood close by the house, Gianetto crouched down in it, and the child covered him up so as to leave a little breathing space, and yet in such a way as to make it impossible for any one to suspect that the hay concealed a man. He acted, further, with the ingenious cunning of the savage. He fetched a cat and her kittens and put them on top of the haystack to make believe that it had not been touched for a long time. Then he carefully covered over

[1] A leather belt which served the joint purposes of a cartridge box and pocket for dispatches and orders.

with dust the blood stains which he had noticed on the path near the house, and, this done, he lay down again in the sun with the utmost sang-froid.

Some minutes later six men with brown uniform with yellow collars, commanded by an adjutant, stood before Mateo's door. This adjutant was a distant relative of the Falcones. (It is said that further degrees of relationship are recognized in Corsica than anywhere else.) His name was Tidora Gamba; he was an energetic man, greatly feared by the banditti, and had already hunted out many of them.

"Good day, youngster," he said, coming up to Fortunato. "How you have grown! Did you see a man pass just now?"

"Oh, I am not yet so tall as you, cousin," the child replied, with a foolish look.

"You soon will be. But tell me, have you not seen a man pass by?"

"Have I seen a man pass by?"

"Yes, a man with a pointed black velvet cap and a waistcoat embroidered in red and yellow."

"A man with a pointed cap and a waistcoat embroidered in scarlet and yellow?"

"Yes; answer sharply, and don't repeat my questions."

"The priest passed our door this morning on his horse Piero. He asked me how papa was, and I replied — "

"You are making game of me, you rascal. Tell me at once, which way Gianetto went, for it is he we are after; I am certain he took this path."

"How do you know that?"

"How do I know that? I know you have seen him."

"How can one see passers-by when one is asleep?"

"You were not asleep, you little demon; the gunshots would wake you."

"You think, then, cousin, that your guns make noise enough? My father's rifle makes much more noise."

"May the devil take you, you young scamp. I am absolutely certain you have seen Gianetto. Perhaps you have hidden him. Here, you fellows, go into the house, and see if our man is not there. He could only walk on one foot, and he has too much common sense, the villain, to have tried to reach the *máquis* limping. Besides, the traces of blood stop here."

"Whatever will papa say?" Fortunato asked, with a chuckle. "What will he say when he finds out that his house has been searched during his absence?"

"Do you know that I can make you change your tune, you scamp?" cried the adjutant Gamba, seizing him by the ear. "Perhaps you will speak when you have had a thrashing with the flat of a sword."

Fortunato kept on laughing derisively.

"My father is Mateo Falcone," he said significantly.

"Do you know, you young scamp, that I can take you away to Corte or to Bastia? I shall put you in a dungeon, on a bed of straw, with your feet in irons, and I shall guillotine you if you do not tell me where Gianetto Sanpiero is."

The child burst out laughing at this ridiculous menace.

"My father is Mateo Falcone," he repeated.

"Adjutant, do not let us embroil ourselves with Mateo," one of the soldiers whispered.

Gamba was evidently embarrassed. He talked in a low

voice with his soldiers, who had already been all over the house. It was not a lengthy operation, for a Corsican hut only consists of a single square room. The furniture comprises a table, benches, boxes, and utensils for cooking and hunting. All this time little Fortunato caressed his cat, and seemed, maliciously, to enjoy the confusion of his cousin and the soldiers.

One soldier came up to the haycock. He looked at the cat and carelessly stirred the hay with his bayonet, shrugging his shoulders as though he thought the precaution ridiculous. Nothing moved, and the face of the child did not betray the least agitation.

The adjutant and his band were in despair; they looked solemnly out over the plain, half inclined to turn the way they had come; but their chief, convinced that threats would produce no effect upon the son of Falcone, thought he would make one last effort by trying the effect of favors and presents.

"My boy," he said, "you are a wide-awake young dog, I can see. You will get on. But you play a dangerous game with me; and, if I did not want to give pain to my cousin Mateo, devil take it! I would carry you off with me."

"Bah!"

"But, when my cousin returns I shall tell him all about it, and he will give you the whip till he draws blood for having told me lies."

"How do you know that?"

"You will see. But, look here, be a good lad, and I will give you something."

"You had better go and look for Gianetto in the

mâquis, cousin, for if you stay any longer it will take a cleverer fellow than you to catch him."

The adjutant drew a watch out of his pocket, a silver watch worth quite ten crowns. He watched how little Fortunato's eyes sparkled as he looked at it, and he held out the watch at the end of its steel chain.

"You rogue," he said, you would like to have such a watch as this hung round your neck, and to go and walk up and down the streets of Porto-Vecchio as proud as a peacock; people would ask you the time, and you would reply, look at my watch!"

"When I am grown up, my uncle the corporal will give me a watch."

"Yes; but your uncle's son has one already — not such a fine one as this, however — for he is younger than you."

The boy sighed.

"Well, would you like this watch, kiddy?"

Fortunato ogled the watch out of the corner of his eyes, just as a cat does when a whole chicken is given to it. It dares not pounce upon the prey, because it is afraid a joke is being played on it, but it turns its eyes away now and then, to avoid succumbing to the temptation, licking its lips all the time as though to say to its master, "What a cruel joke you are playing on me!"

The adjutant Gamba, however, seemed really willing to give the watch. Fortunato did not hold out his hand; but he said to him with a bitter smile : —

"Why do you make fun of me?"

"I swear I am not joking. Only tell me where Gianetto is, and this watch is yours."

Fortunato smiled incredulously, and fixed his black eyes on those of the adjutant. He tried to find in them the faith he would fain have in his words.

"May I lose my epaulets," cried the adjutant, "if I do not give you the watch upon that condition! I call my men to witness, and then I cannot retract."

As he spoke, he held the watch nearer and nearer until it almost touched the child's pale cheeks. His face plainly expressed the conflict going on in his mind between covetousness and the claims of hospitality. His bare breast heaved violently almost to suffocation. All the time the watch dangled and twisted and even hit the tip of his nose. By degrees he raised his right hand toward the watch, his finger ends touched it; and its whole weight rested on his palm, although the adjutant still held the end of the chain loosely. . . . The watch face was blue. . . . The case was newly polished. . . . It seemed blazing in the sun like fire. . . . The temptation was too strong.

Fortunato raised his left hand at the same time, and pointed with his thumb over his shoulder to the haycock against which he was leaning. The adjutant understood him immediately, and let go the end of the chain. Fortunato felt himself sole possessor of the watch. He jumped up with the agility of a deer, and stood ten paces distant from the haycock, which the soldiers at once began to upset.

It was not long before they saw the hay move, and a bleeding man came out, poniard in hand; when, however, he tried to rise to his feet, his stiffening wound prevented him from standing. He fell down. The adjutant threw himself upon him and snatched away his dagger. He was speedily and strongly bound, in spite of his resistance.

Gianetto was bound and laid on the ground like a bundle of fagots. He turned his head toward Fortunato, who had come up to him.

"Son of —," he said to him, more in contempt than in anger.

The boy threw to him the silver piece that he had received from him, feeling conscious that he no longer deserved it; but the outlaw took no notice of the action. He merely said in a low voice to the adjutant: —

"My dear Gamba, I cannot walk; you will be obliged to carry me to the town."

"You could run as fast as a kid just now," his captor retorted brutally. "But don't be anxious; I am glad enough to have caught you; I would carry you for a league on my own back and not feel tired. All the same, my friend, we will make a litter for you out of the branches and your cloak. The farm at Crespoli will provide us with horses."

"All right," said the prisoner; "I hope you will put a little straw on your litter to make it easier for me."

While the soldiers were busy, some making a rough stretcher out of chestnut boughs, and others dressing Gianetto's wound, Mateo Falcone and his wife suddenly appeared in a turning of the path from the *mâquis*. The wife came in, bending laboriously under the weight of a huge sack of chestnuts; while her husband jaunted up, carrying his gun in one hand, and a second gun slung in his shoulder belt. It is considered undignified for a man to carry any other burden but his weapons.

MATEO FALCONE

When he saw the soldiers, Mateo's first thought was that they had come to arrest him. But he had no ground for this fear; he had never quarreled with the law. On the contrary, he bore a good reputation. He was, as the saying is, particularly well thought of. But he was a Corsican, and mountain bred, and there are but few Corsican mountaineers who, if they search their memories sufficiently, cannot recall some little peccadillo, some gunshot, or dagger thrust, or such like bagatelle. Mateo's conscience was clearer than most, for it was fully ten years since he had pointed his gun at any man; yet at the same time he was cautious, and he prepared to make a brave defense if needs be.

"Wife, put down your sack," he said, "and keep yourself in readiness."

She obeyed immediately. He gave her the gun which was slung over his shoulder, as it was likely to be the one that would inconvenience him the most. He held the other gun in readiness and proceeded leisurely toward the house by the side of the trees which bordered the path, ready to throw himself behind the largest trunk for cover, and to fire at the least sign of hostility. His wife walked close behind him, holding her reloaded gun and her cartridges. It was the duty of a good housewife, in case of a conflict, to reload her husband's arms.

On his side, the adjutant was very uneasy at the sight of Mateo advancing thus upon them with measured steps, his gun pointed and finger on trigger.

"If it happens that Gianetto is related to Mateo," thought he, "or he is his friend, and he means to protect him, two of his bullets will be put into two of us as sure as a letter goes to the post, and he will aim at me in spite of our kinship! . . ."

In this perplexity, he put on a bold face and went forward alone toward Mateo to tell him what had happened, greeting him like an old acquaintance. But the brief interval which separated him from Mateo seemed to him of terribly long duration.

"Hullo! Ah! my old comrade," he called out. "How are you, old fellow? I am your cousin Gamba."

Mateo did not say a word, but stood still; and while the other was speaking, he softly raised the muzzle of his rifle in such a manner that by the time the adjutant came up to him it was pointing skyward.

"Good day, brother,"[1] said the adjutant, holding out his hand. "It is a very long time since I saw you."

"Good day, brother."

"I just called in when passing to say 'good day' to you and cousin Pepa. We have done a long tramp to-day; but we must not complain of fatigue, for we have taken a fine catch. We have got hold of Gianetto Sanpiero."

"Thank Heaven!" exclaimed Giuseppa. "He stole one of our milch goats last week."

Gamba rejoiced at these words.

"Poor devil!" said Mateo, "he was hungry."

"The fellow fought like a lion," continued the adjutant, slightly nettled. "He killed one of the men, and, not content to stop there, he broke Corporal Chardon's arm; but that is not of much consequence, for he is only a Frenchman. . . . Then he hid himself so

[1] The ordinary greeting of Corsicans.

cleverly that the devil could not have found him. If it had not been for my little cousin Fortunato, I should never have discovered him."

"Fortunato?" cried Mateo.

"Fortunato?" repeated Giuseppa.

"Yes; Gianetto was concealed in your haycock there, but my little cousin showed me his trick. I will speak of him to his uncle the corporal, who will send him a nice present as a reward. And both his name and yours will be in the report which I shall send to the superintendent."

"Curse you!" cried Mateo under his breath.

By this time they had rejoined the company. Gianetto was already laid on his litter, and they were ready to set out. When he saw Mateo in Gamba's company he smiled a strange smile; then, turning toward the door of the house, he spat on the threshold.

"It is the house of a traitor!" he exclaimed.

No man but one willing to die would have dared to utter the word "traitor" in connection with Falcone. A quick stroke from a dagger, without need for a second, would have immediately wiped out the insult. But Mateo made no other movement beyond putting his hand to his head like a dazed man.

Fortunato went into the house when he saw his father come up. He reappeared shortly, carrying a jug of milk, which he offered with downcast eyes to Gianetto.

"Keep off me!" roared the outlaw.

Then turning to one of the soldiers, he said: —

"Comrade, give me a drink of water."

The soldier placed the flask in his hands, and the

bandit drank the water given him by a man with whom he had but now exchanged gunshots. He then asked that his hands might be tied crossed over his breast instead of behind his back.

"I prefer," he said, "to lie down comfortably."

They granted him his request. Then, at a sign from the adjutant, they set out, first bidding adieu to Mateo, who answered never a word, and descended at a quick pace toward the plain.

Well-nigh ten minutes elapsed before Mateo opened his mouth. The child looked uneasily first at his mother, then at his father, who leant on his gun, looking at him with an expression of concentrated anger.

"Well, you have made a pretty beginning," said Mateo at last in a voice calm, but terrifying to those who knew the man.

"Father," the boy cried out, with tears in his eyes, just ready to fall at his knees.

"Out of my sight!" shouted Mateo.

The child stopped motionless a few steps off from his father, and began to sob.

Giuseppa came near him. She had just seen the end of the watch chain hanging from out his shirt.

"Who gave you that watch?" she asked severely.

"My cousin the adjutant."

Falcone seized the watch and threw it against a stone with such force that it broke into a thousand pieces.

"Woman," he said, "is this my child?"

Giuseppa's brown cheeks flamed brick-red.

"What are you saying, Mateo? Do you know to whom you are speaking?"

"Yes, very well. This child is the first traitor of his race."

Fortunato's sobs and hiccoughs redoubled, and Falcone kept his lynx eyes steadily fixed on him. At length he struck the ground with the butt end of his gun; then he flung it across his shoulder, retook the way to the *mâquis,* and ordered Fortunato to follow him. The child obeyed.

Giuseppa ran after Mateo, and seized him by the arm.

"He is your son," she said in a trembling voice, fixing her black eyes on those of her husband, as though to read all that was passing in his mind.

"Leave go," replied Mateo; "I am his father."

Giuseppa kissed her son, and went back crying into the hut. She threw herself on her knees before an image of the Virgin, and prayed fervently. When Falcone had walked about two hundred yards along the path, he stopped at a little ravine and went down into it. He sounded the ground with the butt end of his gun, and found it soft and easy to dig. The spot seemed suitable to his purpose.

"Fortunato, go near to that large rock."

The boy did as he was told, then knelt down.

"Father, father, do not kill me!"

"Say your prayers!" repeated Mateo in a terrible voice.

The child repeated the Lord's Prayer and the Creed, stammering and sobbing. The father said "Amen!" in a firm voice at the close of each prayer.

"Are those all the prayers you know?"

"I know also the Ave Maria and Litany, that my aunt taught me, father."

"It is long, but never mind."

The child finished the Litany in a faint voice.

"Have you finished?"

"Oh, father, father, forgive me! forgive me! I will never do it again. I will beg my cousin the corporal with all my might to pardon Gianetto!"

He went on imploring. Mateo loaded his rifle and took aim.

"May God forgive you!" he said.

The boy made a frantic effort to get up and clasp his father's knees, but he had no time. Mateo fired, and Fortunato fell stone dead.

Without throwing a single glance at the body, Mateo went back to his house to fetch a spade with which to bury his son. He had only returned a little way along the path when he met Giuseppa, who had run out, alarmed by the sound of the firing.

"What have you done?" she cried.

"Justice!"

"Where is he?"

"In the ravine; I am going to bury him. He died a Christian. I shall have a mass sung for him. Let some one tell my son-in-law Tiodoro Bianchi to come and live with us."

NOTE. — This is at once a story of local color — for it could not have happened outside of Corsica — and a tale of inexorable justice, presented with a total absence of sentimentality. The author tells us that this thing happened in this fashion; and he omits all comment. His attitude appears to be cold and remote, devoid of sympathy; yet his narrative is so devised as to make us feel intensely for the hapless father who cannot but do what seems to him his duty. Especially noteworthy is the skill with which Mérimée, starting with colloquial common-place, steadily stiffens the interest until it culminates in the unexpected catastrophe. Attention should be called also to the reserve with which Mérimée presents the figure of the unfortunate lad's mother, upon whose emotions it would have been easy to dilate — but only to the weakening of the total effect.

VIII. THE SHOT

By Alexander Pushkin (1799-1837)

Pushkin was a Russian poet and playwright, novelist and historian. Exiled for a while to the Caucasus, he was afterward taken into favor by the Czar. He was killed in a duel with his brother-in-law. He is the typical Romanticist poet of Russia, strongly under the influence of Byron. This story was published in 1830.

THE SHOT

I

We were stationed in the little town of N——. The life of an officer in the army is well known. In the morning, drill and the riding school; dinner with the Colonel or at a Jewish restaurant; in the evening, punch and cards. In N—— there was not one open house, not a single marriageable girl. We used to meet in each other's rooms, where, except our uniforms, we never saw anything.

One civilian only was admitted into our society. He was about thirty-five years of age, and therefore we looked upon him as an old fellow. His experience gave him great advantage over us, and his habitual taciturnity,

THE SHOT

stern disposition, and caustic tongue produced a deep impression upon our young minds. Some mystery surrounded his existence; he had the appearance of a Russian, although his name was a foreign one. He had formerly served in the Hussars, and with distinction. Nobody knew the cause that had induced him to retire from the service and settle in a wretched little village, where he lived poorly and, at the same time, extravagantly. He always went on foot, and constantly wore a shabby black overcoat, but the officers of our regiment were ever welcome at his table. His dinners, it is true, never consisted of more than two or three dishes, prepared by a retired soldier, but the champagne flowed like water. Nobody knew what his circumstances were, or what his income was, and nobody dared to question him about them. He had a collection of books, consisting chiefly of works on military matters and a few novels. He willingly lent them to us to read, and never asked for them back; on the other hand, he never returned to the owner the books that were lent to him. His principal amusement was shooting with a pistol. The walls of his room were riddled with bullets, and were as full of holes as a honeycomb. A rich collection of pistols was the only luxury in the humble cottage where he lived. The skill which he had acquired with his favorite weapon was simply incredible; and if he had offered to shoot a pear off somebody's forage cap, not a man in our regiment would have hesitated to place the object upon his head.

Our conversation often turned upon duels. Silvio — so I will call him — never joined in it. When asked if he had ever fought, he dryly replied that he had; but he entered into no particulars, and it was evident that such questions were not to his liking. We came to the conclusion that he had upon his conscience the memory of some unhappy victim of his terrible skill. Moreover, it never entered into the head of any of us to suspect him of anything like cowardice. There are persons whose mere look is sufficient to repel such a suspicion. But an unexpected incident occurred which astounded us all.

One day, about ten of our officers dined with Silvio. They drank as usual, that is to say, a great deal. After dinner we asked our host to hold the bank for a game at faro. For a long time he refused, for he hardly ever played, but at last he ordered cards to be brought, placed half a hundred ducats upon the table, and sat down to deal. We took our places round him, and the play began. It was Silvio's custom to preserve a complete silence when playing. He never disputed, and never entered into explanations. If the punter made a mistake in calculating, he immediately paid him the difference or noted down the surplus. We were acquainted with this habit of his, and we always allowed him to have his own way; but among us on this occasion was an officer who had only recently been transferred to our regiment. During the course of the game, this officer absently scored one point too many. Silvio took the chalk and noted down the correct account according to his usual custom. The officer, thinking that he had made a mistake, began to enter into explanations. Silvio continued dealing in silence. The officer, losing patience, took the brush and rubbed out what he considered was wrong. Silvio took the chalk and corrected the score again. The officer, heated with wine, play, and the

THE SHOT

laughter of his comrades, considered himself grossly insulted, and in his rage he seized a brass candlestick from the table, and hurled it at Silvio, who barely succeeded in avoiding the missile. We were filled with consternation. Silvio rose, white with rage, and with gleaming eyes, said: —

"My dear sir, have the goodness to withdraw, and thank God that this has happened in my house."

None of us entertained the slightest doubt as to what the result would be, and we already looked upon our new comrade as a dead man. The officer withdrew, saying that he was ready to answer for his offense in whatever way the banker liked. The play went on for a few minutes longer, but feeling that our host was no longer interested in the game, we withdrew one after the other, and repaired to our respective quarters, after having exchanged a few words upon the probability of there soon being a vacancy in the regiment.

The next day, at the riding school, we were already asking each other if the poor lieutenant was still alive, when he himself appeared among us. We put the same question to him, and he replied that he had not yet heard from Silvio. This astonished us. We went to Silvio's house and found him in the courtyard, shooting bullet after bullet into an ace pasted upon the gate. He received us as usual, but did not utter a word about the event of the previous evening. Three days passed, and the lieutenant was still alive. We asked each other in astonishment: "Can it be possible that Silvio is not going to fight?"

Silvio did not fight. He was satisfied with a very lame explanation, and became reconciled to his assailant.

This lowered him very much in the opinion of all our

young fellows. Want of courage is the last thing to be pardoned by young men, who usually look upon bravery as the chief of all human virtues, and the excuse for every possible fault. But, by degrees, everything became forgotten, and Silvio regained his former influence.

I alone could not approach him on the old footing. Being endowed by nature with a romantic imagination, I had become attached more than all the others to the man whose life was an enigma, and who seemed to me the hero of some mysterious drama. He was fond of me; at least, with me alone did he drop his customary sarcastic tone, and converse on different subjects in a simple and unusually agreeable manner. But after this unlucky evening, the thought that his honor had been tarnished, and that the stain had been allowed to remain upon it in accordance with his own wish, was ever present in my mind, and prevented me treating him as before. I was ashamed to look at him. Silvio was too intelligent and experienced not to observe this and guess the cause of it. This seemed to vex him; at least I observed once or twice a desire on his part to enter into an explanation with me, but I avoided such opportunities, and Silvio gave up the attempt. From that time forward I saw him only in the presence of my comrades, and our confidential conversations came to an end.

The inhabitants of the capital, with minds occupied by so many matters of business and pleasure, have no idea of the many sensations so familiar to the inhabitants of villages and small towns, as, for instance, the awaiting the arrival of the post. On Tuesdays and Fridays our regimental bureau used to be filled with officers: some

THE SHOT

expecting money, some letters, and others newspapers. The packets were usually opened on the spot, items of news were communicated from one to another, and the bureau used to present a very animated picture. Silvio used to have his letters addressed to our regiment, and he was generally there to receive them.

One day he received a letter, the seal of which he broke with a look of great impatience. As he read the contents, his eyes sparkled. The officers, each occupied with his own letters, did not observe anything.

"Gentlemen," said Silvio, "circumstances demand my immediate departure; I leave to-night. I hope that you will not refuse to dine with me for the last time. I shall expect you, too," he added, turning toward me. "I shall expect you without fail."

With these words he hastily departed, and we, after agreeing to meet at Silvio's, dispersed to our various quarters.

I arrived at Silvio's house at the appointed time, and found nearly the whole regiment there. All his things were already packed; nothing remained but the bare, bullet-riddled walls. We sat down to table. Our host was in an excellent humor, and his gayety was quickly communicated to the rest. Corks popped every moment, glasses foamed incessantly, and, with the utmost warmth, we wished our departing friend a pleasant journey and every happiness. When we rose from the table it was already late in the evening. After having wished everybody good-by, Silvio took me by the hand and detained me just at the moment when I was preparing to depart.

"I want to speak to you," he said in a low voice.

I stopped behind.

The guests had departed, and we two were left alone. Sitting down opposite each other, we silently lit our pipes. Silvio seemed greatly troubled; not a trace remained of his former convulsive gayety. The intense pallor of his face, his sparkling eyes, and the thick smoke issuing from his mouth, gave him a truly diabolical appearance. Several minutes elapsed, and then Silvio broke the silence.

"Perhaps we shall never see each other again," said he; "before we part, I should like to have an explanation with you. You may have observed that I care very little for the opinion of other people, but I like you, and I feel that it would be painful to me to leave you with a wrong impression upon your mind."

He paused, and began to knock the ashes out of his pipe. I sat gazing silently at the ground.

"You thought it strange," he continued, "that I did not demand satisfaction from that drunken idiot R——. You will admit, however, that having the choice of weapons, his life was in my hands, while my own was in no great danger. I could ascribe my forbearance to generosity alone, but I will not tell a lie. If I could have chastised R—— without the least risk of my own life, I should never have pardoned him."

I looked at Silvio with astonishment. Such a confession completely astounded me. Silvio continued: —

"Exactly so: I have no right to expose myself to death. Six years ago I received a slap in the face, and my enemy still lives."

My curiosity was greatly excited.

"Did you not fight with him?" I asked. "Circumstances probably separated you."

"I did fight with him," replied Silvio; "and here is a souvenir of our duel."

Silvio rose and took from a cardboard box a red cap with a gold tassel and embroidery (what the French call a *bonnet de police*); he put it on — a bullet had passed through it about an inch above the forehead.

"You know," continued Silvio, "that I served in one of the Hussar regiments. My character is well known to you: I am accustomed to taking the lead. From my youth this has been my passion. In our time, dissoluteness was the fashion, and I was the most outrageous man in the army. We used to boast of our drunkenness; I beat in a drinking bout the famous Bourtsoff, of whom Denis Davidoff has sung. Duels in our regiment were constantly taking place, and in all of them I was either second or principal. My comrades adored me, while the regimental commanders, who were constantly being changed, looked upon me as a necessary evil.

"I was calmly enjoying my reputation, when a young man belonging to a wealthy and distinguished family — I will not mention his name — joined our regiment. Never in my life have I met with such a fortunate fellow! Imagine to yourself youth, wit, beauty, unbounded gayety, the most reckless bravery, a famous name, untold wealth — imagine all these, and you can form some idea of the effect that he would be sure to produce among us. My supremacy was shaken. Dazzled by my reputation, he began to seek my friendship, but I received him coldly, and without the least regret he held aloof from me. I took a hatred to him. His success in the regiment and in the society of ladies brought me to the verge of despair. I began to seek a quarrel with him; to my epigrams he replied with epigrams which always seemed to me more spontaneous and more cutting than mine, and which were decidedly more amusing, for he joked while I fumed. At last, at a ball given by a Polish landed proprietor, seeing him the object of the attention of all the ladies, and especially of the mistress of the house, with whom I was upon very good terms, I whispered some grossly insulting remark in his ear. He flamed up and gave me a slap in the face. We grasped our swords; the ladies fainted; we were separated; and that same night we set out to fight.

"The dawn was just breaking. I was standing at the appointed place with my three seconds. With inexplicable impatience I awaited my opponent. The spring sun rose, and it was already growing hot. I saw him coming in the distance. He was walking on foot, accompanied by one second. We advanced to meet him. He approached, holding his cap filled with black cherries. The seconds measured twelve paces for us. I had to fire first, but my agitation was so great, that I could not depend upon the steadiness of my hand; and in order to give myself time to become calm, I ceded to him the first shot. My adversary would not agree to this. It was decided that we should cast lots. The first number fell to him, the constant favorite of fortune. He took aim, and his bullet went through my cap. It was now my turn. His life at last was in my hands; I looked at him eagerly, endeavoring to detect if only the faintest shadow of uneasiness. But he stood in front of my pistol, picking out the ripest cherries from his cap and spitting out the stones, which flew almost as far as my feet. His indifference annoyed me beyond measure. 'What is the use,' thought I, 'of depriving him of life, when he attaches no value whatever to it?' A malicious thought flashed through my mind. I lowered my pistol.

"'You don't seem to be ready for death just at present,' I said to him: 'you wish to have your breakfast; I do not wish to hinder you.'

"'You are not hindering me in the least,' replied he. 'Have the goodness to fire, or just as you please— the shot remains yours; I shall always be ready at your service.'

"I turned to the seconds, informing them that I had no intention of firing that day, and with that the duel came to an end.

"I resigned my commission and retired to this little place. Since then not a day has passed that I have not thought of revenge. And now my hour has arrived."

Silvio took from his pocket the letter that he had received that morning, and gave it to me to read. Some one (it seemed to be his business agent) wrote to him from Moscow, that a *certain person* was going to be married to a young and beautiful girl.

"You can guess," said Silvio, "who the certain person is. I am going to Moscow. We shall see if he will look death in the face with as much indifference now, when he is on the eve of being married, as he did once with his cherries!"

With these words, Silvio rose, threw his cap upon the

floor, and began pacing up and down the room like a tiger in his cage. I had listened to him in silence; strange conflicting feelings agitated me.

The servant entered and announced that the horses were ready. Silvio grasped my hand tightly, and we embraced each other. He seated himself in his *telega*, in which lay two trunks, one containing his pistols, the other his effects. We said good-by once more, and the horses galloped off.

II

Several years passed, and family circumstances compelled me to settle in the poor little village of M——. Occupied with agricultural pursuits, I ceased not to sigh in secret for my former noisy and careless life. The most difficult thing of all was having to accustom myself to passing the spring and winter evenings in perfect solitude. Until the hour for dinner I managed to pass away the time somehow or other, talking with the bailiff, riding about to inspect the work, or going round to look at the new buildings; but as soon as it began to get dark, I positively did not know what to do with myself. The few books that I had found in the cupboards and storerooms I already knew by heart. All the stories that my housekeeper Kirilovna could remember I had heard over and over again. The songs of the peasant women made me feel depressed. I tried drinking spirits, but it made my head ache; and moreover, I confess I was afraid of becoming a drunkard from mere chagrin, that is to say, the saddest kind of drunkard, of which I had seen many examples in our district.

THE SHOT

I had no near neighbors, except two or three topers, whose conversation consisted for the most part of hiccoughs and sighs. Solitude was preferable to their society. At last I decided to go to bed as early as possible, and to dine as late as possible; in this way I shortened the evening and lengthened out the day, and I found that the plan answered very well.

Four versts from my house was a rich estate belonging to the Countess B——; but nobody lived there except the steward. The Countess had only visited her estate once, in the first year of her married life, and then she had remained there no longer than a month. But in the second spring of my hermitical life a report was circulated that the Countess, with her husband, was coming to spend the summer on her estate. The report turned out to be true, for they arrived at the beginning of June.

The arrival of a rich neighbor is an important event in the lives of country people. The landed proprietors and the people of their households talk about it for two months beforehand and for three years afterward. As for me, I must confess that the news of the arrival of a young and beautiful neighbor affected me strongly. I burned with impatience to see her, and the first Sunday after her arrival I set out after dinner for the village of A——, to pay my respects to the Countess and her husband, as their nearest neighbor and most humble servant.

A lackey conducted me into the Count's study, and then went to announce me. The spacious apartment was furnished with every possible luxury. Around the walls were cases filled with books and surmounted by bronze busts; over the marble mantelpiece was a large mirror; on the floor was a green cloth covered with carpets. Unaccustomed to luxury in my own poor corner, and not having seen the wealth of other people for a long time, I awaited the appearance of the Count with some little trepidation, as a suppliant from the provinces awaits the arrival of the minister. The door opened, and a handsome-looking man, of about thirty-two years of age, entered the room. The Count approached me with a frank and friendly air; I endeavored to be self-possessed and began to introduce myself, but he anticipated me. We sat down. His conversation, which was easy and agreeable, soon dissipated my awkward bashfulness; and I was already beginning to recover my usual composure, when the Countess suddenly entered, and I became more confused than ever. She was indeed beautiful. The Count presented me. I wished to appear at ease, but the more I tried to assume an air of unconstraint, the more awkward I felt. They, in order to give me time to recover myself and to become accustomed to my new acquaintances, began to talk to each other, treating me as a good neighbor, and without ceremony. Meanwhile, I walked about the room, examining the books and pictures. I am no judge of pictures, but one of them attracted my attention. It represented some view in Switzerland, but it was not the painting that struck me, but the circumstance that the canvas was shot through by two bullets, one planted just above the other.

"A good shot that!" said I, turning to the Count.

"Yes," replied he, "a very remarkable shot. . . . Do you shoot well?" he continued.

"Tolerably," replied I, rejoicing that the conversation had turned at last upon a subject that was familiar to me. "At thirty paces I can manage to hit a card without fail, — I mean, of course, with a pistol that I am used to."

"Really?" said the Countess, with a look of the greatest interest. "And you, my dear, could you hit a card at thirty paces?"

"Some day," replied the Count, "we will try. In my time I did not shoot badly, but it is now four years since I touched a pistol."

"Oh!" I observed, "in that case, I don't mind laying a wager that Your Excellency will not hit the card at twenty paces; the pistol demands practice every day. I know that from experience. In our regiment I was reckoned one of the best shots. It once happened that I did not touch a pistol for a whole month, as I had sent mine to be mended; and would you believe it, Your Excellency, the first time I began to shoot again, I missed a bottle four times in succession at twenty paces. Our captain, a witty and amusing fellow, happened to be standing by, and he said to me: 'It is evident, my friend, that your hand will not lift itself against the bottle.' No, Your Excellency, you must not neglect to practice, or your hand will soon lose its cunning. The best shot that I ever met used to shoot at least three times every day before dinner. It was as much his custom to do this as it was to drink his daily glass of brandy."

The Count and Countess seemed pleased that I had begun to talk.

"And what sort of a shot was he?" asked the Count.

"Well, it was this way with him, Your Excellency: if he saw a fly settle on the wall — you smile, Countess, but, before Heaven, it is the truth — if he saw a fly, he would call out: 'Kouzka, my pistol!' Kouzka would bring him a loaded pistol — bang! and the fly would be crushed against the wall."

"Wonderful!" said the Count. "And what was his name?"

"Silvio, Your Excellency."

"Silvio!" exclaimed the Count, starting up. "Did you know Silvio?"

"How could I help knowing him, Your Excellency: we were intimate friends; he was received in our regiment like a brother officer, but it is now five years since I had any tidings of him. Then Your Excellency also knew him?"

"Oh, yes, I knew him very well. Did he ever tell you of one very strange incident in his life?"

"Does Your Excellency refer to the slap in the face that he received from some blackguard at a ball?"

"Did he tell you the name of this blackguard?"

"No, Your Excellency, he never mentioned his name. . . . Ah! Your Excellency!" I continued, guessing the the truth: "pardon me . . . I did not know . . . could it really have been you?"

"Yes, I myself," replied the Count, with a look of extraordinary agitation; "and that bullet-pierced picture is a memento of our last meeting."

"Ah, my dear," said the Countess, "for Heaven's sake, do not speak about that; it would be too terrible for me to listen to."

THE SHOT

"No," replied the Count: "I will relate everything. He knows how I insulted his friend, and it is only right that he should know how Silvio revenged himself."

The Count pushed a chair toward me, and with the liveliest interest I listened to the following story: —

"Five years ago I got married. The first month — the honeymoon — I spent here, in this village. To this house I am indebted for the happiest moments of my life, as well as for one of its most painful recollections.

"One evening we went out together for a ride on horseback. My wife's horse became restive; she grew frightened, gave the reins to me, and returned home on foot. I rode on before. In the courtyard I saw a traveling carriage, and I was told that in my study sat waiting for me a man, who would not give his name, but who merely said that he had business with me. I entered the room and saw in the darkness a man, covered with dust, and wearing a beard of several days' growth. He was standing there, near the fireplace. I approached him, trying to remember his features.

"'You do not recognize me, Count?' said he, in a quivering voice.

"'Silvio!' I cried, and I confess that I felt as if my hair had suddenly stood on end.

"'Exactly,' continued he. 'There is a shot due to me, and I have come to discharge my pistol. Are you ready?'

"His pistol protruded from a side pocket. I measured twelve paces and took my stand there in that corner, begging him to fire quickly, before my wife arrived. He hesitated, and asked for a light. Candles were brought in.

I closed the doors, gave orders that nobody was to enter, and again begged him to fire. He drew out his pistol and took aim. . . . I counted the seconds. . . . I thought of her. . . . A terrible minute passed! Silvio lowered his hand.

"'I regret,' said he, 'that the pistol is not loaded with cherry stones . . . the bullet is heavy. It seems to me that this is not a duel, but a murder. I am not accustomed to taking aim at unarmed men. Let us begin all over again; we will cast lots as to who shall fire first.'

"My head went round . . . I think I raised some objection. . . . At last we loaded another pistol and rolled up two pieces of paper. He placed these latter in his cap — the same through which I had once sent a bullet — and again I drew the first number.

"'You are devilishly lucky, Count,' said he, with a smile that I shall never forget.

"I don't know what was the matter with me, or how it was that he managed to make me do it . . . but I fired and hit that picture.

The Count pointed with his finger to the perforated picture; his face glowed like fire; the Countess was whiter than her own handkerchief; and I could not restrain an exclamation.

"I fired," continued the Count, "and, thank Heaven, missed my aim. Then Silvio . . . at that moment he was really terrible . . . Silvio raised his hand to take aim at me. Suddenly the door opens, Masha rushes into the room, and with a loud shriek throws herself upon my neck. Her presence restored to me all my courage.

"'My dear,' said I to her, 'don't you see that we are

joking? How frightened you are! Go and drink a glass of water and then come back to us; I will introduce you to an old friend and comrade.'

"Masha still doubted.

"'Tell me, is my husband speaking the truth?' said she, turning to the terrible Silvio: 'is it true that you are only joking?'

"'He is always joking, Countess,' replied Silvio: 'once he gave me a slap in the face in a joke; on another occasion he sent a bullet through my cap in a joke; and just now, when he fired at me and missed me, it was all in a joke. And now I feel inclined for a joke.'

"With these words he raised his pistol to take aim at me — right before her! Masha threw herself at his feet.

"'Rise, Masha; are you not ashamed!' I cried in a rage: 'and you, sir, will you cease to make fun of a poor woman? Will you fire or not?'

"'I will not,' replied Silvio: 'I am satisfied. I have seen your confusion, your alarm. I forced you to fire at me. That is sufficient. You will remember me. I leave you to your conscience.'

"Then he turned to go, but pausing in the doorway, and looking at the picture that my shot had passed through, he fired at it almost without taking aim, and disappeared. My wife had fainted away; the servants did not venture to stop him; the mere look of him filled them with terror. He went out upon the steps, called his coachman, and drove off before I could recover myself."

The Count was silent. In this way I learned the end of the story, whose beginning had once made such a deep impression upon me. The hero of it I never saw again.

It is said that Silvio commanded a detachment of Hetairists during the revolt under Alexander Ipsilanti, and that he was killed in the battle of Skoulana.

NOTE. — This is an anecdote, rather than a true short-story, although it deals with a theme admirably suited for treatment in this form. In Pushkin's telling, the incidents are straggling; and the tale lacks the compression, the swiftness, and the impending terror that later writers would have given to it. If Pushkin had been familiar with the cold condensation of Mérimée's narrative, he might have told this tale with a fuller appreciation of its artistic possibilities.

IX. THE STEADFAST TIN SOLDIER

By Hans Christian Andersen (1805-1875)

Andersen's fairy tales have the quaintness, the simplicity, the naturalness, of the primitive folk story, with a humor, a pleasant irony of their own. He was a born story-teller, and there are a dozen little masterpieces to be selected from his several collections. The "Steadfast Tin Soldier" is one of the earliest as it is one of the best. It was published in 1835, when its author was already a full-grown man, — but a man who had preserved the power to see the world as a little child sees it.

THE STEADFAST TIN SOLDIER

There were once five and twenty tin soldiers, all brothers, for they were the offspring of the same old tin spoon. Each man shouldered his gun, kept his eyes well to the front, and wore the smartest red and blue uniform imaginable. The first thing they heard in their new world, when the lid was taken off the box, was a little boy clapping his hands and crying, "Soldiers, soldiers!" It was his birthday, and they had just been given to him; so he lost no time in setting them up on the table. All the soldiers were exactly alike with one exception, and he differed from the rest in having only one leg. For he was made last, and there was not quite enough tin left to finish him. However, he stood just as well on his one leg as the others on two; in fact he is the very one who is to become famous. On the table where they were being set up were many other toys; but the chief thing which caught the eye was a delightful paper castle. You could see through the tiny windows, right into the rooms. Outside there were some little trees surrounding a small mirror, representing a lake, whose surface reflected the waxen swans which were swimming about on it. It was altogether charming, but the prettiest thing of all was a little maiden standing at the open door of the castle. She, too, was cut out of paper, but she wore a dress of the lightest gauze, with a dainty little blue ribbon over her shoulders, by way of a scarf, set off by a brilliant spangle as big as her whole face. The little maid was stretching out both arms, for she was a dancer, and in the dance, one of her legs was raised so high into the air that the tin soldier could see absolutely nothing of it, and supposed that she, like himself, had but one leg.

"That would be the very wife for me!" he thought; "but she is much too grand; she lives in a palace, while I only have a box, and then there are five and twenty of us to share it. No, that would be no place for her! but I must try to make her acquaintance!" Then he lay down full length behind a snuffbox which stood on the table. From that point he could have a good look at the little lady, who continued to stand on one leg without losing her balance.

THE STEADFAST TIN SOLDIER

Late in the evening the other soldiers were put into their box, and the people of the house went to bed. Now was the time for the toys to play; they amused themselves with paying visits, fighting battles, and giving balls. The tin soldiers rustled about in their box, for they wanted to join the games, but they could not get the lid off. The nutcrackers turned somersaults, and the pencil scribbled nonsense on the slate. There was such a noise that the canary woke up and joined in, but his remarks were in verse. The only two who did not move were the tin soldier and the little dancer. She stood as stiff as ever on tiptoe, with her arms spread out; he was equally firm on his one leg, and he did not take his eyes off her for a moment.

Then the clock struck twelve, when pop! up flew the lid of the snuffbox, but there was no snuff in it, no! There was a little black goblin, a sort of Jack-in-the-box.

"Tin soldier!" said the goblin, "have the goodness to keep your eyes to yourself."

But the tin soldier feigned not to hear.

"Ah! you just wait till to-morrow," said the goblin.

In the morning, when the children got up, they put the tin soldier on the window frame, and whether it was caused by the goblin or by a puff of wind, I do not know, but all at once the window burst open, and the soldier fell head foremost from the third story.

It was a terrific descent, and he landed at last, with his leg in the air, and rested on his cap, with his bayonet fixed between two paving stones. The maidservant and the little boy ran down at once to look for him; but although they almost trod on him, they could not see him. Had the soldier only called, "here I am," they would easily have found him; but he did not think it proper to shout when he was in uniform.

Presently it began to rain, and the drops fell faster and faster, till there was a regular torrent. When it was over, two street boys came along.

"Look out!" said one; "there is a tin soldier! He shall go for a sail."

So they made a boat out of a newspaper and put the soldier into the middle of it, and he sailed away down the gutter; both boys ran alongside, clapping their hands. Good heavens! what waves there were in the gutter, and what a current, but then it certainly had rained cats and dogs. The paper boat danced up and down, and now and then whirled round and round. A shudder ran through the tin soldier, but he remained undaunted, and did not move a muscle, only looked straight before him with his gun shouldered. All at once the boat drifted under a long wooden tunnel, and it became as dark as it was in his box.

"Where on earth am I going to now!" thought he. "Well, well, it is all the fault of that goblin! Oh, if only the little maiden were with me in the boat, it might be twice as dark for all I should care!"

At this moment a big water rat, who lived in the tunnel, came up.

"Have you a pass?" asked the rat. "Hand up your pass!"

The tin soldier did not speak, but clung still tighter to his gun. The boat rushed on, the rat close behind. Phew, how he gnashed his teeth and shouted to the bits of stick and straw.

THE STEADFAST TIN SOLDIER

"Stop him, stop him, he hasn't paid his toll! he hasn't shown his pass!"

But the current grew stronger and stronger; the tin soldier could already see daylight before him at the end of the tunnel; but he also heard a roaring sound, fit to strike terror to the bravest heart. Just imagine! Where the tunnel ended the stream rushed straight into the big canal. That would be just as dangerous for him as it would be for us to shoot a great rapid.

He was so near the end now that it was impossible to stop. The boat dashed out; the poor tin soldier held himself as stiff as he could; no one should say of him that he even winced.

The boat swirled round three or four times, and filled with water to the edge; it must sink. The tin soldier stood up to his neck in water, and the boat sank deeper and deeper. The paper became limper and limper, and at last the water went over his head — then he thought of the pretty little dancer, whom he was never to see again, and this refrain rang in his ears: —

> "Onward! Onward! Soldier!
> For death thou canst not shun."

At last the paper gave way entirely and the soldier fell through — but at the same moment he was swallowed by a big fish.

Oh! how dark it was inside that fish; it was worse than being in the tunnel, even; and then it was so narrow! But the tin soldier was as dauntless as ever, and lay full length, shouldering his gun.

The fish rushed about and made the most frantic movements. At last it became quite quiet, and after a time, a flash like lightning pierced it. The soldier was once more in the broad daylight, and some one called out loudly, "a tin soldier!" The fish had been caught, taken to market, sold, and brought into the kitchen, where the cook cut it open with a large knife. She took the soldier up by the waist, with two fingers, and carried him into the parlor, where every one wanted to see the wonderful man, who had traveled about in the stomach of a fish; but the tin soldier was not at all proud. They set him up on the table, and, wonder of wonders! he found himself in the very same room that he had been in before. He saw the very same children, and the toys were still standing on the table, as well as the beautiful castle with the pretty little dancer.

She still stood on one leg, and held the other up in the air. You see she also was unbending. The soldier was so much moved that he was ready to shed tears of tin, but that would not have been fitting. He looked at her, and she looked at him, but they said never a word. At this moment one of the little boys took up the tin soldier, and without rime or reason, threw him into the fire. No doubt the little goblin in the snuffbox was to blame for that. The tin soldier stood there, lighted up by the flame, and in the most horrible heat; but whether it was the heat of the real fire, or the warmth of his feelings, he did not know. He had lost all his gay color; it might have been from his perilous journey, or it might have been from grief, who can tell?

He looked at the little maiden, and she looked at him; and he felt that he was melting away, but he still managed to keep himself erect, shouldering his gun bravely.

THE STEADFAST TIN SOLDIER 181

A door was suddenly opened, the draught caught the little dancer and she fluttered like a sylph, straight into the fire, to the soldier, blazed up and was gone!

By this time the soldier was reduced to a mere lump, and when the maid took away the ashes next morning she found him, in the shape of a small tin heart. All that was left of the dancer was her spangle, and that was burnt as black as a coal.

NOTE. —This is an apologue, a fable, a parable, if we so choose to take it. But it is real also, however fanciful the invention. It has the child-like ingenuousness of the folk-tale, so rarely caught by writers who have forgotten how they felt when they were young. A large part of the effectiveness of the story is due to the certainty with which the author keeps to the chosen key.

X. THE FALL OF THE HOUSE OF USHER

By Edgar Allan Poe (1809–1849)

Poe is the earliest master of the short-story who was conscious of its possibilities and of its limitations. Whatever perfection may have been achieved before him was almost accidental; but he knew what he was doing and how he meant to do it. His short-stories vary greatly in theme and in manner, ranging from the ingenious but somewhat mechanical detective tale to the imaginative altitude of "Ligeia" and the "Masque of the Red Death." Perhaps no one of them better reveals his sheer power, his command over form, his mastery of verbal music, his ability to suggest far more than he ventures to put into words, than the "Fall of the House of Usher," which was written in 1839, and which he included in his "Tales of the Grotesque and of the Arabesque," published at the end of that year.

THE FALL OF THE HOUSE OF USHER

> Son cœur est un luth suspendu ;
> Sitôt qu'on le touche il résonne.
> — DE BÉRANGER.

During the whole of a dull, dark, and soundless day in the autumn of the year, when the clouds hung oppressively low in the heavens, I had been passing alone, on horseback, through a singularly dreary tract of country; and at length found myself, as the shades of the evening drew on, within view of the melancholy House of Usher. I know not how it was; but, with the first glimpse of the building, a sense of insufferable gloom pervaded my spirit. I say insufferable; for the feeling was unrelieved by any of that half-pleasurable, because poetic, sentiment, with which the mind usually receives even the sternest natural images of the desolate or terrible. I looked upon the scene before me — upon the mere house, and the simple landscape features of the domain — upon the bleak walls — upon the vacant eye-like windows — upon a few rank sedges — and upon a few white trunks of decayed trees — with an utter depression of soul which I can compare to no earthly sensation more properly than to the after-dream of the reveler upon opium — the bitter lapse into every-day life — the hideous dropping off of the veil. There was an iciness, a sinking, a sickening of the heart — an unredeemed dreariness of thought which no goading of the imagination could torture into aught of the sublime. What was it — I paused to think — what was it that so unnerved me in the contemplation of the House of Usher? It was a mystery all insoluble; nor could I grapple with the shadowy fancies that crowded upon me as I pondered. I was forced to fall back upon the unsatisfactory conclusion that while, beyond doubt, there *are* combinations of very simple natural objects which have the power of thus affecting us, still the analysis of this power lies among considerations beyond our depth. It was possible, I reflected, that a mere different arrangement of the particulars of the scene, of the details of the picture, would be sufficient to modify, or perhaps to annihilate its capacity for sorrowful impression; and, acting upon this idea, I reined my horse to the precipitous brink of a black and lurid tarn that lay in unruffled luster by the dwelling, and gazed down — but with a shudder even more thrilling than before — upon the remodeled and inverted images of the gray sedge, and the ghastly tree stems, and the vacant and eye-like windows.

Nevertheless, in this mansion of gloom I now proposed to myself a sojourn of some weeks. Its proprietor, Roderick Usher, had been one of my boon companions in boyhood; but many years had elapsed since our last meeting. A letter, however, had lately reached me in a distant part of the country — a letter from him — which, in its wildly importunate nature, had admitted of no other than a personal reply. The MS. gave evidence of nervous agitation. The writer spoke of acute bodily illness, of a mental disorder which oppressed him, and of an earnest desire to see me, as his best, and indeed his only personal friend, with a view of attempting, by the cheerfulness of my society, some alleviation of his malady. It was the manner in which all this, and much more, was said — it was the apparent *heart* that went with his request — which allowed me no room for hesitation; and I accordingly obeyed forthwith what I still considered a very singular summons.

Although, as boys, we had been even intimate associates, yet I really knew little of my friend. His reserve had been always excessive and habitual. I was aware, however, that his very ancient family had been noted, time out of mind, for a peculiar sensibility of temperament, displaying itself, through long ages, in many works of exalted art, and manifested, of late, in repeated deeds of munificent, yet unobtrusive charity, as well as in a passionate devotion to the intricacies, perhaps even more than to the orthodox and easily recognizable beauties, of musical science. I had learned, too, the very remarkable fact that the stem of the Usher race, all time-honored as it was, had put forth, at no period, any enduring branch; in other words, that the entire family lay in the direct line of descent, and had always, with very trifling and very temporary variation, so lain. It was this deficiency, I considered, while running over in thought the perfect keeping of the character of the premises with the accredited character of the people, and while speculating upon the possible influence which the one, in the long lapse of centuries, might have exercised upon the other — it was this deficiency, perhaps, of collateral issue, and the consequent undeviating transmission, from sire to son, of the patrimony with the name, which had, at length, so identified the two as to merge the original title of the estate in the quaint and equivocal appellation of the "House of Usher" — an appellation which seemed to include, in the minds of the peasantry who used it, both the family and the family mansion.

I have said that the sole effect of my somewhat childish experiment of looking down within the tarn had been to deepen the first singular impression. There can be no doubt that the consciousness of the rapid increase of my superstition — for why should I not so term it? — served mainly to accelerate the increase itself. Such, I have long known, is the paradoxical law of all sentiments having terror as a basis. And it might have been for this reason only, that, when I again uplifted my eyes to the house itself, from its image in the pool, there grew in my mind a strange fancy — a fancy so ridiculous, indeed, that I but mention it to show the vivid force of the sensations which oppressed me. I had so worked upon my imagination as really to believe that about the whole mansion and domain there hung an atmosphere peculiar to themselves and their immediate vicinity — an atmosphere which had no affinity with the air of heaven, but which had reeked up from the decayed trees, and the gray wall, and the silent tarn — a pestilent and mystic vapor, dull, sluggish, faintly discernible, and leaden-hued.

Shaking off from my spirit what *must* have been a dream, I scanned more narrowly the real aspect of the building. Its principal feature seemed to be that of an excessive antiquity. The discoloration of ages had been great. Minute fungi overspread the whole exterior, hanging in a fine, tangled web-work from the eaves. Yet all this was apart from any extraordinary dilapidation. No portion of the masonry had fallen; and there appeared to be a wild inconsistency between its still perfect adaptation of parts, and the crumbling condition of the individual stones. In this there was much that reminded me of the specious totality of old woodwork which has rotted for years in some neglected vault, with no disturbance from the breath of the external air. Beyond this indication of extensive decay, however, the fabric gave little token of instability. Perhaps the eye of a scrutinizing observer might have discovered a barely perceptible fissure, which, extending from the roof of the building in front, made its way down the wall in a zigzag direction, until it became lost in the sullen waters of the tarn.

Noticing these things, I rode over a short causeway to the house. A servant in waiting took my horse, and I entered the Gothic archway of the hall. A valet, of stealthy step, thence conducted me, in silence, through many dark and intricate passages in my progress to the *studio* of his master. Much that I encountered on the way contributed, I know not how, to heighten the vague sentiments of which I have already spoken. While the objects around me — while the carvings of the ceilings, the somber tapestries of the walls, the ebon blackness of the floors, and the phantasmagoric armorial trophies which rattled as I strode, were but matters to which, or to such as which, I had been accustomed from my infancy — while I hesitated not to acknowledge how familiar was all this — I still wondered to find how unfamiliar were the fancies which ordinary images were stirring up. On one of the staircases I met the physician of the family. His countenance, I thought, wore a mingled expression of low cunning and perplexity. He accosted me with trepidation and passed on. The valet now threw open a door and ushered me into the presence of his master.

The room in which I found myself was very large and lofty. The windows were long, narrow, and pointed, and at so vast a distance from the black oaken floor as to be altogether inaccessible from within. Feeble gleams of encrimsoned light made their way through the trellised panes, and served to render sufficiently distinct the more prominent objects around; the eye, however, struggled in vain to reach the remoter angles of the chamber, or the recesses of the vaulted and fretted ceiling. Dark draperies hung upon the walls. The general furniture was profuse, comfortless, antique, and tattered. Many books and musical instruments lay scattered about, but failed to give any vitality to the scene. I felt that I breathed an atmosphere of sorrow. An air of stern, deep, and irredeemable gloom hung over and pervaded all.

Upon my entrance, Usher arose from a sofa on which he had been lying at full length, and greeted me with a vivacious warmth which had much in it, I at first thought, of an overdone cordiality — of the constrained effort of the *ennuyé* man of the world. A glance, however, at his countenance convinced me of his perfect sincerity. We sat down; and for some moments, while he spoke not, I gazed upon him with a feeling half of pity, half of awe. Surely, man had never before so terribly altered, in so brief a period, as had Roderick Usher! It was with difficulty that I could bring myself to admit the identity of the wan being before me with the companion of my early

THE FALL OF THE HOUSE OF USHER

boyhood. Yet the character of his face had been at all times remarkable. A cadaverousness of complexion; an eye large, liquid, and luminous beyond comparison; lips somewhat thin and very pallid, but of a surpassingly beautiful curve; a nose of a delicate Hebrew model, but with a breadth of nostril unusual in similar formations; a finely molded chin, speaking, in its want of prominence, of a want of moral energy; hair of a more than web-like softness and tenuity; these features, with an inordinate expansion above the regions of the temple, made up altogether a countenance not easily to be forgotten. And now in the mere exaggeration of the prevailing character of these features, and of the expression they were wont to convey, lay so much of change that I doubted to whom I spoke. The now ghastly pallor of the skin, and the now miraculous luster of the eye, above all things startled and even awed me. The silken hair, too, had been suffered to grow all unheeded, and as, in its wild gossamer texture, it floated rather than fell about the face, I could not, even with effort, connect its arabesque expression with any idea of simple humanity.

In the manner of my friend I was at once struck with an incoherence — an inconsistency; and I soon found this to arise from a series of feeble and futile struggles to overcome an habitual trepidancy, an excessive nervous agitation. For something of this nature I had indeed been prepared, no less by his letter than by reminiscences of certain boyish traits, and by conclusions deduced from his peculiar physical conformation and temperament. His action was alternately vivacious and sullen. His voice varied rapidly from a tremulous indecision (when the animal spirits seemed utterly in abeyance) to that species of energetic concision — that abrupt, weighty, unhurried, and hollow-sounding enunciation — that leaden, self-balanced, and perfectly modulated guttural utterance, which may be observed in the lost drunkard, or the irreclaimable eater of opium, during the periods of his most intense excitement.

It was thus that he spoke of the object of my visit, of his earnest desire to see me, and of the solace he expected me to afford him. He entered, at some length, into what he conceived to be the nature of his malady. It was, he said, a constitutional and a family evil, and one for which he despaired to find a remedy — a mere nervous affection, he immediately added, which would undoubtedly soon pass off. It displayed itself in a host of unnatural sensations. Some of these, as he detailed them, interested and bewildered me; although, perhaps, the terms and the general manner of the narration had their weight. He suffered much from a morbid acuteness of the senses. The most insipid food was alone endurable; he could wear only garments of certain texture; the odors of all flowers were oppressive; his eyes were tortured by even a faint light; and there were but peculiar sounds, and these from stringed instruments, which did not inspire him with horror.

To an anomalous species of terror I found him a bounden slave. "I shall perish," said he, "I *must* perish in this deplorable folly. Thus, thus, and not otherwise, shall I be lost. I dread the events of the future, not in themselves, but in their results. I shudder at the thought of any, even the most trivial, incident, which may operate upon this intolerable agitation of soul. I have, indeed, no abhorrence of danger, except in its absolute effect — in terror. In this unnerved — in this pitiable condition — I feel that the period will sooner or later arrive when I must abandon life and reason together, in some struggle with the grim phantasm, FEAR."

I learned, moreover, at intervals, and through broken and equivocal hints, another singular feature of his mental condition. He was enchained by certain superstitious impressions in regard to the dwelling which he tenanted, and whence, for many years, he had never ventured forth — in regard to an influence whose supposititious force was conveyed in terms too shadowy here to be restated — an influence which some peculiarities in the mere form and substance of his family mansion, had, by dint of long sufferance, he said, obtained over his spirit — an effect which the *physique* of the gray walls and turrets, and of the dim tarn into which they all looked down, had, at length, brought about upon the *morale* of his existence.

He admitted, however, although with hesitation, that much of the peculiar gloom which thus afflicted him could be traced to a more natural and far more palpable origin — to the severe and long-continued illness — indeed to the evidently approaching dissolution — of a tenderly beloved sister, his sole companion for long years, his last and only relative on earth. "Her decease," he said, with a bitterness which I can never forget, "would leave him (him the hopeless and the frail) the last of the ancient race of the Ushers." While he spoke, the lady Madeline (for so was she called) passed slowly through a remote portion of the apartment, and, without having noticed my presence, disappeared. I regarded her with an utter astonishment not unmingled with dread;[1] and yet I found it impossible to account for such feelings. A sensation of stupor oppressed me, as my eyes followed her retreating steps. When a door, at length, closed upon her, my glance sought instinctively and eagerly the countenance of the brother; but he had buried his face in his hands, and I could only perceive that a far more than ordinary wanness had overspread the emaciated fingers through which trickled many passionate tears.

The disease of the lady Madeline had long baffled the skill of her physicians. A settled apathy, a gradual wasting away of the person, and frequent although transient affections of a partially cataleptical character, were the unusual diagnosis. Hitherto she had steadily borne up against the pressure of her malady, and had not betaken herself finally to bed; but on the closing in of the evening of my arrival at the house, she succumbed (as her brother told me at night with inexpressible agitation) to the prostrating power of the destroyer; and I learned that the glimpse I had obtained of her person would thus probably be the last I should obtain — that the lady, at least while living, would be seen by me no more.

For several days ensuing her name was unmentioned by either Usher or myself; and during this period I was

[[1] In place of this clause the first edition has: " Her figure, her air, her features, — all, in their very minutest development were those — were identically (I can use no other sufficient term), were identically those of the Roderick Usher who sat beside me. A feeling of stupor," etc.]

busied in earnest endeavors to alleviate the melancholy of my friend. We painted and read together; or I listened, as if in a dream, to the wild improvisations of his speaking guitar. And thus, as a closer and still closer intimacy admitted me more unreservedly into the recesses of his spirit, the more bitterly did I perceive the futility of all attempt at cheering a mind from which darkness, as if an inherent positive quality, poured forth upon all objects of the moral and physical universe, in one unceasing radiation of gloom.

I shall ever bear about me a memory of the many solemn hours I thus spent alone with the master of the House of Usher. Yet I should fail in any attempt to convey an idea of the exact character of the studies, or of the occupations in which he involved me, or led me the way. An excited and highly distempered ideality threw a sulphurous luster over all. His long, improvised dirges will ring forever in my ears. Among other things, I hold painfully in mind a certain singular perversion and amplification of the wild air of the last waltz of Von Weber. From the paintings over which his elaborate fancy brooded, and which grew, touch by touch, into vaguenesses at which I shuddered the more thrillingly because I shuddered knowing not why, — from these paintings (vivid as their images now are before me) I would in vain endeavor to educe more than a small portion which should lie within the compass of merely written words. By the utter simplicity, by the nakedness of his designs, he arrested and overawed attention. If ever mortal painted an idea, that mortal was Roderick Usher. For me, at least, in the circumstances then surrounding me, there arose out of the pure abstractions which the hypochondriac contrived to throw upon his canvas, an intensity of intolerable awe, no shadow of which felt I ever yet in the contemplation of the certainly glowing yet too concrete reveries of Fuseli.

One of the phantasmagoric conceptions of my friend, partaking not so rigidly of the spirit of abstraction, may be shadowed forth, although feebly, in words. A small picture presented the interior of an immensely long and rectangular vault or tunnel, with low walls, smooth, white, and without interruption or device. Certain accessory points of the design served well to convey the idea that this excavation lay at an exceeding depth below the surface of the earth. No outlet was observed in any portion of its vast extent, and no torch or other artificial source of light was discernible; yet a flood of intense rays rolled throughout, and bathed the whole in a ghastly and inappropriate splendor.

I have just spoken of that morbid condition of the auditory nerve which rendered all music intolerable to the sufferer, with the exception of certain effects of stringed instruments. It was, perhaps, the narrow limits to which he thus confined himself upon the guitar, which gave birth, in great measure, to the fantastic character of his performances. But the fervid *facility* of his *impromptus* could not be so accounted for. They must have been, and were, in the notes, as well as in the words of his wild fantasias (for he not unfrequently accompanied himself with rimed verbal improvisations), the result of that intense mental collectedness and concentration to which I have previously alluded as observable only in particular moments of the highest artificial excitement. The words of one of these rhapsodies I have easily remembered. I was, perhaps, the more forcibly impressed with it, as he gave it, because, in the under or mystic current of its meaning, I fancied that I perceived, and for the first time, a full consciousness on the part of Usher, of the tottering of his lofty reason upon her throne. The verses, which were entitled "The Haunted Palace," ran very nearly, if not accurately, thus: —

I

In the greenest of our valleys,
   By good angels tenanted,
Once a fair and stately palace —
   Radiant palace — reared its head.
In the monarch Thought's dominion —
   It stood there!
Never seraph spread a pinion
   Over fabric half so fair.

II

Banners yellow, glorious, golden,
   On its roof did float and flow;
(This — all this — was in the olden
   Time long ago)
And every gentle air that dallied,
   In that sweet day,
Along the ramparts plumed and pallid,
   A wingèd odor went away.

III

Wanderers in that happy valley
   Through two luminous windows saw
Spirits moving musically
   To a lute's well-tunèd law,

Round about a throne, where sitting
  (Porphyrogene!)
In state his glory well befitting,
  The ruler of the realm was seen.

IV

And all with pearl and ruby glowing
  Was the fair palace door,
Through which came flowing, flowing, flowing,
  And sparkling evermore,
A troop of Echoes whose sweet duty
  Was but to sing,
In voices of surpassing beauty,
  The wit and wisdom of their king.

V

But evil things, in robes of sorrow,
  Assailed the monarch's high estate
(Ah, let us mourn, for never morrow
  Shall dawn upon him, desolate!);
And, round about his home, the glory
  That blushed and bloomed
Is but a dim-remembered story
  Of the old time entombed.

VI

And travelers now within that valley,
  Through the red-litten windows, see
Vast forms that move fantastically
  To a discordant melody;
While, like a rapid ghastly river,
  Through the pale door,
A hideous throng rush out forever,
  And laugh — but smile no more.

I well remember that suggestions arising from this ballad led us into a train of thought wherein there became manifest an opinion of Usher's which I mention not so much on account of its novelty (for other men [1] have thought thus) as on account of the pertinacity with which he maintained it. This opinion, in its general form, was that of the sentience of all vegetable things. But, in his disordered fancy, the idea had assumed a more daring character, and trespassed, under certain conditions, upon the kingdom of inorganization. I lack words to express the full extent or the earnest *abandon* of his persuasion. The belief, however, was connected (as I have previously hinted) with the gray stones of the home of his forefathers. The conditions of the sentience had been here, he imagined, fulfilled in the method of collocation of these stones — in the order of their arrangement, as well as in that of the many *fungi* which overspread them, and of the decayed trees which stood around — above all, in the long-undisturbed endurance of this arrangement, and in its reduplication in the still waters of the tarn. Its evidence — the evidence of the sentience — was to be seen, he said (and I here started as he spoke), in the gradual yet certain condensation of an atmosphere of their own about the waters and the walls. The result was discoverable, he added, in that silent, yet importunate and terrible influence which for centuries had molded the destinies of his family, and which made *him* what I now saw him — what he was. Such opinions need no comment, and I will make none.

Our books — the books which, for years, had formed no small portion of the mental existence of the invalid —

[1] Watson, Dr. Percival, Spallanzani, and especially the Bishop of Llandaff. See "Chemical Essays," Vol. V.

were, as might be supposed, in strict keeping with this character of phantasm. We pored together over such works as the "Ververt et Chartreuse" of Gresset; the "Belphegor" of Machiavelli; the "Heaven and Hell" of Swedenborg; the "Subterranean Voyage of Nicholas Klimm" by Holberg; the "Chiromancy" of Robert Flud, of Jean D'Indaginé, and of De la Chambre; the "Journey into the Blue Distance" of Tieck; and the "City of the Sun" of Campanella. One favorite volume was a small octavo edition of the "Directorium Inquisitorium," by the Dominican Eymeric de Cironne; and there were passages in Pomponius Mela, about the old African Satyrs and Œgipans, over which Usher would sit dreaming for hours. His chief delight, however, was found in the perusal of an exceedingly rare and curious book in quarto Gothic — the manual of a forgotten church — the "Vigiliæ Mortuorum secundum Chorum Ecclesiæ Maguntinæ."

I could not help thinking of the wild ritual of this work, and of its probable influence upon the hypochondriac, when, one evening, having informed me abruptly that the lady Madeline was no more, he stated his intention of preserving her corpse for a fortnight (previously to its final interment) in one of the numerous vaults within the main walls of the building. The worldly reason, however, assigned for this singular proceeding, was one which I did not feel at liberty to dispute. The brother had been led to his resolution, so he told me, by consideration of the unusual character of the malady of the deceased, of certain obtrusive and eager inquiries on the part of her medical men, and of the remote and exposed situation of the burial ground of the family. I will not deny that when I called to mind the sinister countenance of the person whom I met upon the staircase, on the day of my arrival at the house, I had no desire to oppose what I regarded as at best but a harmless, and by no means an unnatural precaution.

At the request of Usher, I personally aided him in the arrangements for the temporary entombment. The body having been encoffined, we two alone bore it to its rest. The vault in which we placed it (and which had been so long unopened that our torches, half smothered in its oppressive atmosphere, gave us little opportunity for investigation) was small, damp, and entirely without means of admission for light; lying, at great depth, immediately beneath that portion of the building in which was my own sleeping apartment. It had been used, apparently, in remote feudal times, for the worst purposes of a donjon-keep, and in later days, as a place of deposit for powder, or some other highly combustible substance, as a portion of its floor, and the whole interior of a long archway through which we reached it, were carefully sheathed with copper. The door, of massive iron, had been also similarly protected. Its immense weight caused an unusually sharp grating sound, as it moved upon its hinges.

Having deposited our mournful burden upon tressels within this region of horror, we partially turned aside the yet unscrewed lid of the coffin, and looked upon the face of the tenant. A striking similitude between the brother and sister now first arrested my attention; and Usher, divining, perhaps, my thoughts, murmured out some few words from which I learned that the deceased and himself had been twins, and that sympathies of a scarcely intelligible nature had always existed between them. Our glances, however, rested not long upon the dead — for we could not regard her unawed. The disease which had thus entombed the lady in the maturity of youth, had left, as usual in all maladies of a strictly cataleptical character, the mockery of a faint blush upon the bosom and the face, and that suspiciously lingering smile upon the lip which is so terrible in death. We replaced and screwed down the lid, and having secured the door of iron, made our way, with toil, into the scarcely less gloomy apartments of the upper portion of the house.

And now, some days of bitter grief having elapsed, an observable change came over the features of the mental disorder of my friend. His ordinary manner had vanished. His ordinary occupations were neglected or forgotten. He roamed from chamber to chamber with hurried, unequal, and objectless step. The pallor of his countenance had assumed, if possible, a more ghastly hue — but the luminousness of his eye had utterly gone out. The once occasional huskiness of his tone was heard no more; and a tremulous quaver, as if of extreme terror, habitually characterized his utterance. There were times, indeed, when I thought his unceasingly agitated mind was laboring with some oppressive secret, to divulge which he struggled for the necessary courage. At times, again, I was obliged to resolve all into the mere inexplicable vagaries of madness; for I beheld him gazing upon vacancy for long hours, in an attitude of the profoundest attention, as if listening to some imaginary sound. It was no wonder that his condition terrified — that it infected me. I felt creeping upon me, by slow yet certain degrees, the wild influence of his own fantastic yet impressive superstitions.

It was, especially, upon retiring to bed late in the night of the seventh or eighth day after the placing of the lady Madeline within the donjon, that I experienced the full power of such feelings. Sleep came not near my couch, while the hours waned and waned away. I struggled to reason off the nervousness which had dominion over me. I endeavored to believe that much, if not all of what I felt, was due to the bewildering influence of the gloomy furniture of the room — of the dark and tattered draperies, which, tortured into motion by the breath of a rising tempest, swayed fitfully to and fro upon the walls, and rustled uneasily about the decorations of the bed. But my efforts were fruitless. An irrepressible tremor gradually pervaded my frame; and, at length, there sat upon my very heart an incubus of utterly causeless alarm. Shaking this off with a gasp and a struggle, I uplifted myself upon the pillows, and peering earnestly within the intense darkness of the chamber, hearkened — I know not why, except that an instinctive spirit prompted me — to certain low and indefinite sounds which came, through the pauses of the storm, at long intervals, I knew not whence. Overpowered by an intense sentiment of horror, unaccountable yet unendurable, I threw on my clothes with haste (for I felt that I should sleep no more during the night), and endeavored to arouse myself from the pitiable condition into which I had fallen, by pacing rapidly to and fro through the apartment.

I had taken but few turns in this manner, when a light step on an adjoining staircase arrested my attention. I presently recognized it as that of Usher. In an instant afterward he rapped, with a gentle touch, at my door, and entered, bearing a lamp. His countenance was, as usual, cadaverously wan — but, moreover, there was a species of mad hilarity in his eyes — and evidently restrained hysteria in his whole demeanor. His air appalled me — but anything was preferable to the solitude which I had so long endured, and I even welcomed his presence as a relief.

"And you have not seen it?" he said abruptly, after having stared about him for some moments in silence — "you have not then seen it? — but stay! you shall." Thus speaking, and having carefully shaded his lamp, he hurried to one of the casements, and threw it freely open to the storm.

The impetuous fury of the entering gust nearly lifted us from our feet. It was, indeed, a tempestuous yet sternly beautiful night, and one wildly singular in its terror and its beauty. A whirlwind had apparently collected its force in our vicinity; for there were frequent and violent alterations in the direction of the wind; and the exceeding density of the clouds (which hung so low as to press upon the turrets of the house) did not prevent our perceiving the lifelike velocity with which they flew careering from all points against each other, without passing away into the distance. I say that even their exceeding density did not prevent our perceiving this — yet we had no glimpse of the moon or stars — nor was there any flashing forth of the lightning. But the under surfaces of the huge masses of agitated vapor, as well as all terrestrial objects immediately around us, were glowing in the unnatural light of a faintly luminous and distinctly visible gaseous exhalation which hung about and enshrouded the mansion.

"You must not — you shall not behold this!" said I, shudderingly, to Usher, as I led him, with a gentle violence, from the window to a seat. "These appearances, which bewilder you, are merely electrical phenomena not uncommon — or it may be that they have their ghastly origin in the rank miasma of the tarn. Let us close this casement — the air is chilling and dangerous to your frame. Here is one of your favorite romances. I will read and you shall listen; and so we will pass away this terrible night together."

The antique volume which I had taken up was the "Mad Trist" of Sir Launcelot Canning; but I had called it a favorite of Usher's more in sad jest than in earnest; for, in truth, there is little in its uncouth and unimaginative prolixity which could have had interest for the lofty and spiritual ideality of my friend. It was, however, the only book immediately at hand; and I indulged a vague hope that the excitement which now agitated the hypochondriac, might find relief (for the history of mental disorder is full of similar anomalies) even in the extremeness of the folly which I should read. Could I have judged, indeed, by the wild, overstrained air of vivacity with which he hearkened, or apparently harkened, to the words of the tale, I might well have congratulated myself upon the success of my design.

I had arrived at that well-known portion of the story where Ethelred, the hero of the "Trist," having sought in vain for peaceable admission into the dwelling of the hermit, proceeds to make good an entrance by force. Here, it will be remembered, the words of the narrative run thus: —

"And Ethelred, who was by nature of a doughty heart, and who was now mighty withal, on account of the powerfulness of the wine which he had drunken, waited no longer to hold parley with the hermit, who, in sooth, was of an obstinate and maliceful turn; but, feeling the rain upon his shoulders, and fearing the rising of the tempest, uplifted his mace outright, and, with blows, made quickly room in the plankings of the door for his gauntleted hand; and now pulling therewith sturdily, he so cracked, and ripped, and tore all asunder, that the noise of the dry and hollow-sounding wood alarummed and reverberated throughout the forest."

At the termination of this sentence I started, and for a moment paused; for it appeared to me (although I at once concluded that my excited fancy had deceived me) — it appeared to me that, from some very remote portion of the mansion, there came, indistinctly, to my ears what might have been, in its exact similarity of character, the echo (but a stifled and dull one certainly) of the very cracking and ripping sound which Sir Launcelot had so particularly described. It was, beyond doubt, the coincidence alone which had arrested my attention; for, amid the rattling of the sashes of the casements, and the ordinary commingled noises of the still increasing storm, the sound, in itself, had nothing, surely, which should have interested or disturbed me. I continued the story: —

"But the good champion Ethelred, now entering within the door, was soar enraged and amazed to perceive no signal of the maliceful hermit; but, in the stead thereof, a dragon of a scaly and prodigious demeanor, and of a fiery tongue, which sate in guard before a palace of gold, with a floor of silver; and upon the wall there hung a shield of shining brass with this legend enwritten:—

> Who entereth herein, a conqueror hath been;
> Who slayeth the dragon, the shield he shall win.

And Ethelred uplifted his mace, and struck upon the head of the dragon, which fell before him, and gave up his pesty breath, with a shriek so horrid and harsh, and withal so piercing, that Ethelred had fain to close his ears with his hands against the dreadful noise of it, the like whereof was never before heard."

Here again I paused abruptly, and now with a feeling of wild amazement — for there could be no doubt whatever that, in this instance, I did actually hear (although from what direction it proceeded I found it impossible to say) a low and apparently distant, but harsh, protracted, and most unusual screaming or grating sound — the exact counterpart of what my fancy had already conjured up for the dragon's unnatural shriek as described by the romancer.

Oppressed, as I certainly was, upon the occurrence of this second and most extraordinary coincidence, by a thousand conflicting sensations, in which wonder and extreme terror were predominant, I still retained sufficient presence of mind to avoid exciting, by any observation, the sensitive nervousness of my companion. I was by no means certain that he had noticed the sounds in question; although, assuredly, a strange alteration had, during the last few minutes, taken place in his demeanor. From a position fronting my own, he had gradually brought round his chair, so as to sit with his face to the door of the chamber; and thus I could but partially perceive his features, although I saw that his lips trembled as if he were murmuring inaudibly. His head had dropped upon his breast — yet I knew that he was not asleep, from the wide and rigid opening of the eye as I caught a glance of it in profile. The motion of his body, too, was at variance with this idea — for he rocked from side to side with a gentle yet constant and uniform sway. Having rapidly taken notice of all this, I resumed the narrative of Sir Launcelot, which thus proceeded : —

"And now the champion, having escaped from the terrible fury of the dragon, bethinking himself of the brazen shield, and of the breaking up of the enchantment which was upon it, removed the carcass from out of the way before him, and approached valorously over the silver pavement of the castle to where the shield was upon the wall ; which in sooth tarried not for his full coming, but fell down at his feet upon the silver floor, with a mighty great and terrible ringing sound."

No sooner had these syllables passed my lips, than — as if a shield of brass had indeed, at the moment, fallen heavily upon a floor of silver — I became aware of a distinct, hollow, metallic and clangorous, yet apparently muffled reverberation. Completely unnerved, I leaped to my feet ; but the measured rocking movement of Usher was undisturbed. I rushed to the chair in which he sat. His eyes were bent fixedly before him, and throughout his whole countenance there reigned a stony rigidity. But, as I placed my hand upon his shoulder, there came a strong shudder over his whole person ; a sickly smile quivered about his lips ; and I saw that he spoke in a low, hurried, and gibbering murmur, as if unconscious of my presence. Bending closely over him, I at length drank in the hideous import of his words.

"Not hear it? — yes, I hear it, and *have* heard it. Long — long — long — many minutes, many hours, many days, have I heard it — yet I dared not — oh, pity me, miserable wretch that I am ! — I dared not — I *dared* not speak ! *We have put her living in the tomb !* Said I not that my senses were acute? I *now* tell you that I heard her first feeble movements in the hollow coffin. I heard them — many, many days ago — yet I dared not — *I dared not speak !* And now — to-night — Ethelred — ha ! ha ! — the breaking of the hermit's door, and the death-cry of the dragon, and the clangor of the shield ! — say, rather, the rending of her coffin, and the grating of the iron hinges of her prison, and her struggles within the coppered archway of the vault ! Oh, whither shall I fly ? Will she not be here anon ? Is she not hurrying to upbraid me for my haste ? Have I not heard her footstep on the stair ? Do I not distinguish that heavy and horrible beating of her heart? Madman!" — here he sprang furiously to his feet, and shrieked out his syllables, as if in the effort he were giving up his soul — " *Madman! I tell you that she now stands without the door!* "

As if in the superhuman energy of his utterance there had been found the potency of a spell — the huge antique panels to which the speaker pointed threw slowly back, upon the instant, their ponderous and ebony jaws. It was the work of the rushing gust — but then without those doors there *did* stand the lofty and enshrouded figure of the lady Madeline of Usher. There was blood upon her white robes, and the evidence of some bitter struggle upon every portion of her emaciated frame. For a moment she remained trembling and reeling to and fro upon the threshold — then, with a low, moaning cry, fell heavily inward upon the person of her brother, and in her violent and now final death-agonies, bore him to the floor a corpse, and a victim to the terrors he had anticipated.

From that chamber, and from that mansion, I fled aghast. The storm was still abroad in all its wrath as I found myself crossing the old causeway. Suddenly there shot along the path a wild light, and I turned to see whence a gleam so unusual could have issued; for the vast house and its shadows were alone behind me. The radiance was that of the full, setting, and blood-red moon, which now shone vividly through that once barely discernible fissure, of which I have before spoken as extending from the roof of the building, in a zigzag direction, to the base. While I gazed, this fissure rapidly widened — there came a fierce breath of the whirlwind — the entire orb of the satellite burst at once upon my sight — my brain reeled as I saw the mighty walls rushing asunder — there was a long tumultuous shouting sound like the voice of a thousand waters — and the deep and dank tarn at my feet closed sullenly and silently over the fragments of the "*House of Usher.*"

NOTE. — In none of his short-stories has Poe been more successful than in this in centering the interest of the reader upon a single theme and in giving to his narrative the unity of impression that he aimed at. He achieves this partly by his rigid exclusion of any suggestion, of any word even, which does not help to complete his picture, — which does not lend its own vague detail to the vision he wished to evoke. From the first note to the last, all is in keeping; there is a consummate harmony of tone. What he had determined to do that he did; by the aid of a thousand artifices of phrasing he accomplished an implacable directness. Attention may be called to the fact that this is rather a story of atmosphere, of a special destiny, than of character or incident, and that therefore Poe begins by description and continues with description, to which he keeps incident and character subordinate.

XI. THE AMBITIOUS GUEST

By Nathaniel Hawthorne (1804-1864)

Hawthorne was a less conscious artist than Poe, and less interested in technic. Although the best of his short-stories achieve essential unity, he seems not to have striven for it; and it is the result not so much of intention as of his instinctive artistic feeling. He was a moralist who did not parade his moral, but who used it as the sustaining skeleton of his narrative. There is an ethical problem at the core of most of his narratives, novels, or brief tales. "The Ambitious Guest" is not the greatest of his short-stories, but it is one of the most characteristic in its quaint simplicity and in its wide application. It was included in the second series of "Twice Told Tales" published in 1845; but it had been written several years earlier.

THE AMBITIOUS GUEST[1]

One September night a family had gathered round their hearth, and piled it high with the driftwood of mountain

[1] Printed by permission of and special arrangement with the authorized publishers, Houghton, Mifflin & Co.

streams, the dry cones of the pine, and the splintered ruins of great trees that had come crashing down the precipice. Up the chimney roared the fire, and brightened the room with its broad blaze. The faces of the father and mother had a sober gladness; the children laughed; the eldest daughter was the image of Happiness at seventeen; and the aged grandmother, who sat knitting in the warmest place, was the image of Happiness grown old. They had found the "herb, heart's-ease," in the bleakest spot of all New England. This family were situated in the Notch of the White Hills, where the wind was sharp throughout the year, and pitilessly cold in the winter, — giving their cottage all its fresh inclemency before it descended on the valley of the Saco. They dwelt in a cold spot and a dangerous one; for a mountain towered above their heads, so steep that the stones would often rumble down its sides and startle them at midnight.

The daughter had just uttered some simple jest that filled them all with mirth, when the wind came through the Notch and seemed to pause before their cottage — rattling the door, with a sound of wailing and lamentation, before it passed into the valley. For a moment it saddened them, though there was nothing unusual in the tones. But the family were glad again when they perceived that the latch was lifted by some traveler, whose footsteps had been unheard amid the dreary blast which heralded his approach, and wailed as he was entering, and went moaning away from the door.

Though they dwelt in such a solitude, these people held daily converse with the world. The romantic pass of the Notch is a great artery, through which the life-blood of internal commerce is continually throbbing between Maine, on one side, and the Green Mountains and the shores of the St. Lawrence, on the other. The stagecoach always drew up before the door of the cottage. The wayfarer, with no companion but his staff, paused here to exchange a word, that the sense of loneliness might not utterly overcome him ere he could pass through the cleft of the mountain, or reach the first house in the valley. And here the teamster, on his way to Portland market, would put up for the night; and, if a bachelor, might sit an hour beyond the usual bedtime, and steal a kiss from the mountain maid at parting. It was one of those primitive taverns where the traveler pays only for food and lodging, but meets with a homely kindness beyond all price. When the footsteps were heard, therefore, between the outer door and the inner one, the whole family rose up, grandmother, children, and all, as if about to welcome some one who belonged to them, and whose fate was linked with theirs.

The door was opened by a young man. His face at first wore the melancholy expression, almost despondency, of one who travels a wild and bleak road, at nightfall and alone, but soon brightened up when he saw the kindly warmth of his reception. He felt his heart spring forward to meet them all, from the old woman, who wiped a chair with her apron, to the little child that held out its arms to him. One glance and smile placed the stranger on a footing of innocent familiarity with the eldest daughter.

"Ah, this fire is the right thing!" cried he; "especially when there is such a pleasant circle round it. I am quite benumbed; for the Notch is just like the pipe of a great pair of bellows; it has blown a terrible blast in my face all the way from Bartlett."

"Then you are going toward Vermont?" said the master of the house, as he helped to take a light knapsack off the young man's shoulders.

"Yes; to Burlington, and far enough beyond," replied he. "I meant to have been at Ethan Crawford's to-night; but a pedestrian lingers along such a road as this. It is no matter; for, when I saw this good fire, and all your cheerful faces, I felt as if you had kindled it on purpose for me, and were waiting my arrival. So I shall sit down among you, and make myself at home."

The frank-hearted stranger had just drawn his chair to the fire when something like a heavy footstep was heard without, rushing down the steep side of the mountain, as with long and rapid strides, and taking such a leap in passing the cottage as to strike the opposite precipice. The family held their breath, because they knew the sound, and their guest held his by instinct.

"The old mountain has thrown a stone at us, for fear we should forget him," said the landlord, recovering himself. "He sometimes nods his head and threatens to come down; but we are old neighbors, and agree together pretty well upon the whole. Besides, we have a sure place of refuge hard by if he should be coming in good earnest."

Let us now suppose the stranger to have finished his supper of bear's meat; and, by his natural felicity of manner, to have placed himself on a footing of kindness with the whole family, so that they talked as freely together as if he belonged to their mountain brood. He was of a proud, yet gentle spirit — haughty and reserved among the rich and great; but ever ready to stoop his head to the lowly cottage door, and be like a brother or a son at the poor man's fireside. In the household of the Notch he found warmth and simplicity of feeling, the pervading intelligence of New England, and a poetry, of native growth, which they had gathered when they little thought of it from the mountain peaks and chasms, and at the very threshold of their romantic and dangerous abode. He had traveled far and alone; his whole life, indeed, had been a solitary path; for, with the lofty caution of his nature, he had kept himself apart from those who might otherwise have been his companions. The family, too, though so kind and hospitable, had that consciousness of unity among themselves, and separation from the world at large, which, in every domestic circle, should still keep a holy place where no stranger may intrude. But this evening a prophetic sympathy impelled the refined and educated youth to pour out his heart before the simple mountaineers, and constrained them to answer him with the same free confidence. And thus it should have been. Is not the kindred of a common fate a closer tie than that of birth?

The secret of the young man's character was a high and abstracted ambition. He could have borne to live an undistinguished life, but not to be forgotten in the grave. Yearning desire had been transformed to hope; and hope, long cherished, had become like certainty that, obscurely as he journeyed now, a glory was to beam on all his pathway, — though not, perhaps, while he was treading it. But when posterity should gaze back into the gloom of what was now the present, they would trace the brightness of his footsteps, brightening as meaner glories faded, and confess that a gifted one had passed from his cradle to his tomb with none to recognize him.

"As yet," cried the stranger,—his cheek glowing and his eye flashing with enthusiasm,—"as yet, I have done nothing. Were I to vanish from the earth to-morrow, none would know so much of me as you: that a nameless youth came up at nightfall from the valley of the Saco, and opened his heart to you in the evening, and passed through the Notch by sunrise, and was seen no more. Not a soul would ask, 'Who was he? Whither did the wanderer go?' But I cannot die till I have achieved my destiny. Then, let Death come! I shall have built my monument!"

There was a continual flow of natural emotion, gushing forth amid abstracted revery, which enabled the family to understand this young man's sentiments, though so foreign from their own. With quick sensibility of the ludicrous, he blushed at the ardor into which he had been betrayed.

"You laugh at me," said he, taking the eldest daughter's hand, and laughing himself. "You think my ambition as nonsensical as if I were to freeze myself to death on the top of Mount Washington, only that people might spy at me from the country round about. And, truly, that would be a noble pedestal for a man's statue!"

"It is better to sit here by this fire," answered the girl, blushing, "and be comfortable and contented, though nobody thinks about us."

"I suppose," said her father, after a fit of musing,

"there is something natural in what the young man says; and if my mind had been turned that way, I might have felt just the same. It is strange, wife, how his talk has set my head running on things that are pretty certain never to come to pass."

"Perhaps they may," observed the wife. "Is the man thinking what he will do when he is a widower?"

"No, no!" cried he, repelling the idea with reproachful kindness. "When I think of your death, Esther, I think of mine, too. But I was wishing we had a good farm in Bartlett, or Bethlehem, or Littleton, or some other township round the White Mountains; but not where they could tumble on our heads. I should want to stand well with my neighbors and be called Squire, and sent to General Court for a term or two; for a plain, honest man may do as much good there as a lawyer. And when I should be grown quite an old man and you an old woman, so as not to be long apart, I might die happy enough in my bed, and leave you all crying around me. A slate gravestone would suit me as well as a marble one — with just my name and age, and a verse of a hymn, and something to let people know that I lived an honest man and died a Christian."

"There now!" exclaimed the stranger; "it is our nature to desire a monument, be it slate or marble, or a pillar of granite, or a glorious memory in the universal heart of man."

"We're in a strange way to-night," said the wife, with tears in her eyes. "They say it's a sign of something, when folks' minds go a-wandering so. Hark to the children!"

THE AMBITIOUS GUEST

They listened accordingly. The younger children had been put to bed in another room, but with an open door between them, so that they could be heard talking busily among themselves. One and all seemed to have caught the infection from the fireside circle, and were outvying each other in wild wishes, and childish projects of what they would do when they came to be men and women. At length a little boy, instead of addressing his brothers and sisters, called out to his mother.

"I'll tell you what I wish, mother," cried he. "I want you and father and grandma'm, and all of us, and the stranger, too, to start right away, and go and take a drink out of the basin of the Flume!"

Nobody could help laughing at the child's notion of leaving a warm bed, and dragging them from a cheerful fire, to visit the basin of the Flume, — a brook which tumbles over the precipice, deep within in the Notch. The boy had hardly spoken when a wagon rattled along the road, and stopped a moment before the door. It appeared to contain two or three men, who were cheering their hearts with the rough chorus of a song, which resounded, in broken notes, between the cliffs, while the singers hesitated whether to continue their journey or put up here for the night."

"Father," said the girl, "they are calling you by name."

But the good man doubted whether they had really called him, and was unwilling to show himself too solicitous of gain by inviting people to patronize his house. He therefore did not hurry to the door; and the lash being soon applied, the travelers plunged into the Notch, still singing and laughing, though their music and mirth came back drearily from the heart of the mountain.

"There, mother!" cried the boy again. "They'd have given us a ride to the Flume."

Again they laughed at the child's pertinacious fancy for a night ramble. But it happened that a light cloud passed over the daughter's spirit; she looked gravely into the fire, and drew a breath that was almost a sigh. It forced its way in spite of the struggle to repress it. Then, starting and blushing, she looked quickly round the circle, as if they had caught a glimpse into her bosom. The stranger asked what she had been thinking of.

"Nothing," answered she, with a downcast smile. "Only I felt lonesome just then."

"Oh, I have always had a gift of feeling what is in other people's hearts," said he, half seriously. "Shall I tell the secrets of yours? For I know what to think when a young girl shivers by a warm hearth, and complains of lonesomeness at her mother's side. Shall I put these feelings into words?"

"They would not be a girl's feelings any longer if they could be put into words," replied the mountain nymph, laughing, but avoiding his eye.

All this was said apart. Perhaps a germ of love was springing in their hearts, so pure that it might blossom in Paradise, since it could not be matured on earth; for women worship such gentle dignity as his; and the proud, contemplative, yet kindly soul is oftenest captivated by simplicity like hers. But while they spoke softly, and he was watching the happy sadness, the lightsome shadows, the shy yearnings of a maiden's nature, the wind through

THE AMBITIOUS GUEST

the Notch took a deeper and drearier sound. It seemed, as the fanciful stranger said, like the choral strain of the spirits of the past, who in old Indian times had their dwelling among these mountains, and made their heights and recesses a sacred region. There was a wail along the road, as if a funeral were passing. To chase away the gloom, the family threw pine branches on their fire, till the dry leaves crackled and the flame arose, discovering once again a scene of peace and humble happiness. The light hovered about them fondly, and caressed them all. There were the little faces of the children, peeping from their bed apart, and here the father's frame of strength, the mother's subdued and careful mien, the high-browed youth, the budding girl, and the good old grandma, still knitting in the warmest place. The aged woman looked up from her task, and, with fingers ever busy, was the next to speak.

"Old folks have their notions," said she, "as well as young ones. You've been wishing and planning, and letting your heads run on one thing and another, till you've set my mind a-wandering too. Now what should an old woman wish for, when she can go but a step or two before she comes to her grave? Children, it will haunt me night and day till I tell you."

"What is it, mother?" cried the husband and wife at once.

Then the old woman, with an air of mystery which drew the circle closer round the fire, informed them that she had provided her grave-clothes some years before,—a nice linen shroud, a cap with a muslin ruff, and everything of a finer sort than she had worn since her wedding day. But this evening an old superstition had strangely recurred to her. It used to be said, in her younger days, that if anything were amiss with a corpse, if only the ruff were not smooth, or the cap did not set right, the corpse in the coffin and beneath the clods would strive to put up its cold hands and arrange it. The bare thought made her nervous.

"Don't talk so, grandmother!" said the girl, shuddering.

"Now," — continued the old woman, with singular earnestness, yet smiling strangely at her own folly, — "I want one of you, my children, — when your mother is dressed in the coffin — I want one of you to hold a looking-glass over my face. Who knows but I may take a glimpse at myself, and see whether all's right."

"Old and young, we dream of graves and monuments," murmured the stranger youth. "I wonder how mariners feel when the ship is sinking, and they, unknown and undistinguished, are to be buried together in the ocean — that wide and nameless sepulcher?"

For a moment, the old woman's ghastly conception so engrossed the minds of her hearers that a sound abroad in the night, rising like the roar of a blast, had grown broad, deep, and terrible, before the fated group were conscious of it. The house and all within it trembled; the foundations of the earth seemed to be shaken, as if this awful sound were the peal of the last trump. Young and old exchanged one wild glance, and remained an instant, pale, affrighted, without utterance, or power to move. Then the same shriek burst simultaneously from all their lips. "The Slide! The Slide!"

The simplest words must intimate, but not portray, the unutterable horror of the catastrophe. The victims rushed from their cottage, and sought refuge in what they deemed a safer spot — where, in contemplation of such an emergency, a sort of barrier had been reared. Alas! they had quitted their security, and fled right into the pathway of destruction. Down came the whole side of the mountain, in a cataract of ruin. Just before it reached the house, the stream broke into two branches — shivered not a window there, but overwhelmed the whole vicinity, blocked up the road, and annihilated everything in its dreadful course. Long ere the thunder of the great Slide had ceased to roar among the mountains, the mortal agony had been endured, and the victims were at peace. Their bodies were never found.

The next morning, the light smoke was seen stealing from the cottage chimney up the mountain side. Within, the fire was yet smoldering on the hearth, and the chairs in a circle around it, as if the inhabitants had but gone forth to view the devastation of the Slide and would shortly return, to thank Heaven for their miraculous escape. All had left separate tokens, by which those who had known the family were made to shed a tear for each. Who has not heard their name? The story has been told far and wide, and will forever be a legend of these mountains. Poets have sung their fate.

There were circumstances which led some to suppose that a stranger had been received into the cottage on this awful night, and had shared the catastrophe of all its inmates. Others denied that there were sufficient grounds for such a conjecture. Woe for the high-souled youth, with his dream of Earthly Immortality! His name and person utterly unknown; his history, his way of life, his plans, a mystery never to be solved, his death and his existence equally a doubt! Whose was the agony of that death moment?

NOTE. — The perfect harmony of the narrative, the commonplace persons presented, the unexpectedness of the appalling catastrophe, — these are the obvious characteristics of this story. As we read the unpretending recital we feel that this is what might have happened — indeed, that this is what must have happened. The art of the narrator is so perfect here, his adjustment of his characters to his theme is so complete, that we do not always perceive the adroitness of the craftsman, and we may even overlook momentarily the application of the moral which underlies the fiction. In no other short-story of Hawthorne's is his transparent simplicity more evident. And here attention may be called to the fact that as Hawthorne wanted us to be interested in the characters rather than in the scene he begins at once with his personages, reserving till later his description of the place where they all gathered.

XII. A CHILD'S DREAM OF A STAR

By Charles Dickens (1812–1870)

Like Scott, Dickens preferred the long story to the short. He unrolled the panorama of life as he saw it, with its contrasts of broad humor and of pathetic sentiment. Although he took great pains with the plots of his novels, they are ill-shaped for the most part, sprawling and invertebrate. He had not the power of building a story boldly yet simply. The brief tales which he inserted in the early " Pickwick Papers " lack distinction; and the short-stories written long after are often marred by the hard artificiality which characterized much of his later work. But this little tale, written in 1850 on a sudden impulse, is simple and unpretending; and it gains its beauty from this unpretentious simplicity.

A CHILD'S DREAM OF A STAR

There was once a child, and he strolled about a good deal, and thought of a number of things. He had a sister, who was a child, too, and his constant companion. These two used to wonder all day long. They wondered at the beauty of the flowers; they wondered at the height and blueness of the sky; they wondered at the depth of the bright water; they wondered at the goodness and the power of God who made the lovely world.

They used to say to one another sometimes, Supposing all the children upon earth were to die, would the flowers, and the water, and the sky be sorry? They believed they would be sorry. For, said they, the buds are the children of the flowers, and the little playful streams that gambol down the hillsides are the children of the water; and the smallest bright specks playing at hide-and-seek in the sky all night, must surely be the children of the stars; and they would all be grieved to see their playmates, the children of men, no more.

There was one clear shining star that used to come out in the sky before the rest, near the church spire, above the graves. It was larger and more beautiful, they thought, than all others, and every night they watched for it, standing hand in hand at the window. Whoever saw it first, cried out, "I see the star!" And often they cried out both together, knowing so well when it would rise, and where. So they grew to be such friends with it, that before lying down in their beds, they always looked out once again, to bid it good night; and when they were turning around to sleep, they used to say, "God bless the star!"

But while she was very young, oh, very, very young, the sister drooped, and came to be so weak that she could no longer stand in the window at night; and then the child looked sadly out by himself, and when he saw the star, turned round and said to the patient, pale face on the bed, "I see the star!" and then a smile would come upon

A CHILD'S DREAM OF A STAR

the face, and a little weak voice used to say, "God bless my brother and the star!"

And so the time came, all too soon! when the child looked out alone, and when there was no face on the bed; and when there was a little grave among the graves, not there before; and when the star made long rays down toward him, as he saw it through his tears.

Now, these rays were so bright, and they seemed to make such a shining way from earth to heaven, that when the child went to his solitary bed, he dreamed about the star; and dreamed that, lying where he was, he saw a train of people taken up that sparkling road by angels. And the star, opening, showed him a great world of light, where many more such angels waited to receive them.

All these angels who were waiting turned their beaming eyes upon the people who were carried up into the star; and some came out from the long rows in which they stood, and fell upon the people's necks, and kissed them tenderly, and went away with them down avenues of light, and were so happy in their company, that lying in his bed he wept for joy.

But there were many angels who did not go with them, and among them one he knew. The patient face that once had lain upon the bed was glorified and radiant, but his heart found out his sister among all the host.

His sister's angel lingered near the entrance of the star, and said to the leader among those who had brought the people thither —

"Is my brother come?"

And he said, "No."

She was turning hopefully away, when the child stretched

out his arms, and cried, "O sister, I am here! Take me!" And then she turned her beaming eyes upon him and it was night; and the star was shining into the room, making long rays down toward him as he saw it through his tears.

From that hour forth the child looked out upon the star as on the home he was to go to, when his time should come; and he thought that he did not belong to the earth alone, but to the star, too, because of his sister's angel gone before.

There was a baby born to be a brother to the child; and while he was so little that he never yet had spoken word, he stretched his tiny form out on his bed and died.

Again the child dreamed of the opened star, and of the company of angels, and the train of people, and the rows of angels with their beaming eyes all turned upon those people's faces.

Said his sister's angel to the leader: —

"Is my brother come?"

And he said, "Not that one, but another."

As the child beheld his brother's angel in her arms, he cried: "O sister, I am here! Take me!" And she turned and smiled upon him, and the star was shining.

He grew to be a young man, and was busy at his books, when an old servant came to him and said: —

"Thy mother is no more. I bring her blessing on her darling son!"

Again at night he saw the star, and all that former company. Said his sister's angel to the leader: —

"Is my brother come?"

And he said, "Thy mother!"

A CHILD'S DREAM OF A STAR

A mighty cry of joy went forth through all the star, because the mother was reunited to her two children. And he stretched out his arms and cried: "O mother, sister, and brother, I am here! Take me!" And they answered him, "Not yet." And the star was shining.

He grew to be a man whose hair was turning gray, and he was sitting in his chair by the fireside, heavy with grief, and with his face bedewed with tears, when the star opened once again.

Said his sister's angel to the leader, "Is my brother come?"

And he said, "Nay, but his maiden daughter."

And the man who had been the child saw his daughter, newly lost to him, a celestial creature among those three, and he said, "My daughter's head is on my sister's bosom, and her arm is round my mother's neck, and at her feet there is the baby of old time, and I can bear the parting from her, God be praised!"

And the star was shining.

Thus the child came to be an old man, and his once smooth face was wrinkled, and his steps were slow and feeble, and his back was bent. And one night as he lay upon his bed, his children standing round, he cried, as he had cried so long ago: —

"I see the star!"

They whispered one another, "He is dying."

And he said: "I am. My age is falling from me like a garment, and I move toward the star as a child. And, O my Father, now I thank thee that it has so often opened to receive those dear ones who await me!"

And the star was shining; and it shines upon his grave.

NOTE. — Dickens told one of his biographers that as a child he used to wander at night about a churchyard, near their home, with his sister. This sister died only two years before this poetic fantasy was written. Perhaps it was the sincerity of his grief for this lost sister which keeps this story as simple as it is in its sentiment. It is a fable, a lovely apologue, slight in substance and yet adequate in itself. This story of Dickens's may be compared profitably with Lamb's "Dream-Children" and with Andersen's "Steadfast Tin Soldier." All three are fantasies; all three deal with childhood; all three are poetic, each in its own fashion. They all fall well within the frame of the true short-story because the several authors sought to present a single theme with the clearest simplicity.

XIII. WHAT WAS IT? A MYSTERY

By Fitz-James O'Brien (1828–1862)

This brilliant Irish-American was killed in the Civil War before he was thirty-five. He left a group of striking tales, akin to those of Poe, by whom he had been chiefly influenced; and yet he had originality of his own and abundant invention. He lacked the swiftness, the directness, and the certainty of his master; and the short-story here selected has a compactness not always found in his other efforts. It was written in 1859; and it seems to have suggested to Guy de Maupassant his even more powerful "Le Horla." To adjust O'Brien's narrative to the plan of this volume a few omissions have been made.

WHAT WAS IT? A MYSTERY

It is, I confess, with considerable diffidence that I approach the strange narrative which I am about to relate. The events which I purpose detailing are of so extraordinary and unheard-of a character that I am quite prepared to meet with an unusual amount of incredulity and scorn. I accept all such beforehand. I have, I trust, the literary courage to face unbelief. I have, after mature consideration, resolved to narrate, in as simple and straightforward a manner as I can compass, some facts that passed under my observation in the month of July last, and which, in the annals of the mysteries of physical science, are wholly unparalleled.

I live at No. — Twenty-sixth Street, in this city. The house is in some respects a curious one. It has enjoyed for the last two years the reputation of being haunted. It is a large and stately residence, surrounded by what was once a garden, but which is now only a green inclosure used for bleaching clothes. The dry basin of what has been a fountain, and a few fruit-trees, ragged and unpruned, indicate that this spot, in past days, was a pleasant, shady retreat, filled with fruits and flowers and the sweet murmur of waters.

The house is very spacious. A hall of noble size leads to a vast spiral staircase winding through its center, while the various apartments are of imposing dimensions. It was built some fifteen or twenty years since by Mr. A——, the well-known New York merchant, who five years ago threw the commercial world into convulsions by a stupendous bank fraud. Mr. A——, as every one knows, escaped to Europe, and died not long after of a broken heart. Almost immediately after the news of his decease reached this country, and was verified, the report spread in Twenty-sixth Street that No. — was haunted. Legal measures had dispossessed the widow of its former owner, and it was inhabited merely by a care taker and his wife, placed there by the house agent into whose hands it had passed for purposes of renting or sale. These people declared that they were troubled with unnatural noises.

WHAT WAS IT? A MYSTERY

Doors were opened without any visible agency. The remnants of furniture scattered through the various rooms were, during the night, piled one upon the other by unknown hands. Invisible feet passed up and down the stairs in broad daylight, accompanied by the rustle of unseen silk dresses, and the gliding of viewless hands along the massive balusters. The care taker and his wife declared that they would live there no longer. The house agent laughed, dismissed them, and put others in their place. The noises and supernatural manifestations continued. The neighborhood caught up the story, and the house remained untenanted for three years. Several persons negotiated for it; but somehow, always before the bargain was closed, they heard the unpleasant rumors, and declined to treat any further.

It was in this state of things that my landlady — who at that time kept a boarding-house in Bleecker Street, and who wished to move farther up town — conceived the bold idea of renting No. — Twenty-sixth Street. Happening to have in her house rather a plucky and philosophical set of boarders, she laid down her scheme before us, stating candidly everything she had heard respecting the ghostly qualities of the establishment to which she wished to remove us. With the exception of two timid persons, — a sea captain and a returned Californian, who immediately gave notice that they would leave, — all of Mrs. Moffat's guests declared that they would accompany her in her chivalric incursion into the abode of spirits.

Our removal was effected in the month of May, and we were all charmed with our new residence. The portion of Twenty-sixth Street where our house is situated — between Seventh and Eighth Avenues — is one of the pleasantest localities in New York. The gardens back of the houses, running down nearly to the Hudson, form, in the summer time, a perfect avenue of verdure. The air is pure and invigorating, sweeping, as it does, straight across the river from the Weehawken heights, and even the ragged garden which surrounded the house on two sides, although displaying on washing days rather too much clothesline, still gave us a piece of greensward to look at, and a cool retreat in the summer evenings, where we smoked our cigars in the dusk, and watched the fireflies flashing their dark-lanterns in the long grass.

Of course we had no sooner established ourselves at No. — than we began to expect the ghosts. We absolutely awaited their advent with eagerness. Our dinner conversation was supernatural. One of the boarders, who had purchased Mrs. Crowe's "Night Side of Nature" for his own private delectation, was regarded as a public enemy by the entire household for not having bought twenty copies. The man led a life of supreme wretchedness while he was reading this volume. A system of espionage was established, of which he was the victim. If he incautiously laid the book down for an instant and left the room, it was immediately seized and read aloud in secret places to a select few. I found myself a person of immense importance, it having leaked out that I was tolerably well versed in the history of supernaturalism, and had once written a story, entitled "The Pot of Tulips," for *Harper's Monthly*, the foundation of which was a ghost. If a table or a wainscot panel happened to warp when we were assembled in the large drawing-room, there was an instant

WHAT WAS IT? A MYSTERY

silence, and every one was prepared for an immediate clanking of chains and a spectral form.

After a month of psychological excitement, it was with the utmost dissatisfaction that we were forced to acknowledge that nothing in the remotest degree approaching the supernatural had manifested itself. Once the black butler asseverated that his candle had been blown out by some invisible agency while he was undressing himself for the night; but as I had more than once discovered this colored gentleman in a condition when one candle must have appeared to him like two, I thought it possible that, by going a step farther in his potations, he might have reversed his phenomenon, and seen no candle at all where he ought to have beheld one.

Things were in this state when an incident took place so awful and inexplicable in its character that my reason fairly reels at the bare memory of the occurrence. It was the tenth of July. After dinner was over I repaired with my friend, Dr. Hammond, to the garden to smoke my evening pipe. The Doctor and myself found ourselves in an unusually metaphysical mood. We lit our large meerschaums, filled with fine Turkish tobacco; we paced to and fro, conversing. A strange perversity dominated the currents of our thought. They would *not* flow through the sun-lit channels into which we strove to divert them. For some unaccountable reason they constantly diverged into dark and lonesome beds, where a continual gloom brooded. It was in vain that, after our old fashion, we flung ourselves on the shores of the East, and talked of its gay bazaars, of the splendors of the time of Haroun, of harems and golden palaces. Black afreets continually arose from the depths of our talk, and expanded, like the one the fisherman released from the copper vessel, until they blotted everything bright from our vision. Insensibly, we yielded to the occult force that swayed us, and indulged in gloomy speculation. We had talked some time upon the proneness of the human mind to mysticism, and the almost universal love of the Terrible, when Hammond suddenly said to me, "What do you consider to be the greatest element of Terror?"

The question, I own, puzzled me. That many things were terrible, I knew. Stumbling over a corpse in the dark; beholding, as I once did, a woman floating down a deep and rapid river, with wildly lifted arms, and awful, upturned face, uttering, as she sank, shrieks that rent one's heart, while we, the spectators, stood frozen at a window which overhung the river at a height of sixty feet, unable to make the slightest effort to save her, but dumbly watching her last supreme agony and her disappearance. A shattered wreck, with no life visible, encountered floating listlessly on the ocean, is a terrible object, for it suggests a huge terror, the proportions of which are veiled. But it now struck me for the first time that there must be one great and ruling embodiment of fear, a King of Terrors to which all others must succumb. What might it be? To what train of circumstances would it owe its existence?

"I confess, Hammond," I replied to my friend, "I never considered the subject before. That there must be one Something more terrible than any other thing, I feel. I cannot attempt, however, even the most vague definition."

"I am somewhat like you, Harry," he answered. "I feel my capacity to experience a terror greater than anything yet conceived by the human mind, — something combining in fearful and unnatural amalgamation hitherto supposed incompatible elements. The calling of the voices in Brockden Brown's novel of 'Wieland' is awful; so is the picture of the Dweller of the Threshold, in Bulwer's 'Zanoni'; "but," he added, shaking his head gloomily, "there is something more horrible still than these."

"Look here, Hammond," I rejoined, "let us drop this kind of talk, for Heaven's sake!"

"I don't know what's the matter with me to-night," he replied, "but my brain is running upon all sorts of weird and awful thoughts. I feel as if I could write a story like Hoffman to night, if I were only master of a literary style."

"Well, if we are going to be Hoffmanesque in our talk, I'm off to bed. How sultry it is! Good night, Hammond."

"Good night, Harry. Pleasant dreams to you."

"To you, gloomy wretch, afreets, ghouls, and enchanters."

We parted, and each sought his respective chamber. I undressed quickly and got into bed, taking with me, according to my usual custom, a book, over which I generally read myself to sleep. I opened the volume as soon as I had laid my head upon the pillow, and instantly flung it to the other side of the room. It was Goudon's "History of Monsters"—a curious French work, which I had lately imported from Paris, but which, in the state of mind I had then reached, was anything but an agreeable companion. I resolved to go to sleep at once; so, turning down my gas until nothing but a little blue point of light glimmered on the top of the tube, I composed myself to rest.

The room was in total darkness. The atom of gas that still remained lighted did not illuminate a distance of three inches round the burner. I desperately drew my arm across my eyes, as if to shut out even the darkness, and tried to think of nothing. It was in vain. The confounded themes touched on by Hammond in the garden kept obtruding themselves on my brain. I battled against them. I erected ramparts of would-be blankness of intellect to keep them out. They still crowded upon me. While I was lying still as a corpse, hoping that by a perfect physical inaction I should hasten mental repose, an awful incident occurred. A Something dropped, as it seemed, from the ceiling, plumb upon my chest, and the next instant I felt two bony hands encircling my throat, endeavoring to choke me.

I am no coward, and am possessed of considerable physical strength. The suddenness of the attack, instead of stunning me, strung every nerve to its highest tension. My body acted from instinct, before my brain had time to realize the terrors of my position. In an instant I wound two muscular arms around the creature, and squeezed it, with all the strength of despair, against my chest. In a few seconds the bony hands that had fastened on my throat loosened their hold, and I was free to breathe once more. Then commenced a struggle of awful intensity. Immersed in the most profound darkness, totally ignorant of the nature of the Thing by

WHAT WAS IT? A MYSTERY

which I was so suddenly attacked, finding my grasp slipping every moment, by reason, it seemed to me, of the entire nakedness of my assailant, bitten with sharp teeth in the shoulder, neck, and chest, having every moment to protect my throat against a pair of sinewy, agile hands, which my utmost efforts could not confine — these were a combination of circumstances to combat which required all the strength and skill and courage that I possessed.

At last, after a silent, deadly, exhausting struggle, I got my assailant under by a series of incredible efforts of strength. Once pinned, with my knee on what I made out to be its chest, I knew that I was victor. I rested for a moment to breathe. I heard the creature beneath me panting in the darkness, and felt the violent throbbing of a heart. It was apparently as exhausted as I was; that was one comfort. At this moment I remembered that I usually placed under my pillow, before going to bed, a large yellow silk pocket handkerchief, for use during the night. I felt for it instantly; it was there. In a few seconds more I had, after a fashion, pinioned the creature's arms.

I now felt tolerably secure. There was nothing more to be done but to turn on the gas, and, having first seen what my midnight assailant was like, arouse the household. I will confess to being actuated by a certain pride in not giving the alarm before; I wished to make the capture alone and unaided.

Never losing my hold for an instant, I slipped from the bed to the floor, dragging my captive with me. I had but a few steps to make to reach the gas-burner;

these I made with the greatest caution, holding the creature in a grip like a vice. At last I got within arm's-length of the tiny speck of blue light which told me where the gas-burner lay. Quick as lightning I released my grasp with one hand and let on the full flood of light. Then I turned to look at my captive.

I cannot even attempt to give any definition of my sensations the instant after I turned on the gas. I suppose I must have shrieked with terror, for in less than a minute afterward my room was crowded with the inmates of the house. I shudder now as I think of that awful moment. *I saw nothing!* Yes; I had one arm firmly clasped round a breathing, panting, corporeal shape, my other hand gripped with all its strength a throat as warm, and apparently fleshly, as my own; and yet, with this living substance in my grasp, with its body pressed against my own, and all in the bright glare of a large jet of gas, I absolutely beheld nothing! Not even an outline, — a vapor!

I do not, even at this hour, realize the situation in which I found myself. I cannot recall the astounding incident thoroughly. Imagination in vain tries to compass the awful paradox.

It breathed. I felt its warm breath upon my cheek. It struggled fiercely. It had hands. They clutched me. Its skin was smooth, like my own. There it lay, pressed close up against me, solid as stone, — and yet utterly invisible!

I wonder that I did not faint or go mad on the instant. Some wonderful instinct must have sustained me; for, absolutely, in place of loosening my hold on the terrible Enigma, I seemed to gain an additional strength in my moment of horror, and tightened my grasp with such wonderful force that I felt the creature shivering with agony.

Just then Hammond entered my room at the head of the household. As soon as he beheld my face — which, I suppose, must have been an awful sight to look at — he hastened forward, crying, "Great heaven, Harry! what has happened?"

"Hammond! Hammond!" I cried, "come here. Oh! this is awful! I have been attacked in bed by something or other, which I have hold of; but I can't see it — I can't see it!"

Hammond, doubtless struck by the unfeigned horror expressed in my countenance, made one or two steps forward with an anxious yet puzzled expression. A very audible titter burst from the remainder of my visitors. This suppressed laughter made me furious. To laugh at a human being in my position! It was the worst species of cruelty. *Now*, I can understand why the appearance of a man struggling violently, as it would seem, with an airy nothing, and calling for assistance against a vision, should have appeared ludicrous. *Then*, so great was my rage against the mocking crowd that had I the power I would have stricken them dead where they stood.

"Hammond! Hammond!" I cried again, despairingly, "for God's sake come to me. I can hold the — the Thing but a short while longer. It is overpowering me. Help me! Help me!"

"Harry," whispered Hammond, approaching me, "you have been smoking too much."

"I swear to you, Hammond, that this is no vision," I answered, in the same low tone. "Don't you see how it shakes my whole frame with its struggles? If you don't believe me, convince yourself. Feel it, — touch it."

Hammond advanced and laid his hand on the spot I indicated. A wild cry of horror burst from him. He had felt it!

In a moment he had discovered somewhere in my room a long piece of cord, and was the next instant winding it and knotting it about the body of the unseen being that I clasped in my arms.

"Harry," he said, in a hoarse, agitated voice, for, though he preserved his presence of mind, he was deeply moved, "Harry, it's all safe now. You may let go, old fellow, if you're tired. The Thing can't move."

I was utterly exhausted, and I gladly loosed my hold.

Hammond stood holding the ends of the cord that bound the Invisible, twisted round his hand, while before him, self-supporting as it were, he beheld a rope laced and interlaced, and stretching tightly round a vacant space. I never saw a man look so thoroughly stricken with awe. Nevertheless his face expressed all the courage and determination which I knew him to possess. His lips, although white, were set firmly, and one could perceive at a glance that, although stricken with fear, he was not daunted.

The confusion that ensued among the guests of the house who were witnesses of this extraordinary scene between Hammond and myself, — who beheld the pantomime of binding this struggling Something, — who beheld me almost sinking from physical exhaustion when my task

WHAT WAS IT? A MYSTERY

of jailer was over — the confusion and terror that took possession of the bystanders, when they saw all this, was beyond description. The weaker ones fled from the apartment. The few who remained clustered near the door, and could not be induced to approach Hammond and his Charge. Still incredulity broke out through their terror. They had not the courage to satisfy themselves, and yet they doubted. It was in vain that I begged of some of the men to come near and convince themselves by touch of the existence in that room of a living being which was invisible. They were incredulous, but did not dare to undeceive themselves. How could a solid, living, breathing body be invisible, they asked. My reply was this. I gave a sign to Hammond, and both of us — conquering our fearful repugnance to touch the invisible creature — lifted it from the ground, manacled as it was, and took it to my bed. Its weight was about that of a boy of fourteen.

"Now, my friends," I said, as Hammond and myself held the creature suspended over the bed, "I can give you self-evident proof that here is a solid, ponderable body which, nevertheless, you cannot see. Be good enough to watch the surface of the bed attentively."

I was astonished at my own courage in treating this strange event so calmly; but I had recovered from my first terror, and felt a sort of scientific pride in the affair which dominated every other feeling.

The eyes of the bystanders were immediately fixed on my bed. At a given signal Hammond and I let the creature fall. There was the dull sound of a heavy body alighting on a soft mass. The timbers of the bed creaked.

A deep impression marked itself distinctly on the pillow, and on the bed itself. The crowd who witnessed this gave a sort of low, universal cry, and rushed from the room. Hammond and I were left alone with our Mystery.

We remained silent for some time, listening to the low, irregular breathing of the creature on the bed, and watching the rustle of the bedclothes as it impotently struggled to free itself from confinement. Then Hammond spoke.

"Harry, this is awful."

"Aye, awful."

"But not unaccountable."

"Not unaccountable! What do you mean? Such a thing has never occurred since the birth of the world. I know not what to think, Hammond. God grant that I am not mad, and that this is not an insane fantasy!"

"Let us reason a little, Harry. Here is a solid body which we touch, but which we cannot see. The fact is so unusual that it strikes us with terror. Is there no parallel, though, for such a phenomenon? Take a piece of pure glass. It is tangible and transparent. A certain chemical coarseness is all that prevents its being so entirely transparent as to be totally invisible. It is not *theoretically impossible*, mind you, to make a glass which shall not reflect a single ray of light — a glass so pure and homogeneous in its atoms that the rays from the sun shall pass through it as they do through the air, refracted but not reflected. We do not see the air, and yet we feel it."

"That's all very well, Hammond, but these are inanimate substances. Glass does not breathe, air does not breathe. *This* thing has a heart that palpitates, — a will that moves it, — lungs that play, and inspire and respire."

"You forget the strange phenomena of which we have so often heard of late," answered the Doctor, gravely. "At the meetings called 'spirit circles,' invisible hands have been thrust into the hands of those persons round the table — warm, fleshly hands that seemed to pulsate with mortal life."

"What? Do you think, then, that this thing is — "

"I don't know what it is," was the solemn reply; "but please the gods I will, with your assistance, thoroughly investigate it."

We watched together, smoking many pipes, all night long, by the bedside of the unearthly being that tossed and panted until it was apparently wearied out. Then we learned by the low, regular breathing that it slept.

The next morning the house was all astir. The boarders congregated on the landing outside my room, and Hammond and myself were lions. We had to answer a thousand questions as to the state of our extraordinary prisoner, for as yet not one person in the house except ourselves could be induced to set foot in the apartment.

The creature was awake. This was evidenced by the convulsive manner in which the bedclothes were moved in its efforts to escape. There was something truly terrible in beholding, as it were, those second-hand indications of the terrible writhings and agonized struggles for liberty which themselves were invisible.

Hammond and myself had racked our brains during the long night to discover some means by which we might realize the shape and general appearance of the Enigma.

As well as we could make out by passing our hands over the creature's form, its outlines and lineaments were human. There was a mouth; a round, smooth head without hair; a nose, which, however, was little elevated above the cheeks; and its hands and feet felt like those of a boy. At first we thought of placing the being on a smooth surface and tracing its outline with chalk, as shoemakers trace the outline of the foot. This plan was given up as being of no value. Such an outline would give not the slightest idea of its conformation.

A happy thought struck me. We would take a cast of it in plaster of Paris. This would give us the solid figure, and satisfy all our wishes. But how to do it? The movements of the creature would disturb the setting of the plastic covering, and distort the mold. Another thought. Why not give it chloroform? It had respiratory organs — that was evident by its breathing. Once reduced to a state of insensibility, we could do with it what we would. Doctor X—— was sent for; and after the worthy physician had recovered from the first shock of amazement, he proceeded to administer the chloroform. In three minutes afterward we were enabled to remove the fetters from the creature's body, and a well-known modeler of this city was busily engaged in covering the invisible form with the moist clay. In five minutes more we had a mold, and before evening a rough *fac simile* of the mystery. It was shaped like a man,— distorted, uncouth, and horrible, but still a man. It was small, not over four feet and some inches in height, and its limbs revealed a muscular development that was unparalleled. Its face surpassed in hideousness anything I had ever seen. Gustave Doré, or Callot, or Tony

Johannot, never conceived anything so horrible. There is a face in one of the latter's illustrations to "Un Voyage où il vous plaira," which somewhat approaches the countenance of this creature, but does not equal it. It was the physiognomy of what I should have fancied a ghoul to be. It looked as if it was capable of feeding on human flesh.

Having satisfied our curiosity, and bound every one in the house to secrecy, it became a question what was to be done with our Enigma. It was impossible that we should keep such a horror in our house; it was equally impossible that such an awful being should be let loose upon the world. I confess that I would have gladly voted for the creature's destruction. But who would shoulder the responsibility? Who would undertake the execution of this horrible semblance of a human being? Day after day this question was deliberated gravely. The boarders all left the house. Mrs. Moffat was in despair, and threatened Hammond and myself with all sorts of legal penalties if we did not remove the Horror. Our answer was, "We will go if you like, but we decline taking this creature with us. Remove it yourself if you please. It appeared in your house. On you the responsibility rests." To this there was, of course, no answer. Mrs. Moffat could not obtain for love or money a person who would even approach the Mystery.

The most singular part of the transaction was that we were entirely ignorant of what the creature habitually fed on. Everything in the way of nutriment that we could think of was placed before it, but was never touched. It was awful to stand by, day after day, and see the clothes toss, and hear the hard breathing, and know that it was starving.

Ten, twelve days, a fortnight passed, and it still lived. The pulsations of the heart, however, were daily growing fainter, and had now nearly ceased altogether. It was evident that the creature was dying for want of sustenance. While this terrible life struggle was going on, I felt miserable. I could not sleep of nights. Horrible as the creature was, it was pitiful to think of the pangs it was suffering.

At last it died. Hammond and I found it cold and stiff one morning in the bed. The heart had ceased to beat, the lungs to inspire. We hastened to bury it in the garden. It was a strange funeral, the dropping of that viewless corpse into the damp hole. The cast of its form I gave to Dr. X——, who keeps it in his museum in Tenth Street.

As I am on the eve of a long journey from which I may not return, I have drawn up this narrative of an event the most singular that has ever come to my knowledge.

NOTE. — It was rumored that the proprietors of a well-known museum in this city had made arrangements with Dr. X —— to exhibit to the public the singular cast which Mr. Escott deposited with him. So extraordinary a history cannot fail to attract universal attention.

NOTE. — The originality of the invention is most evident, and there is a realism in the story-form which is more than mere similitude. The matter-of-fact telling of the tale recalls De Foe, while the theme itself suggests Poe. But Poe would never have condescended to the prosaic plaster cast at the end.

XIV. THE FATHER

By Björnstjerne Björnson (1832-   )

Björnson is the most intensely Norwegian of all Norwegian writers; he delights in setting before his readers the accent of his beloved fatherland. And yet his themes transcend the local interests of Norway, and have often a universal application. In "The Father," for example, the setting is full of local color and the successive incidents are strictly Scandinavian; but the theme is not limited to any one country. This story was written in 1860.

THE FATHER [1]

The man whose story is here to be told was the wealthiest and most influential person in his parish; his name was Thord Overaas. He appeared in the priest's study one day, tall and earnest.

"I have gotten a son," said he, "and I wish to present him for baptism."

[1] This translation, by Professor R. B. Anderson, is printed by permission of Houghton, Mifflin & Co.

"What shall his name be?"

"Finn, — after my father."

"And the sponsors?"

They were mentioned, and proved to be the best men and women of Thord's relations in the parish.

"Is there anything else?" inquired the priest, and looked up.

The peasant hesitated a little.

"I should like very much to have him baptized by himself," said he finally.

"That is to say on a week day?"

"Next Saturday, at twelve o'clock noon."

"Is there anything else?" inquired the priest.

"There is nothing else;" and the peasant twirled his cap, as though he were about to go.

Then the priest arose. "There is yet this, however," said he, and walking toward Thord, he took him by the hand and looked gravely into his eyes: "God grant that the child may become a blessing to you!"

One day sixteen years later, Thord stood once more in the priest's study.

"Really, you carry your age astonishingly well, Thord," said the priest; for he saw no change whatever in the man.

"That is because I have no troubles," replied Thord.

To this the priest said nothing, but after a while he asked: "What is the pleasure this evening?"

"I have come this evening about that son of mine who is to be confirmed to-morrow."

"He is a bright boy."

"I did not wish to pay the priest until I heard what

THE FATHER

number the boy would have when he takes his place in church to-morrow."

"He will stand number one."

"So I have heard; and here are ten dollars for the priest."

"Is there anything else I can do for you?" inquired the priest, fixing his eyes on Thord.

"There is nothing else."

Thord went out.

Eight years more rolled by, and then one day a noise was heard outside of the priest's study, for many men were approaching, and at their head was Thord, who entered first.

The priest looked up and recognized him.

"You come well attended this evening, Thord," said he.

"I am here to request that the banns may be published for my son; he is about to marry Karen Storliden, daughter of Gudmund, who stands here beside me."

"Why, that is the richest girl in the parish."

"So they say," replied the peasant, stroking back his hair with one hand.

The priest sat awhile as if in deep thought, then entered the names in his book, without making any comments, and the men wrote their signatures underneath. Thord laid three dollars on the table.

"One is all I am to have," said the priest.

"I know that very well; but he is my only child; I want to do it handsomely."

The priest took the money.

"This is now the third time, Thord, that you have come here on your son's account."

"But now I am through with him," said Thord, and folding up his pocket-book he said farewell and walked away.

The men slowly followed him.

A fortnight later, the father and son were rowing across the lake, one calm, still day, to Storliden to make arrangements for the wedding.

"This thwart is not secure," said the son, and stood up to straighten the seat on which he was sitting.

At the same moment the board he was standing on slipped from under him; he threw out his arms, uttered a shriek, and fell overboard.

"Take hold of the oar!" shouted the father, springing to his feet and holding out the oar.

But when the son had made a couple of efforts he grew stiff.

"Wait a moment!" cried the father, and began to row toward his son.

Then the son rolled over on his back, gave his father one long look, and sank.

Thord could scarcely believe it; he held the boat still, and stared at the spot where his son had gone down, as though he must surely come to the surface again. There rose some bubbles, then some more, and finally one large one that burst; and the lake lay there as smooth and bright as a mirror again.

For three days and three nights people saw the father rowing round and round the spot, without taking either food or sleep; he was dragging the lake for the body of his son. And toward morning of the third day he found it, and carried it in his arms up over the hills to his gard.

THE FATHER

It might have been about a year from that day, when the priest, late one autumn evening, heard some one in the passage outside of the door, carefully trying to find the latch. The priest opened the door, and in walked a tall, thin man, with bowed form and white hair. The priest looked long at him before he recognized him. It was Thord.

"Are you out walking so late?" said the priest, and stood still in front of him.

"Ah, yes! it is late," said Thord, and took a seat.

The priest sat down also, as though waiting. A long, long silence followed. At last Thord said: —

"I have something with me that I should like to give to the poor; I want it to be invested as a legacy in my son's name."

He rose, laid some money on the table, and sat down again. The priest counted it.

"It is a great deal of money," said he.

"It is half the price of my gard. I sold it to-day."

The priest sat long in silence. At last he asked, but gently: —

"What do you propose to do now, Thord?"

"Something better."

They sat there for a while, Thord with downcast eyes, the priest with his eyes fixed on Thord. Presently the priest said, slowly and softly: —

"I think your son has at last brought you a true blessing."

"Yes, I think so myself," said Thord, looking up, while two big tears coursed slowly down his cheeks.

NOTE. — There is a Biblical largeness in this story, with all its brevity and its directness. It is a parable, if one so chooses to regard it, with a tragedy in the middle of it, out of which there comes peace at the end. The pathos is all the more powerful for being implied rather than stated. The Scandinavian author displays here one of the finest characteristics of all imaginative writing — the ability to suggest far more than he has chosen to put into words.

XV. TENNESSEE'S PARTNER

By Bret Harte (1839-1902)

Bret Harte derived his method from Dickens as Dickens had derived his from Smollett; but the American author had a finer sense of form than his British master. His stories present not so much novel situation as eccentric character. Their center of interest is in a strange human being of unexpected characteristics. What interests us in one of his vignettes of California in the days of the Argonauts of '49 is not so much what happens, as the creature to whom it happens. Whether or not these curious beings are really characteristic of California cannot be asserted with certainty. But it is a fact that Bret Harte captured the romance of those days, the glamour of the quest of gold, the atmosphere of the time and the place. This story was written about 1870.

TENNESSEE'S PARTNER [1]

I do not think that we ever knew his real name. Our ignorance of it certainly never gave us any social incon-

[1] Copyright, 1899, by Bret Harte. Printed by permission of Houghton, Mifflin & Co.

venience, for at Sandy Bar in 1854 most men were christened anew. Sometimes these appellatives were derived from some distinctiveness of dress, as in the case of "Dungaree Jack"; or from some peculiarity of habit, as shown in "Saleratus Bill," so called from an undue proportion of that chemical in his daily bread; or from some unlucky slip, as exhibited in "The Iron Pirate," a mild, inoffensive man, who earned that baleful title by his unfortunate mispronunciation of the term "iron pyrites." Perhaps this may have been the beginning of a rude heraldry; but I am constrained to think that it was because a man's real name in that day rested solely upon his own unsupported statement. "Call yourself Clifford, do you?" said Boston, addressing a timid newcomer with infinite scorn; "hell is full of such Cliffords!" He then introduced the unfortunate man, whose name happened to be really Clifford, as "Jay-bird Charley," — an unhallowed inspiration of the moment, that clung to him ever after.

But to return to Tennessee's Partner, whom we never knew by any other than this relative title; that he had ever existed as a separate and distinct individuality we only learned later. It seems that in 1853 he left Poker Flat to go to San Francisco, ostensibly to procure a wife. He never got any farther than Stockton. At that place he was attracted by a young person who waited upon the table at the hotel where he took his meals. One morning he said something to her which caused her to smile not unkindly, to somewhat coquettishly break a plate of toast over his upturned, serious, simple face, and to retreat to the kitchen. He followed her, and emerged a few moments later, covered with more toast and victory. That day week they were married by a Justice of the Peace, and returned to Poker Flat. I am aware that something more might be made of this episode, but I prefer to tell it as it was current at Sandy Bar, — in the gulches and barrooms, — where all sentiment was modified by a strong sense of humor.

Of their married felicity but little is known, perhaps for the reason that Tennessee, then living with his partner, one day took occasion to say something to the bride on his own account, at which, it is said, she smiled not unkindly and chastely retreated, — this time as far as Marysville, where Tennessee followed her, and where they went to housekeeping without the aid of a Justice of the Peace. Tennessee's Partner took the loss of his wife simply and seriously, as was his fashion. But to everybody's surprise, when Tennessee one day returned from Marysville, without his partner's wife, — she having smiled and retreated with somebody else, — Tennessee's Partner was the first man to shake his hand and greet him with affection. The boys who had gathered in the cañon to see the shooting were naturally indignant. Their indignation might have found vent in sarcasm but for a certain look in Tennessee's Partner's eye that indicated a lack of humorous appreciation. In fact, he was a grave man, with a steady application to practical detail which was unpleasant in a difficulty.

Meanwhile a popular feeling against Tennessee had grown up on the Bar. He was known to be a gambler; he was suspected to be a thief. In these suspicions Tennessee's Partner was equally compromised; his continued intimacy with Tennessee after the affair above quoted could only be accounted for on the hypothesis of a co-partnership of crime. At last Tennessee's guilt became flagrant. One day he overtook a stranger on his way to Red Dog. The stranger afterward related that Tennessee beguiled the time with interesting anecdote and reminiscence, but illogically concluded the interview in the following words: " And now, young man, I'll trouble you for your knife, your pistols, and your money. You see your weppings might get you into trouble at Red Dog, and your money's a temptation to the evilly disposed. I think you said your address was San Francisco. I shall endeavor to call." It may be stated here that Tennessee had a fine flow of humor, which no business preoccupation could wholly subdue.

This exploit was his last. Red Dog and Sandy Bar made common cause against the highwayman. Tennessee was hunted in very much the same fashion as his prototype, the grizzly. As the toils closed around him, he made a desperate dash through the Bar, emptying his revolver at the crowd before the Arcade Saloon, and so on up Grizzly Cañon; but at its farther extremity he was stopped by a small man on a gray horse. The men looked at each other a moment in silence. Both were fearless, both self-possessed and independent; and both types of a civilization that in the seventeenth century would have been called heroic, but, in the nineteenth, simply "reckless." "What have you got there? — I call," said Tennessee, quietly. "Two bowers and an ace," said the stranger, as quietly, showing two revolvers and a bowie knife. "That takes me," returned Ten-

TENNESSEE'S PARTNER

nessee; and with this gamblers' epigram, he threw away his useless pistol, and rode back with his captor.

It was a warm night. The cool breeze which usually sprang up with the going down of the sun behind the *chaparral*-crested mountain was that evening withheld from Sandy Bar. The little cañon was stifling with heated resinous odors, and the decaying driftwood on the Bar sent forth faint, sickening exhalations. The feverishness of day, and its fierce passions, still filled the camp. Lights moved restlessly along the bank of the river, striking no answering reflection from its tawny current. Against the blackness of the pines the windows of the old loft above the express office stood out staringly bright; and through their curtainless panes the loungers below could see the forms of those who were even then deciding the fate of Tennessee. And above all this, etched on the dark firmament, rose the Sierra, remote and passionless, crowned with remoter passionless stars.

The trial of Tennessee was conducted as fairly as was consistent with a judge and jury who felt themselves to some extent obliged to justify, in their verdict, the previous irregularities of arrest and indictment. The law of Sandy Bar was implacable, but not vengeful. The excitement and personal feeling of the chase were over; with Tennessee safe in their hands they were ready to listen patiently to any defense, which they were already satisfied was insufficient. There being no doubt in their own minds, they were willing to give the prisoner the benefit of any that might exist. Secure in the hypothesis that he ought to be hanged, on general principles, they indulged him with more latitude of defense than his

SHORT-STORY — 17

reckless hardihood seemed to ask. The Judge appeared to be more anxious than the prisoner, who, otherwise unconcerned, evidently took a grim pleasure in the responsibility he had created. "I don't take any hand in this yer game," had been his invariable, but good-humored reply to all questions. The Judge — who was also his captor — for a moment vaguely regretted that he had not shot him "on sight," that morning, but presently dismissed this human weakness as unworthy of the judicial mind. Nevertheless, when there was a tap at the door, and it was said that Tennessee's Partner was there on behalf of the prisoner, he was admitted at once without question. Perhaps the younger members of the jury, to whom the proceedings were becoming irksomely thoughtful, hailed him as a relief.

For he was not, certainly, an imposing figure. Short and stout, with a square face, sunburned into a preternatural redness, clad in a loose duck "jumper," and trousers streaked and splashed with red soil, his aspect under any circumstances would have been quaint, and was now even ridiculous. As he stooped to deposit at his feet a heavy carpetbag he was carrying, it became obvious, from partially developed legends and inscriptions, that the material with which his trousers had been patched had been originally intended for a less ambitious covering. Yet he advanced with great gravity, and after having shaken the hand of each person in the room with labored cordiality, he wiped his serious, perplexed face on a red bandanna handkerchief, a shade lighter than his complexion, laid his powerful hand upon the table to steady himself, and thus addressed the Judge : —

"I was passin' by," he began, by way of apology, "and I thought I'd just step in and see how things was gittin' on with Tennessee thar, — my pardner. It's a hot night. I disremember any sich weather before on the Bar."

He paused a moment, but nobody volunteering any other meteorological recollection, he again had recourse to his pocket handkerchief, and for some moments mopped his face diligently.

"Have you anything to say in behalf of the prisoner?" said the Judge, finally.

"Thet's it," said Tennessee's Partner, in a tone of relief. "I come yar as Tennessee's pardner, — knowing him nigh on four year, off and on, wet and dry, in luck and out o' luck. His ways ain't allers my ways, but thar ain't any p'ints in that young man, thar ain't any liveliness as he's been up to, as I don't know. And you sez to me, sez you, — confidential-like, and between man and man, — sez you, 'Do you know anything in his behalf?' and I sez to you, sez I, — confidential-like, as between man and man, — 'What should a man know of his pardner?'"

"Is this all you have to say?" asked the Judge, impatiently, feeling, perhaps, that a dangerous sympathy of humor was beginning to humanize the Court.

"Thet's so," continued Tennessee's Partner. "It ain't for me to say anything agin' him. And now, what's the case? Here's Tennessee wants money, wants it bad, and doesn't like to ask it of his old pardner. Well, what does Tennessee do? He lays for a stranger, and he fetches that stranger. And you lays for *him*, and you fetches *him;* and the honors is easy. And I put it to you, bein' a far-minded man, and to you, gentlemen, all, as far-minded men, ef this isn't so."

"Prisoner," said the Judge, interrupting, "have you any questions to ask this man?"

"No! no!" continued Tennessee's Partner, hastily. "I play this yer hand alone. To come down to the bed rock, it's just this: Tennessee, thar, has played it pretty rough and expensive-like on a stranger, and on this yer camp. And now, what's the fair thing? Some would say more; some would say less. Here's seventeen hundred dollars in coarse gold and a watch, it's about all my pile, — and call it square!" And before a hand could be raised to prevent him, he had emptied the contents of the carpetbag upon the table.

For a moment his life was in jeopardy. One or two men sprang to their feet, several hands groped for hidden weapons, and a suggestion to "throw him from the window" was only overridden by a gesture from the Judge. Tennessee laughed. And apparently oblivious of the excitement, Tennessee's Partner improved the opportunity to mop his face again with his handkerchief.

When order was restored, and the man was made to understand, by the use of forcible figures and rhetoric, that Tennessee's offense could not be condoned by money, his face took a more serious and sanguinary hue, and those who were nearest to him noticed that his rough hand trembled slightly on the table. He hesitated a moment as he slowly returned the gold to the carpetbag, as if he had not yet entirely caught the elevated sense of justice which swayed the tribunal, and was perplexed with the belief that he had not offered enough. Then he turned to the Judge, and saying, "This yer is a lone hand, played alone, and without my pardner," he bowed to the jury and was about to withdraw, when the Judge called him back. "If you have anything to say to Tennessee, you had better say it now." For the first time that evening the eyes of the prisoner and his strange advocate met. Tennessee smiled, showed his white teeth, and, saying, "Euchred, old man!" held out his hand. Tennessee's Partner took it in his own, and saying, "I just dropped in as I was passin' to see how things was gettin' on," let the hand passively fall, and adding that "it was a warm night," again mopped his face with his handkerchief, and without another word withdrew.

The two men never again met each other alive. For the unparalleled insult of a bribe offered to Judge Lynch — who, whether bigoted, weak, or narrow, was at least incorruptible — firmly fixed in the mind of that mythical personage any wavering determination of Tennessee's fate; and at the break of day he was marched, closely guarded, to meet it at the top of Marley's Hill.

How he met it, how cool he was, how he refused to say anything, how perfect were the arrangements of the committee, were all duly reported, with the addition of a warning moral and example to all future evil doers, in the Red Dog *Clarion*, by its editor, who was present, and to whose vigorous English I cheerfully refer the reader. But the beauty of that midsummer morning, the blessed amity of earth and air and sky, the awakened life of the free woods and hills, the joyous renewal and promise of Nature, and above all, the infinite serenity that thrilled through each, was not reported, as not being a part of the social lesson. And yet, when the weak and foolish deed was done, and a life, with its possibilities and responsibilities, had passed out of the misshapen thing that dangled between earth and sky, the birds sang, the flowers bloomed, the sun shone, as cheerily as before; and possibly the Red Dog *Clarion* was right.

Tennessee's Partner was not in the group that surrounded the ominous tree. But as they turned to disperse, attention was drawn to the singular appearance of a motionless donkey cart halted at the side of the road. As they approached, they at once recognized the venerable "Jenny" and the two-wheeled cart as the property of Tennessee's Partner, — used by him in carrying dirt from his claim; and a few paces distant the owner of the equipage himself, sitting under a buckeye tree, wiping the perspiration from his glowing face. In answer to an inquiry, he said he had come for the body of the "diseased," "if it was all the same to the committee." He didn't wish to "hurry anything"; he could "wait." He was not working that day; and when the gentlemen were done with the "diseased," he would take him. "Ef thar is any present," he added, in his simple, serious way, "as would care to jine in the fun'l, they kin come." Perhaps it was from a sense of humor, which I have already intimated was a feature of Sandy Bar, — perhaps it was from something even better than that; but two thirds of the loungers accepted the invitation at once.

It was noon when the body of Tennessee was delivered into the hands of his partner. As the cart drew up to the fatal tree, we noticed that it contained a rough, oblong box, — apparently made from a section of sluicing, — and half filled with bark and the tassels of pine. The cart was further decorated with slips of willow, and made fragrant with buckeye blossoms. When the body was deposited in the box, Tennessee's Partner drew over it a piece of tarred canvas, and gravely mounting the narrow seat in front, with his feet upon the shafts, urged the little donkey forward. The equipage moved slowly on, at that decorous pace which was habitual with "Jenny" even under less solemn circumstances. The men — half curiously, half jestingly, but all good-humoredly — strolled along beside the cart; some in advance, some a little in the rear of the homely catafalque. But, whether from the narrowing of the road or some present sense of decorum, as the cart passed on, the company fell to the rear in couples, keeping step, and otherwise assuming the external show of a formal procession. Jack Folinsbee, who had at the outset played a funeral march in dumb show upon an imaginary trombone, desisted, from a lack of sympathy and appreciation, — not having, perhaps, your true humorist's capacity to be content with the enjoyment of his own fun.

The way led through Grizzly Cañon, — by this time clothed in funereal drapery and shadows. The redwoods, burying their moccasined feet in the red soil, stood in Indian file along the track, trailing an uncouth benediction from their bending boughs upon the passing bier. A hare, surprised into helpless inactivity, sat upright and pulsating in the ferns by the roadside, as the *cortége* went by. Squirrels hastened to gain a secure outlook from higher boughs; and the blue jays, spreading their wings, fluttered before them like outriders, until the outskirts of Sandy Bar were reached, and the solitary cabin of Tennessee's Partner.

Viewed under more favorable circumstances, it would not have been a cheerful place. The unpicturesque site, the rude and unlovely outlines, the unsavory details, which distinguish the nest-building of the California miner, were all here, with the dreariness of decay superadded. A few paces from the cabin there was a rough inclosure, which, in the brief days of Tennessee's Partner's matrimonial felicity, had been used as a garden, but was now overgrown with fern. As we approached it we were surprised to find that what we had taken for a recent attempt at cultivation was the broken soil about an open grave.

The cart was halted before the inclosure; and rejecting the offers of assistance with the same air of simple self-reliance he had displayed throughout, Tennessee's Partner lifted the rough coffin on his back, and deposited it, unaided, within the shallow grave. He then nailed down the board which served as a lid; and mounting the little mound of earth beside it, took off his hat, and slowly mopped his face with his handkerchief. This the crowd felt was a preliminary to speech; and they disposed themselves variously on stumps and bowlders, and sat expectant.

"When a man," began Tennessee's Partner, slowly, "has been running free all day, what's the natural thing for him to do? Why, to come home. And if he ain't in a condition to go home, what can his best friend do?

Why, bring him home! And here's Tennessee has been running free, and we brings him home from his wandering." He paused, and picked up a fragment of quartz, rubbed it thoughtfully on his sleeve, and went on: "It ain't the first time that I've packed him on my back, as you see'd me now. It ain't the first time that I brought him to this yer cabin when he couldn't help himself; it ain't the first time that I and 'Jinny' have waited for him on yon hill, and picked him up and so fetched him home, when he couldn't speak, and didn't know me. And now that it's the last time, why, — " he paused, and rubbed the quartz gently on his sleeve, — "you see it's sort of rough on his pardner. And now, gentlemen," he added, abruptly, picking up his long-handled shovel, "the fun'l's over; and my thanks, and Tennessee's thanks, to you for your trouble."

Resisting any proffers of assistance, he began to fill in the grave, turning his back upon the crowd, that after a few moments' hesitation gradually withdrew. As they crossed the little ridge that hid Sandy Bar from view, some, looking back, thought they could see Tennessee's Partner, his work done, sitting upon the grave, his shovel between his knees, and his face buried in his red bandanna handkerchief. But it was argued by others that you couldn't tell his face from his handkerchief at that distance; and this point remained undecided.

In the reaction that followed the feverish excitement of that day, Tennessee's Partner was not forgotten. A secret investigation had cleared him of any complicity in Tennessee's guilt, and left only a suspicion of his general sanity. Sandy Bar made a point of calling on him and proffering various uncouth but well-meant kindnesses. But from that day his rude health and great strength seemed visibly to decline; and when the rainy season fairly set in, and the tiny grass-blades were beginning to peep from the rocky mound above Tennessee's grave, he took to his bed.

One night, when the pines beside the cabin were swaying in the storm, and trailing their slender fingers over the roof, and the roar and rush of the swollen river were heard below, Tennessee's Partner lifted his head from the pillow, saying, "It is time to go for Tennessee; I must put 'Jinny' in the cart"; and would have risen from his bed but for the restraint of his attendant. Struggling, he still pursued his singular fancy: "There, now, steady, 'Jinny,' — steady, old girl. How dark it is! Look out for the ruts, — and look out for him, too, old gal. Sometimes, you know, when he's blind drunk, he drops down right in the trail. Keep on straight up to the pine on the top of the hill. Thar — I told you so! — thar he is, — coming this way, too, — all by himself sober, and his face a-shining. Tennessee! Pardner!"

And so they met.

NOTE. — Bret Harte's sentiment is obvious, yet restrained. His pathos is not paraded and insisted upon as Dickens's was. For all the variety of incident, there is a controlling unity of theme and of tone.

XVI. THE SIEGE OF BERLIN

By Alphonse Daudet (1840–1897)

Daudet is like Dickens in his sentiment and in his sympathy with the humble. He came from Provence to Paris; he began as a poet and he ended as a realistic novelist. But there is a lyric grace in his prose even when he is dealing with the lower realities of life in Paris. His short-stories have often a ballad-like quality as though they might have been told in verse. They deal with his native South often but almost as frequently with his adopted Paris, and especially with the capital when it was besieged by the Prussians. The "Siege of Berlin" was written about 1872.

THE SIEGE OF BERLIN[1]

We were going up the Champs Elysées with Dr. V——, gathering from the walls pierced by shell, the pavement plowed by grape shot, the history of the besieged Paris, when just before reaching the Place de l'Etoile, the Doctor stopped and pointed out to me one of those large corner houses, so pompously grouped around the Arc de Triomphe.

[1] From "Tales from Many Sources," printed by permission of Dodd, Mead & Co.

"Do you see," said he, "those four closed windows on the balcony up there? In the beginning of August, that terrible month of August of '70, so laden with storm and disaster, I was summoned there to attend a case of apoplexy. The sufferer was Colonel Jouve, an old Cuirassier of the First Empire, full of enthusiasm for glory and patriotism, who, at the commencement of the war, had taken an apartment with a balcony in the Champs Elysées — for what do you think? To assist at the triumphal entry of our troops! Poor old man! The news of Wissembourg arrived as he was rising from table. On reading the name of Napoleon at the foot of that bulletin of defeat he fell senseless.

"I found the old Cuirassier stretched upon the floor, his face bleeding and inert as from the blow of a club. Standing, he would have been very tall; lying, he looked immense; with fine features, beautiful teeth, and white curling hair, carrying his eighty years as though they had been sixty. Beside him knelt his granddaughter in tears. She resembled him. Seeing them side by side, they reminded me of two Greek medallions stamped with the same impress, only the one was antique, earth-stained, its outlines somewhat worn; the other beautiful and clear, in all the luster of freshness.

"The child's sorrow touched me. Daughter and granddaughter of soldiers, — for her father was on MacMahon's staff, — the sight of this old man stretched before her evoked in her mind another vision no less terrible. I did my best to reassure her, though in reality I had but little hope. We had to contend with hæmoptysis, from which at eighty there is small chance of recovery.

THE SIEGE OF BERLIN

"For three days the patient remained in the same condition of immobility and stupor. Meanwhile came the news of Reichshofen — you remember how strangely? Till the evening we all believed in a great victory — twenty thousand Prussians killed, the Crown Prince prisoner.

"I cannot tell by what miracle, by what magnetic current, an echo of this national joy can have reached our poor invalid, hitherto deaf to all around him; but that evening, on approaching the bed, I found a new man. His eye was almost clear, his speech less difficult, and he had the strength to smile and to stammer : —

"'Victory, victory.'

"'Yes, Colonel, a great victory.' And as I gave the details of MacMahon's splendid success I saw his features relax and his countenance brighten.

"When I went out his granddaughter was waiting for me, pale and sobbing. —

"'But he is saved,' said I, taking her hands.

"The poor child had hardly courage to answer me. The true Reichshofen had just been announced, MacMahon a fugitive, the whole army crushed. We looked at each other in consternation, she anxious at the thought of her father, I trembling for the grandfather. Certainly he would not bear this new shock. And yet what could we do? Let him enjoy the illusion which had revived him? But then we should have to deceive him.

"'Well, then, I will deceive him,' said the brave girl, and hastily wiping away her tears she reëntered her grandfather's room with a beaming face.

"It was a hard task she had set herself. For the first few days it was comparatively easy, as the old man's head was weak, and he was as credulous as a child. But with returning health came clearer ideas. It was necessary to keep him *au courant* with the movements of the army and to invent military bulletins. It was pitiful to see that beautiful girl bending night and day over her map of Germany, marking it with little flags, forcing herself to combine the whole of a glorious campaign — Bazaine on the road to Berlin, Frossard in Bavaria, MacMahon on the Baltic. In all this she asked my counsel, and I helped her as far as I could, but it was the grandfather who did the most for us in this imaginary invasion. He had conquered Germany so often during the First Empire. He knew all the moves beforehand. 'Now they should go there. This is what they will do,' and his anticipations were always realized, not a little to his pride. Unfortunately, we might take towns and gain battles, but we never went fast enough for the Colonel. He was insatiable. Every day I was greeted with a fresh feat of arms.

"'Doctor, we have taken Mayence,' said the young girl, coming to meet me with a heartrending smile, and through the door I heard a joyous voice crying:—

"'We are getting on. We are getting on. In a week we shall enter Berlin.'

"At that moment the Prussians were but a week from Paris. At first we thought it might be better to move to the provinces, but once out of doors, the state of the country would have told him all, and I thought him still too weak, too enervated, to know the truth. It was therefore decided that they should stay where they were.

"On the first day of the investment I went to see my patient — much agitated, I remember, and with that pang in my heart which we all felt at knowing that the gates of Paris were shut, that the war was under our walls, that our suburbs had become our frontiers.

"I found the old man jubilant and proud.

"'Well,' said he, 'the siege has begun.'

"I looked at him stupefied.

"'How, Colonel, do you know?'

"His granddaughter turned to me, 'Oh, yes, Doctor, it is great news. The siege of Berlin has commenced.'

"She said this composedly, while drawing out her needle. How could he suspect anything? He could not hear the cannon nor see that unhappy Paris, so sullen and disorderly. All that he saw from his bed was calculated to keep up his delusion. Outside was the Arc de Triomphe, and in the room quite a collection of souvenirs of the First Empire. Portraits of marshals, engravings of battles, the King of Rome in his baby robes; the stiff consoles, ornamented with trophies in brass, were covered with Imperial relics, medals, bronzes; a stone from St. Helena under a glass shade; miniatures all representing the same becurled lady, in ball dress, in a yellow gown with leg-of-mutton sleeves, and light eyes; and all — the consoles, the King of Rome, the medals, the yellow ladies with short waists and sashes under their arms — in that style of awkward stiffness which was the grace of 1806. — Good Colonel! it was this atmosphere of victory and conquest, rather than all we could say, which made him believe so naïvely in the siege of Berlin.

"From that day our military operations became much simpler. Taking Berlin was merely a matter of patience. Every now and then, when the old man was tired of waiting, a letter from his son was read to him — an imaginary letter, of course, as nothing could enter Paris, and as, since Sedan, MacMahon's aid-de-camp had been sent to a German fortress. Can you not imagine the despair of the poor girl, without tidings of her father, knowing him to be a prisoner, deprived of all comforts, perhaps ill, and yet obliged to make him speak in cheerful letters, somewhat short, as from a soldier in the field, always advancing in a conquered country. Sometimes, when the invalid was weaker than usual, weeks passed without fresh news. But was he anxious and unable to sleep, suddenly a letter arrived from Germany which she read gayly at his bedside, struggling hard with her tears. The Colonel listened religiously, smiling with an air of superiority, approving, criticising, explaining; but it was in the answers to his son that he was at his best. ' Never forget that you are a Frenchman,' he wrote; 'be generous to those poor people. Do not make the invasion too hard for them.' His advice was never ending; edifying sermons about respect of property, the politeness due to ladies, — in short, quite a code of military honor for the use of conquerors. With all this he put in some general reflections on politics and the conditions of the peace to be imposed on the vanquished. With regard to the latter, I must say he was not exacting: —

"'The war indemnity and nothing else. It is no good to take provinces. Can one turn Germany into France?'"

THE SIEGE OF BERLIN

"He dictated this with so firm a voice, and one felt so much sincerity in his words, so much patriotic faith, that it was impossible to listen to him unmoved.

"Meanwhile the siege went on — not the siege of Berlin, alas! We were at the worst period of cold, of bombardment, of epidemic, of famine. But, thanks to our care, and the indefatigable tenderness which surrounded him, the old man's serenity was never for a moment disturbed. Up to the end I was able to procure white bread and fresh meat for him, but for him only. You could not imagine anything more touching than those breakfasts of the grandfather, so innocently egotistic, sitting up in bed, fresh and smiling, the napkin tied under his chin, at his side his granddaughter, pale from her privations, guiding his hands, making him drink, helping him to eat all these good, forbidden things. Then, revived by the repast, in the comfort of his warm room with the wintry wind shut out and the snow eddying about the window, the old Cuirassier would recall his Northern campaigns and would relate to us that disastrous retreat in Russia where there was nothing to eat but frozen biscuit and horseflesh.

"'Can you understand that, little one? We ate horseflesh.'

"I should think she did understand it. For two months she had tasted nothing else. As convalescence approached, our task increased daily in difficulty. The numbness of the Colonel's senses, as well as of his limbs, which had hitherto helped us so much, was beginning to pass away. Once or twice already, those terrible volleys at the Porte Maillot had made him start and prick up his ears like a war horse; we were obliged to invent a recent victory of Bazaine's before Berlin and salvoes fired from the Invalides in honor of it. Another day (the Thursday of Buzenval, I think it was) his bed had been pushed to the window, whence he saw some of the National Guard massed upon the Avenue de la Grande Armée.

"'What soldiers are those?' he asked, and we heard him grumbling beneath his teeth: —

"'Badly drilled, badly drilled.'

"Nothing came of this, but we understood that henceforth greater precautions were necessary. Unfortunately, we were not careful enough.

"One evening I was met by the child in much trouble.

"'It is to-morrow they make their entry,' she said.

"Could the grandfather's door have been opened? In thinking of it since, I remember that all that evening his face wore an extraordinary expression. Probably he had overheard us; only we spoke of the Prussians and he thought of the French, of the triumphal entry he had so long expected, MacMahon descending the Avenue amidst flowers and flourish of trumpets, his own son riding beside the marshal, and he himself on his balcony, in full uniform as at Lützen, saluting the ragged colors and the eagles blackened by powder.

"Poor Colonel Jouve! He no doubt imagined that we wished to prevent his assisting at the defile of our troops, lest the emotion should prove too much for him, and therefore took care to say nothing to us; but the next day, just at the time the Prussian battalions cautiously entered the long road leading from the Porte Maillot to the Tuileries, the window up there was softly opened and

THE SIEGE OF BERLIN

the Colonel appeared on the balcony with his helmet, his sword, all his long unused, but glorious apparel of Milhaud's Cuirassiers.

"I often ask myself what supreme effort of will, what sudden impulse of fading vitality, had placed him thus erect in harness.

"All we know is that he was there, standing at the railing, wondering to find the wide avenue so silent, the shutters all closed, Paris like a great lazaret, flags everywhere, but such strange ones, white with red crosses, and no one to meet our soldiers.

"For a moment he may have thought himself mistaken.

"But no! there, behind the Arc de Triomphe, there was a confused sound, a black line advancing in the growing daylight — then, little by little, the spikes of the helmets glisten, the little drums of Jena begin to beat, and under the Arc de l'Etoile, accompanied by the heavy tramp of the troops, by the clatter of sabers, bursts forth Schubert's Triumphal March.

"In the dead silence of the streets was heard a cry, a terrible cry: —

"'To arms! — to arms! — the Prussians.' And the four Uhlans of the advance guard might have seen up there, on the balcony, a tall old man stagger, wave his arms, and fall. This time Colonel Jouve was dead."

NOTE. — This is the simplest of tales, scarcely more than an anecdote, but it is told with tender irony and with patriotic pathos. There is a directness, a sense of reality, due to the device of putting the narrative into the mouth of the attending physician, who tells merely what he saw.

XVII. THE INSURGENT

By Ludovic Halévy (1834–   )

BETTER known as a dramatist, — he was the joint-author of "Frou-frou" and of the "Grande Duchesse de Geroldstein," — the writer of this vigorous portrait has won fame also as a novelist, and his charming novel, the "Abbé Constantin," has had thousands of readers. But his short-stories are better than his longer novels; they have the clearness of structure and the sharpness of outline which we are wont to find in the best plays. "The Insurgent," written in 1872, has been translated for this volume by the editor.

THE INSURGENT

"Prisoner," said the president of the military tribunal, "have you anything to add in your own defense?"

"Yes, Colonel," answered the prisoner. "You assigned me a little lawyer who has defended me in his fashion. I want to defend myself in my own.

"My name is Martin, — Louis Joseph. I'm fifty-five. My father was a locksmith. He had a little shop up in the St. Martin quarter, and he had only a little business. We were able to live. I learned to read in the *National*, which was, I believe, Monsieur Thiers's newspaper.

"The 27th of July, 1830, my father went out early in the

morning. That evening, at ten o'clock, they brought him back to us, dying on a litter; he had received a bullet in the chest. By his side, on the litter, was his gun.

"'Take it,' he said to me; 'I give it to you, — and whenever there shall be an insurrection against the government, — always, always, always!'

"An hour after he was dead. I went out into the night. At the first barricade, I stopped and offered myself. A man examined me by the light of a lantern. 'A child,' he cried. I was not yet fifteen. I was very small, very undersized. I answered, 'A child, that's possible; but my father was killed two hours ago. He gave me his gun. Teach me how to use it.'

"From that moment I became what I have always been for forty years — an insurgent! If I fought under the Commune, it was not because I was forced for the thirty cents. It was from liking, for pleasure, by habit, by routine.

"In 1830, I behaved myself bravely enough in the attack on the Louvre. That boy who first climbed the iron fence under the fire of the Swiss, that was I. I received the Medal of July; but the shopkeepers gave us a king. We had all our work to do over again. I joined a secret society; I learned how to cast bullets, to make powder. In a word, I completed my education, — and I waited.

"I had to wait nearly two years. June 5, 1832, at noon, before the Madeleine, I was the first to unhitch one of the horses from the hearse of General Lamarque. I spent the day crying, 'Hurrah for La Fayette!' and the night making barricades. The next morning we were attacked by the regulars. That afternoon, about four o'clock, we were shut in, bombarded, swept with grape-shot, crushed in the church of St. Méry. I had a ball in my body and three bayonet wounds when the regulars picked me up, on the steps of a little chapel on the right, — St. John's chapel. I used to go back often to that little chapel, — not to pray, for I hadn't been brought up in those ideas, — but to see the stains of my blood which still mark those stones.

"On account of my youth I had only ten years of prison. I was sent to Mont-St.-Michel. That's why I didn't have a hand in the risings of 1834. If I had been out, I should have been fighting in the rue Transnonain, as I had fought in the rue St. Méry, against the government, — always, always, always. That was my father's last word, my evangel, my religion. I called that my catechism in six words. I got out of prison in 1842, and I began again to wait.

"The Revolution of 1848 made itself. The shopkeepers were stupid and cowardly. They didn't go with us, nor against us. Only the city guards defended themselves. We had a little trouble in capturing the post of the Chateau-d'Eau. The night of the 24th of February, I stayed three or four hours on the Place de la Hôtel de Ville. The members of the provisional government, one after another, made speeches to us; they told us we were heroes, great citizens, the foremost people in the world, — that we had thrown off the yoke of tyranny. After having fed us on these fine words, they gave us a Republic which wasn't any better than the Monarchy we had upset.

"In June, I took up my gun again, but this time it didn't succeed. I was arrested, condemned, sent to Cayenne. It seems that I behaved myself out there. One day, I saved a captain of marines who was drowning. They thought that was very fine. Remember that I'd have shot that captain, if he'd been on one side of a barricade and I on the other, but a man who is drowning, who is going to die — well, I was pardoned. I got back to France in 1852, after the Coup d'État; I had missed the insurrection of 1851.

"At Cayenne, I had made a friend, a tailor named Bernard. Six months after I left for France, Bernard was dead. I went to see his widow. She was in dire poverty. I married her. We had a son in 1854. You will understand soon why I speak of my wife and my son. Only you ought to doubt already whether an insurgent who marries the widow of an insurgent has royalist children.

"Under the Empire there was nothing doing. The police had a hard hand. We were dispersed, disarmed. I worked, I brought up my son in the ideas that my father had given me. It was a long time waiting. Rochefort, Gambetta, the public meetings, all that started us up again.

"At the first serious chance I showed myself. I was one of the little group that assaulted the barracks of the firemen of La Villette. Only there there was a fool thing done. They killed a fireman without necessity. I was taken, thrown in prison; but the government of the 4th of September let us out, from which I concluded that we had done right in attacking the barracks and killing the fireman, even without necessity.

"The siege began. From the start I was against the government, for the Commune. I marched against the Hôtel de Ville the 31st of October and the 22d of January. I loved revolt for the revolt itself. An insurgent, I told you at the start; I am an insurgent. I can't see a political club without going in, an insurrection without running to it, a barricade without taking my stone to it. That has passed with my blood.

"And then, besides, I wasn't altogether ignorant; and I said to myself, 'We've only got to succeed one day, down to the bottom, and then in our town, we shall be the government; and things will go a little better than with all the lawyers who get behind us during the fight and go ahead of us after the victory.'

"The 18th of March came, and naturally I took part. I cried 'Hurrah for the regulars!' I fraternized with them. I went to the Hôtel de Ville. I found there a government at work — absolutely, as on the 24th of February.

"Now you tell me that this insurrection was not lawful. That's possible, but I don't know quite why. I begin to get muddled between these insurrections which are a duty and these insurrections which are a crime. I don't see any great difference.

"I fired on the Versailles troops in 1871 as I had fired on the Royal Guard in 1830 and on the City Guard in 1848. After 1830 I had the Medal of July. After 1848 I had the compliments of Monsieur de Lamertine. This time, I'm going to have transportation or death.

"Some insurrections seem to please you. You put up columns to them, you name streets after them; and you give yourselves the places, the offices, the big salaries; and we others, who made the revolution, you call us 'great citizens,' 'heroes,' 'brave people,' etc., etc. It is with that sort of small change that you pay us.

"And then, some other insurrections don't seem to please you. After those, you distribute exile, transportation, death. Well, now, if you had not paid us so many compliments after the first lot, perhaps we might not have made the second. If you had not put up the Column of July in our quarter, perhaps we might not have gone to your quarters to pull down the Vendôme Column. Those twopenny trumpets didn't agree. One had to upset the other; and that's what happened.

"Now, why I threw in a corner of the street my captain's uniform on the 26th of May, why I was in my blouse when I was taken, I'll tell you. When I learned that those fellows of the Commune, instead of standing up to the fire with us on the barricades, were distributing thousand-franc notes to themselves at the Hôtel de Ville, shaving their beards, dyeing their hair, and going to hide themselves in cellars, I wasn't willing to keep the epaulets they had given me.

"Besides, these epaulets annoyed me. 'Captain Martin' was all foolishness. The 'insurgent Martin,' if you like. I wanted to end as I had begun, to die as my father had died, like an insurrectionist in an insurrection, a barricader in a barricade.

"I wasn't able to get myself killed. I was taken. I belong to you. Only I'd like to ask one favor. I've a son, a boy of seventeen; he's at Cherbourg, on the hulks. He's been fighting, that's true, and he won't deny it; but it was I who put the gun in his hand; it was I who told him that his duty was there. He listened to me. He obeyed me. That's all his crime. Don't condemn him too harshly.

"As for me, you've got me; don't let me go, — that's the advice I give you. I'm too old to change, and besides, what would you have? Nothing can alter what is; I was born on the wrong side of the barricade."

NOTE. — Perhaps the most noticeable characteristic of this story is the sympathetic understanding of the central figure. With what the man has done, and with the type to which he belongs, the author has obviously no sympathy; but the man himself the author understands and makes the reader understand. This effect is achieved partly by the device of making the story a monologue and thus letting the man speak for himself and say all that lies close to his heart. And our interest is aroused by the first sentence, which reveals to us that the man is on trial for his life.

XVIII. THE SUBSTITUTE

By François Coppée (1842-   )

It is as a poet that this author is best known, yet he has written many prose stories with a poetic insight and sympathy. He deals with humble characters chiefly, with types of the plain people, with those who have not had a fair chance in life, or with those who, having had it, have let it slip through their fingers. His pathos is manly and simple and unstrained. His interest is rather in character than in action; and yet he can tell a story in straightforward fashion. The present example of his narrative art was written in the early eighties, after Daudet and Halévy had revived the short-story in France, and before Maupassant had come forward. The present translation is by the editor.

THE SUBSTITUTE

He was scarcely ten years old when he was arrested for the first time for vagabondage.

This is what he said to the judges:—

"My name is Jean François Leturc, and for the last six months I've been with the man who sings between two lanterns on the Place de la Bastille, scraping on a bit of catgut. I say the chorus with him, and then I cry out, 'Ask for the new song book, ten centimes, two sous!' He was always drunk, and he beat me. That's how the police found me the other night, in these ruined houses. Before that, I used to be with the man who sells brushes. My mother was a washerwoman; her name is Adèle. A gentleman had set her up on a ground floor, at Montmartre, long ago. She was a good worker and very fond of me. She made money because she had the custom of the café waiters, and they need lots of linen. Sundays, she put me to bed early to go to the ball; but week days, she sent me to the Brothers' school, where I learned to read. Well, at last the policeman whose beat was up our street used to stop before her window to talk to her, — a big man, with the Crimean medal. They got married, and all went wrong. He took a dislike to me, and set mamma against me. Everybody had a slap for me; and it was then that to get away I spent my days on the Place Clichy, where I got acquainted with the mountebanks. My stepfather lost his job, mamma lost her customers, so she went to the washhouse to support her husband. It was there she got consumption, from the dampness. She died at Lariboisière. She was a good woman. Since then I've lived with the brush seller and the catgut scraper. Am I going to be put in prison?"

He talked this way openly, cynically, like a man. He was a ragged little rascal, as tall as a top-boot, with his forehead hidden under a strange yellow mop of hair.

Nobody claiming him, they sent him to the reform school.

THE SUBSTITUTE

Not intelligent, lazy, especially clumsy with his hands, he could learn there only a poor trade, — to reseat straw chairs. Yet he was obedient, naturally quiet and taciturn; and he did not seem to be too profoundly corrupted by that school of vice. But when he was seventeen, and set free in the streets of Paris, he found there, for his misfortune, his prison comrades, wretched creatures, plying the lowest callings. Some were trainers of dogs for rat-catching in the sewers; some shined shoes in the Passage de l'Opéra, on the nights when there were balls; some were amateur wrestlers, letting themselves be thrown by the Hercules of the side shows; some used to fish from rafts out in the river. He tried one of these things and another; and a few months after he had left the house of correction, he was arrested again for a petty theft, — a pair of old shoes picked from out an open show window. Result: a year of imprisonment at Sainte-Pélagie, where he served as valet to the political prisoners.

He lived, astonished, among this group of prisoners, all very young and carelessly dressed, who talked loudly and carried themselves in such a solemn way. They used to meet in the cell of the eldest of them, a fellow of thirty locked up for a long time already and as though settled at Sainte-Pélagie, — a big cell, papered with colored caricatures, out of whose windows could be seen the whole of Paris, its roofs, its steeples, its domes, and far off, the distant line of the hills, blue and vague against the sky. On the walls there were a few shelves filled with books and all the old apparatus of a fencing school, — broken masks, rusty foils, leather jackets and gloves with the stuffing half out. It was there that the political prisoners had dinner together, adding to the inevitable soup and beef, fruit, cheese, and quarts of wine that Jean François was sent to buy at the canteen, — tumultuous repasts, interrupted by violent disputes, and with songs sung in chorus at the dessert, the "Carmagnole" and "Ça ira." But they took on an air of dignity the days when they made room for a newcomer, who was at first solemnly greeted as "citizen," but who was the next day called by his nickname. They made use of big words, Corporation, Solidarity, and phrases quite unintelligible to Jean François, such as this for example, that he once heard uttered imperiously by a hideous little hunchback who spent his nights scribbling: —

"Then it's settled. The cabinet is to be composed of Raymond in the Department of Education, Martial in the Interior, and I in Foreign Affairs."

When his time was up, he wandered again about Paris, with the eye of the police on him, much like the cockchafers that cruel children keep flying tied to a string. He had become one of those fugitive and timid beings whom the law, with a coquetry of its own, arrests and releases, turn and turn about, a little like those platonic fishermen who throw back into the water the fish just out of the net so as not to empty the pond. Without his suspecting that so much honor was done to so feeble a personality, he had a special docket in the mysterious archives of police headquarters; his name and surnames were written in a large backhand on the gray paper of the cover, and the notes and reports, carefully classified, gave him these graduated appellations: "the man named Leturc," "the accused Leturc," and finally, "the convicted Leturc."

He stayed out of prison two years, eating as best he could, sleeping in lodging houses, or sometimes in kilns, and taking part with his fellows in endless games of pitch and toss, on the Boulevards, out near the gates. He wore a greasy cap on the back of his head, carpet slippers, and a short white blouse. When he had five sous, he had his hair curled. He danced at Constant's at Montparnasse; for two sous he bought the knave of hearts or the ace of spades, used as return checks, to sell them again for four sous at the entrance to Bobino; he opened carriage doors when the chance came; he led broken-down horses to the market. He always had bad luck, — in the conscription he drew a good number. Who knows whether the atmosphere of honor which is breathed in the barracks, whether military discipline, might not have saved him? Caught in a haul, with a lot of vagabonds who used to rob the drunkards asleep in the streets, he denied energetically having taken part in their expeditions. Perhaps it was true. But his antecedents were accepted as proof, and he was sent up for three years to Poissy. There he had to make rough toys; he had himself tattooed on the chest; and he learned thieves' slang and the penal code. Another release, another plunge into the Parisian sewer, but this time very short, for at the end of scarce six weeks, he was again compromised in a theft by night, aggravated by violence, a doubtful case in which he played an obscure part, half dupe and half receiver. At the end his complicity seemed evident, and he was condemned to five years' hard labor.

His sorrow in this adventure was to be separated from an old dog that he had picked up on a pile of rubbish and cured of the mange. This beast loved him.

Toulon, the ball on his ankle, work in the harbor, blows, wooden shoes without straw, soup of black beans dating from Trafalgar, no money for tobacco, and the horrible sleep on the filthy iron bed of the convict, that is what he knew for five horrid summers and five winters with the whistling wind. He came out stunned, and was sent under surveillance to Vernon, where he worked for a while on the river; and then, incorrigible vagabond as he was, he broke bounds and came back again to Paris.

He had his savings, fifty-six francs that is to say, time to reflect. During his long absence his old, horrible comrades had been scattered. He was well hidden; he slept in an attic, at an old woman's, to whom he had given himself out as a sailor, weary of the sea, having lost his papers in a recent shipwreck, and wanting to try another trade. His tanned face, his calloused hands, and a few sea phrases he let drop from time to time, made this tale fairly probable.

One day when he had risked a saunter along the streets and when the chance of his walk brought him to Montmarte, where he had been born, an unexpected memory stopped him before the door of the Brothers' school, in which he had learned to read. As it was very warm, the door was open; and with a single look the hesitating passer could recognize the schoolroom. Nothing was changed, not the crucifix over the desk, nor the regular rows of seats, with their leaden inkstands, nor the table of weights and measures, nor the map on which

THE SUBSTITUTE

were still the pins pointing out the operations of some old war. Heedlessly, and without reflecting, Jean François read on the blackboard these words of Scripture, which a well-trained hand had traced as an example of handwriting: —

"Joy shall be in heaven over one sinner that repenteth, more than over ninety and nine just persons, who need no repentance."

It must have been the hour for recreation, for the teaching Brother had left his chair, and sitting on the edge of a table, he seemed to be telling a story to all the children who surrounded him, attentive and raising their eyes. What an innocent and gay expression was that of the beardless young man, in long black robe, with white cravat, with coarse, ugly shoes, and with brown hair badly cut rising up at the back. All those pallid faces of children of the populace which were looking at him, seemed less infantine than his, especially when, charmed with a candid, priestly pleasantry, he broke out with a good and frank laugh, which showed his teeth sound and well-ordered, — a laugh so contagious that all the scholars broke out noisily in their turn, — and it was simple and sweet, this group in the joyous sunlight that made the clear eyes and the blond hair shine.

Jean François looked at it some time in silence, and, for the first time, in this savage nature, all instinct and appetite, there awoke a mysterious and sweet emotion. His heart, that rough and hardened heart, which did not start when the heavy cudgel or the weight of the whip fell on his shoulders, beat almost to oppression. Before this spectacle, in which he saw again his childhood, his eyes closed sorrowfully, and restraining a violent gesture, he moved away with large strides.

The words written on the blackboard came back to him.

"If it was not too late, after all?" he murmured. "If I could once more, like the others, eat my white bread honestly, sleep my sleep out with no nightmare? The police spy would be very clever to recognize me now. My beard, that I shaved down there, has grown again, thick and strong. A man can hide himself in this big ant-heap, and work is not lacking. Whoever does not break down soon in the hell of the prison, comes out agile and robust; and I have learned how to climb ladders with a load on my back. There is building going on everywhere, and the masons need helpers. Three francs a day, — I have never earned so much. If they will only forget me, that is all I ask."

He followed his courageous resolutions; he was faithful to it; and three months later, he was another man. The master for whom he labored cited him as his best workman. After a long day passed on the ladder, in the full sun, in the dust, bending and straightening his back to take the stones from the hands of the man below him and to pass them to the man above him, he came home to get a meal at the cheap eating house, dead tired, his legs heavy, his hands burning, and his eyelashes stuck together by the plaster, but satisfied with himself, and carrying his well-earned money in the knot of his handkerchief. He went out now with no fear of anything, for his white mask made him unrecognizable; and then he had observed that the suspicious glance of the policeman does not often fall on the real worker. He was silent and sober. He slept the good sleep of fatigue. He was free.

At last — a supreme reward — he had a friend.

It was a mason like himself, called Savinien, a little peasant from Limoges, red-cheeked, having came to Paris with his bundle on the end of the stick over his shoulder, who kept away from the liquor dealers and went to mass on Sunday. Jean François liked him for his wholesomeness, for his innocence, for his honesty, for all that he himself had lost long ago. It was a deep passion, reserved, and betraying itself by the care and forethought of a father. Savinien, himself easy-going and selfish, let things take their course, glad only that he had found a comrade who shared his horror of the saloon. The two friends lived together in a furnished room, fairly clean, but their means were very limited; and they had to take in a third companion, an old man from Auvergne, somber and rapacious, who found a way of saving out of his meager wages to buy land at home.

Jean François and Savinien scarcely ever left each other. The days of rest they went on long walks in the environs of Paris to dine in the open air in one of those little country inns where there are many mushrooms in the sauces and innocent enigmas on the bottoms of the plates. Jean François then had his friend tell him all the things which are unknown to those born in cities. He learned the names of the trees, the flowers, the plants, the date of the different harvests; he listened greedily to the thousand details of a farmer's labors, the autumn sowing, the winter work, the splendid feasts of harvest home and vintage, the flails beating the floor, and the sound of the mills by the edge of the water, the tired horses led to the trough, and the morning hunting in the mists, and above all, the long evenings around the fire, shortened by tales of marvel. He discovered in himself springs of an imagination hitherto unsuspected, finding a singular pleasure in the mere recital of these things, so sweet, calm, and monotonous.

One fear troubled him, however, that Savinien might come to know his past. Sometimes there escaped him a shady word of slang, an ignoble gesture, survivals of his former horrible existence; and then he felt the pain of a man whose old wounds open again, — the more particularly as he then thought he saw in Savinien the awakening of an unhealthy curiosity. When the young man, already tempted by the pleasures which Paris offered even to the poorest, asked him about the mysteries of the great city, Jean François feigned ignorance and turned the conversation; but he had then a vague doubt as to the future of his friend.

This was not without foundation; and Savinien could not long remain the innocent countryman he had been on his arrival in Paris. If the gross and noisy pleasures of the saloon were still repugnant to him, he was deeply troubled by other desires full of danger for the inexperience of his twenty years. When the spring came, he began to seek solitude, and he wandered at first before the gayly lighted entrance to the dancing halls, through which he saw the girls going in couples, without bonnets — and whispering with their arms around each other. Then one evening, when the lilacs were in bloom, and when the appeal of the music was more entrancing, he crossed the threshold. And after that Jean François saw him change little by little in his manners and in his looks. Savinien became more careful of his dress and he spent more; often he borrowed from the poor savings of his friend, which he forgot to return. Jean François, feeling himself deserted, was both indulgent and jealous; he suffered and kept silent. He believed he had no right to reproach, but his penetrating friendship had cruel and unconquerable forebodings.

One night when he was climbing the stairs of his lodging, absorbed in his preoccupations, he heard a dialogue of irritated voices in the room he was about to enter, and he recognized one as that of the old man from Auvergne, who shared the room with him and Savinien. An old habit of suspicion made him wait on the landing, and he listened to learn the cause of the trouble.

"Yes," the man from Auvergne was saying angrily, "I am sure that somebody has broken open my trunk and stolen the three louis which I had hidden in a little box; and the man who did the trick can only be one of the two companions who sleep here, unless it is Maria, the servant. This is your business as much as mine, since you are the master of the house; and I will hale you to court if you do not let me at once go through the valises of the two masons. My poor savings! they were in their place only yesterday; and I will tell you what the louis were, so that, if you find them, you will not accuse me of lying. Oh, I know them, my three fine gold pieces. One was a little more worn than the others, of a gold a little greener, and that had the portrait of the great Emperor; another had that of a fat old fellow with a pigtail and epaulets; and the third had a Philip with side whiskers — I had marked it with my teeth. I am not to be cheated, not I. Do you know I need only two more to pay for my vineyard? Come, let us look through the duds of these two comrades, or I will call the police."

"Very well," said the voice of the man who kept the house. "We'll search with Maria. So much the worse if you find nothing and if the masons get angry. It will be because you forced me to it."

Jean François had his heart filled with fear. He recalled the poverty of Savinien, the petty borrowings, the somber manner observed the last few days. Yet he did not want to believe in any theft. He heard the hard breathing of the man from Auvergne in the ardor of the search; and he clenched his hands against his breast as though to repress the beatings of his heart.

"There they are!" suddenly screamed the miser, victorious. "There they are, the louis, my dear treasure! And in the Sunday waistcoat of that little hypocrite from Limoges. See there, boss! They are just as I told you. There's the Napoleon, and the man with the pigtail, and the Philip I had bitten. See the mark. Ah, the little rascal, with his air of innocence. I should more likely have suspected the other. Ah, the villain. He will have to go to prison!"

At this moment Jean François heard the well-known step of Savinien, who was slowly coming upstairs.

"He will betray himself," he thought. "Three flights. I have the time!"

And pushing the door, and pale as death, he entered

the room, where he saw the man who kept the house and the stupefied servant in a corner, and the man from Auvergne on his knees amid the scattered clothes, lovingly kissing his gold pieces.

"Enough of this," he said in a dull voice. "It was I who took the money and put it in the comrade's trunk. But that is too disgusting. I am a thief and not a Judas. Go get the police. I shall not run. Only I must say a word in private to Savinien, — who is here."

The little man from Limoges had in fact just arrived, and seeing his crime discovered and believing himself lost, he stood still, with his eyes fixed and his arms falling.

Jean François sprang to his neck, as though to embrace him; he glued his mouth to Savinien's ear, and said to him in a low and beseeching voice: —

"Hold your tongue!"

Then, turning to the others: —

"Leave me alone with him. I shall not go away, I tell you. Shut us up, if you like, but leave us alone together."

And with a gesture of command, he showed them the door. They went out.

Savinien, broken with anguish, had seated himself on a bed, and had dropped his eyes without understanding.

"Listen," said Jean François, who came to take his hands. "I understand. You stole the three gold pieces to buy some trifle for a girl. That would have been worth six months of prison for you. But you do not get out of that except to go back again; and you would have become a pillar of the police courts and criminal trials. I know all about them. I have done seven years in the reform school, one at Sainte-Pélagie, three at Poissy, and five at Toulon. Now, do not get scared. It is all settled. I have taken it on my shoulders."

"Poor fellow," cried Savinien; but hope was coming back to his cowardly heart.

"When the elder brother is serving with the colors, the younger stays at home," Jean François went on. "I'm your substitute, that is all. You love me a little, do you not? I am paid. Do not be a baby. You cannot refuse. They would have caught me one of these days, for I have broken my leave. And then, you see, that life out there will not be so hard for me as for you; I know it, and shall not complain if I do not render you this service in vain and if you swear to me that you will not do it again. Savinien, I have loved you dearly, and your friendship has made me very happy, for it is thanks to my knowing you that I have kept honest and straight, as I might always have been, if I had had a father to put a tool in my hands, a mother to teach me my prayers. My only regret was that I was useless to you and that I was deceiving you about my past. To-day I lay aside the mask in saving you. It is all right. Come, now, good-by! Do not weep; and embrace me, for I hear the big boots on the stairs. They are coming back with the police; and we must not seem to know each other too well before these fellows."

He hugged Savinien hurriedly to his breast, and then he pushed him away as the door opened wide.

It was the man who kept the house and the man from Auvergne who were bringing the police. Jean François went out on the landing and held out his hands for the handcuffs and said, laughing:—

"Forward, bad lot!"

To-day he is at Cayenne, a prisoner for life, as incorrigible.

NOTE. — Compassion is the chief quality of this little masterpiece, — compassion and understanding of a primitive type of character. The author shows us the good in a character not altogether bad; and he almost makes us feel that the final sacrifice was justifiable. He succeeds in doing this chiefly because he shows us the other characters only as they appeared to Jean François, thus focusing the interest of the reader on this single character.

XIX. MRS. KNOLLYS

By Frederic J. Stimson (1855–   )

The author of this story is a lawyer of distinction who has written several works of fiction having each of them a flavor of its own. "Mrs. Knollys" was written in 1883.

MRS. KNOLLYS[1]

The great Pasterzen glacier rises in Western Austria, and flows into Carinthia, and is fourteen or seventeen miles long, as you measure it from its birth in the snow field, or from where it begins to move from the higher snows and its active course is marked by the first wrinkle. It flows in a straight, steady sweep, a grand avenue, guarded by giant mountains, steep and wide; a prototype, huge and undesigned, of the giants' stairway in the Venice palace. No known force can block its path; it would need a cataclysm to reverse its progress. What falls upon it moves with it, what lies beneath it moves with it — down to the polished surface of the earth's frame, laid bare; no blade of grass grows so slowly as it moves, no meteor of the air is so irresistible. Its substant ice curls freely,

[1] Printed by permission of the author and of the publishers, Charles Scribner's Sons.

molds, and breaks itself like water, — breaks in waves, plastic like honey, crested lightly with a frozen spray; it winds tenderly about the rocky shore, and the granite, distintegrated into crumbs, flows on with it. All this so quietly that busy, officious little Man lived a score of thousand years before he noticed even that the glacier moved.

Now, however, men have learned to congregate upon its shores, and admire. Scientists stick staves in the ground (not too near, lest the earth should move with it), and appraise the majesty of its motion; ladies, politely mystified, give little screams of pleased surprise; young men, secretly exultant, pace the yard or two between the sticks, a distance that takes the frozen stream a year to compass, and look out upon it half contemptuously. Then they cross it — carefully, they have enough respect left for that — with their cunningly nailed shoes and a rope; an hour or two they dally with it, till at last, being hungry and cold, they walk to the inn for supper. At supper they tell stories of their prowess, pay money to the guides who have protected them, and fall asleep after tea with weariness. Meantime, the darkness falls outside; but the white presence of the glacier breaks the night, and strange shapes unseen of men dance in its ashen hollows. It is so old that the realms of death and life conflict; change is on the surface, but immortality broods in the deeper places. The moon rises and sinks; the glacier moves silently, like a timepiece marking the centuries, grooving the record of its being on the world itself, — a feature to be read and studied by far-off generations of some other world. The glacier has a light of its own, and gleams to stars above, and the great Glockner mountain flings his shadow of the planets in its face.

Mrs. Knollys was a young English bride, sunny-haired, hopeful-eyed, with lips that parted to make you love them, — parted before they smiled, and all the soft regions of her face broke into attendant dimples. And then, lest you should think it meant for you, she looked quickly up to "Charles," as she would then call him even to strangers, and Charles looked down to her. Charles was a short foot taller, with much the same hair and eyes, thick flossy whiskers, broad shoulders, and a bass voice. This was in the days before political economy cut Hymen's wings. Charles, like Mary, had little money, but great hopes; and he was clerk in a government office, with a friendly impression of everybody and much trust in himself. And old Harry Colquhoun, his chief, had given them six weeks to go to Switzerland and be happy in, all in celebration of Charles Knollys's majority and marriage to his young wife. So they had both forgotten heaven for the nonce, having a passable substitute; but the powers divine overlooked them pleasantly and forgave it. And even the phlegmatic driver of their *Einspänner* looked back from the corner of his eye at the *schöne Engländerin*, and compared her mentally with the far-famed beauty of the Königssee. So they rattled on in their curious conveyance, with the pole in the middle and the one horse out on one side, and still found more beauty in each other's eyes than in the world about them. Although Charles was only one and twenty, Mary Knollys was barely eighteen, and to her he seemed godlike in his age, as in all other things. Her life had been as simple as it had been short. She remembered being a little girl, and then the next thing that occurred was Charles Knollys, and positively the next thing she remembered of importance was being Mrs. Charles Knollys; so that old Mrs. Knollys, her guardian aunt and his, had first called her a love of a baby, and then but a baby in love. All this, of course, was five and forty years ago, for you know how old she was when she went again to Switzerland last summer — three and sixty.

They first saw the great mountains from the summit of the Schafberg. This is a little height, three-cornered between three lakes; a natural Belvedere for Central Europe. Mr. and Mrs. Knollys were seated on a couch of Alpine roses behind a rhododendron bush watching the sunset; but as Charles was desirous of kissing Mrs. Knollys, and the rhododendron bush was not thick enough, they were waiting for the sun to go down. He was very slow in doing this, and by way of consolation Knollys was keeping his wife's hand hidden in the folds of her dress. Undoubtedly a modern lady would have been talking of the scenery, giving word-color pictures of the view; but I am afraid Mrs. Knollys had been looking at her husband, and talking with him of the cottage they had bought in a Surrey village, not far from Box Hill, and thinking how the little carvings and embroideries would look there which they had bought abroad. And, indeed, Mrs. Charles secretly thought Box Hill an eminence far preferable to the Venediger, and Charles's face an infinitely more interesting sight than any lake, however expressive. But the sun, looking askance at them through the lower mist, was not jealous; all the same he spread his glory lavishly for them, and the bright little mirror of a lake twinkled cannily upward from below. Finally it grew dark; then there was less talking. It was full night when they went in, she leaning on his arm and looking up; and the moonbeam on the snowy shoulder of the Glockner, twenty leagues away, came over, straightway, from the mountain to her face. Three days later, Charles Knollys, crossing with her the lower portion of the Pasterzen glacier, slipped into a crevasse, and vanished utterly from the earth.

II

All this you know. And I was also told more of the girl, bride and widow at eighteen; how she sought to throw herself into the clear blue gulf; how she refused to leave Heiligenblut; how she would sit, tearless, by the rim of the crevasse, day after day, and gaze into its profundity. A guide or man was always with her at these times, for it was still feared she would follow her young husband to the depths of that still sea. Her aunt went over from England to her; the summer waxed; autumn storms set in; but no power could win her from the place whence Charles had gone.

If there was a time worse for her than that first moment, it was when they told her that his body never could be found. They did not dare to tell her this for many days, but busied themselves with idle cranes and ladders, and made futile pretenses with ropes. Some of the big, simple-hearted guides even descended into the chasm, absenting themselves for an hour or so, to give her an idea that something was being done. Poor Mrs. Knollys would have followed them had she been allowed, to wander through the purple galleries, calling Charles. It was well she could not; for all Kaspar could do was to lower himself a hundred yards or so, chisel out a niche, and stand in it, smoking his honest pipe to pass the time, and trying to fancy he could hear the murmur of the waters down below. Meantime Mrs. Knollys strained her eyes, peering downward from above, leaning on the rope about her waist, looking over the clear brink of the bergschrund.

It was the Herr Doctor Zimmermann who first told her the truth. Not that the good Doctor meant to do so. The Herr Doctor had had his attention turned to glaciers by some rounded stones in his garden by the Traunsee, and more particularly by the Herr Privatdocent Splüthner. Splüthner, like Uncle Toby, had his hobby horse, his pet conjuring words, his gods *ex machinâ*, which he brought upon the field in scientific emergencies; and these gods, as with Thales, were Fire and Water. Craters and flood were his accustomed scapegoats, upon whose heads were charged all things unaccountable; and the Herr Doctor, who had only one element left to choose from, and that a passive one, but knew, on general principles, that Splüthner must be wrong, got as far off as he could and took Ice. And Splüthner having pooh-poohed this, Zimmermann rode his hypothesis with redoubled zeal. He became convinced that ice was the embodiment of orthodoxy. Fixing his professional spectacles on his substantial nose, he went into Carinthia and ascended the great Venice mountains, much as he would have performed any other scientific experiment. Then he encamped on the shores of the Pasterzen glacier, and proceeded to make a study of it.

So it happened that the Doctor, taking a morning stroll over the subject of his experiment, in search of small things which might verify his theory, met Mrs. Knollys sitting in her accustomed place. The Doctor had been much puzzled, that morning, on finding in a rock at the foot of the glacier the impression, or sign-manual as it were, of a certain fish, whose acquaintance the Doctor had previously made only in tropical seas. This fact seeming, superficially, to chime in with Splüthnerian mistakes in a most heterodox way, the Doctor's mind had for a moment been diverted from the ice; and he was wondering what the fish had been going to do in that particular gallery, and secretly doubting whether it had known its own mind, and gone thither with the full knowledge and permission of its maternal relative. Indeed, the good Doctor would probably have ascribed its presence to the malicious and personal causation of the devil, but that the one point on which he and Splüthner were agreed was the ignoring of unscientific hypotheses. The Doctor's objections to the devil were none the less strenuous for being purely scientific.

Thus ruminating, the Doctor came to the crevasse where Mrs. Knollys was sitting, and to which a little path had now been worn from the inn. There was nothing of scientific interest about the fair young English girl, and the Doctor did not notice her; but he took from his waistcoat pocket a leaden bullet, molded by himself, and marked "Johannes Carpentarius, Juvavianus, A. U. C. 2590," and dropped it, with much satisfaction, into the crevasse. Mrs. Knollys gave a little cry; the bullet was heard for some seconds tinkling against the sides of the chasm; the tinkles grew quickly fainter, but they waited in vain for the noise of the final fall. "May the Splüthner live that he may learn by it," muttered the Doctor; "I can never recover it."

Then he remembered that the experiment had been attended with a sound unaccounted for by the conformity of the bullet to the laws of gravitation; and looking up he saw Mrs. Knollys in front of him, no longer crying, but very pale. Zimmermann started, and in his confusion dropped his best brass registering thermometer, which also rattled down the abyss.

"You say," whispered Mrs. Knollys, "that it can never be recovered!"

"Madam," spoke the Doctor, doffing his hat, "how would you recofer from a blace when the smallest approximation which I haf yet been able to make puts the depth from the surface to the bed of the gletscher at vrom sixteen hundred to sixteen hundred and sixty *meters* in distance?" Doctor Zimmermann spoke very good English; and he pushed his hat upon the back of his head, and assumed his professional attitude.

"But they all were trying—" Mrs. Knollys spoke faintly. "They said that they hoped he could be recovered." The stranger was the oldest gentleman she had seen, and Mrs. Knollys felt almost like confiding in him. "Oh, I must have the—the body." She closed in a sob; but the Herr Doctor caught at the last word, and this suggested to him only the language of scientific experiment.

"Recofer it? If, madam," Zimmermann went on with all the satisfaction attendant on the enunciation of a scientific truth, "we take a body and drop it in the schrund of this gletscher; and the ice stream moves so slower at its base than on the upper part, and the ice will cover it, efen if we could reach the base, which is a mile in depth. Then, see you, it is all caused by the motion of the ice—"

But at this Mrs. Knollys had given a faint cry, and her guide rushed up angrily to the old professor, who stared helplessly forward. "God will help me, sir," said she to the Doctor, and she gave the guide her arm and walked wearily away.

The professor still stared in amazement at her enthusiasm for scientific experiment and the passion with which she greeted his discoveries. Here was a person who utterly refused to be referred to the agency of ice, or even, like Splüthner, of Fire and Water; and went out of the range of allowable hypotheses to call upon a Noumenon. Now both Splüthner and Zimmermann had studied all natural agencies and made allowance for them, but for the Divine they had always hitherto proved an alibi. The Doctor could make nothing of it.

At the inn that evening he saw Mrs. Knollys with swollen eyes; and remembering the scene of the afternoon, he made inquiries about her of the innkeeper. The latter had heard the guide's account of the meeting; and as soon as Zimmermann had made plain what he had told her of the falling body, "Triple blockhead!"

said he. *"Es war ihr Mann."* The Herr Professor staggered back into his seat; and the kindly innkeeper ran upstairs to see what had happened to his poor young guest.

Mrs. Knollys had recovered from the first shock by this time, but the truth could no longer be withheld. The innkeeper could but nod his head sadly, when she told him that to recover her Charles was hopeless. All the guides said the same thing. The poor girl's husband had vanished from the world as utterly as if his body had been burned to ashes and scattered in the pathway of the winds. Charles Knollys was gone, utterly gone; no more to be met with by his girl-wife, save as spirit to spirit, soul to soul, in ultramundane place. The fair-haired young Englishman lived but in her memory, as his soul, if still existent, lived in places indeterminate, unknowable to Doctor Zimmermann and his compeers. Slowly Mrs. Knollys acquired the belief that she was never to see her Charles again. Then, at last, she resolved to go — to go home. Her strength now gave way; and when her aunt left she had with her but the ghost of Mrs. Knollys — a broken figure, drooping in the carriage, veiled in black. The innkeeper and all the guides stood bareheaded, silent, about the door, as the carriage drove off, bearing the bereaved widow back to England.

III

When the Herr Doctor had heard the innkeeper's answer, he sat for some time with his hands planted on his knees, looking through his spectacles at the opposite wall. Then he lifted one hand and struck his brow impatiently. It was his way, when a chemical reaction had come out wrong.

"Triple blockhead!" said he; "triple blockhead, thou art so bad as Splüthner." No self-condemnation could have been worse to him than this. Thinking again of Mrs. Knollys, he gave one deep, gruff sob. Then he took his hat, and going out, wandered by the shore of the glacier in the night, repeating to himself the Englishwoman's words: "*They said that they hoped he could be recovered.*" Zimmermann came to the tent where he kept his instruments, and stood there, looking at the sea of ice. He went to his measuring pegs, two rods of iron: one sunk deep and frozen in the glacier, the other drilled into a rock on the shore. "Triple blockhead!" said he again, "thou art worse than Splüthner. The Splüthner said the glacier did not move; thou, thou knowest that it does." He sighted from his rods to the mountain opposite. There was a slight and all but imperceptible change of direction from the day before.

He could not bear to see the English girl again, and all the next day was absent from the inn. For a month he stopped at Heiligenblut, and busied himself with his instruments. The guides of the place greeted him coldly every day, as they started on their glacier excursions or their chamois hunting. But none the less did Zimmermann return the following summer, and work upon his great essay in refutation of the Splüthner.

Mrs. Knollys went back to the little cottage in Surrey, and lived there. The chests and cases she brought back lay unopened in the storeroom; the little rooms of the cottage that was to be their home remained bare and unadorned as Charles had seen them last. She could not bring herself to alter them now. What she had looked forward to do with him she had no strength to do alone. She rarely went out. There was no place where she could go to think of him. He was gone; gone from England, gone from the very surface of the earth. If he had only been buried in some quiet English churchyard, she thought, — some green place lying open to the sun, where she could go and scatter flowers on his grave, where she could sit and look forward amid her tears to the time when she should lie side by side with him, — they would then be separated for her short life alone. Now it seemed to her that they were far apart forever.

But late the next summer she had a letter from the place. It was from Dr. Zimmermann. There is no need here to trace the quaint German phrases, the formalism, the cold terms of science in which he made his meaning plain. It spoke of erosion; of the movement of the summer; of the action of the under-waters on the ice. And it told her, with tender sympathy oddly blended with the pride of scientific success, that he had given a year's most careful study to the place; with all his instruments of measurement he had tested the relentless glacier's flow; and it closed by assuring her that her husband might be found — in five and forty years. In five and forty years — the poor professor staked his scientific reputation on the fact — in five and forty years she might return, and the glacier would give up its dead.

This letter made Mrs. Knollys happier. It made her willing to live; it made her almost long to live until old age — that her Charles's body might be given back. She took heart to beautify her little home. The trifling articles she had bought with Charles were now brought out, — the little curiosities and pictures he had given her on their wedding journey. She would ask how such and such a thing looked, turning her pretty head to some kind visitor, as she ranged them on the walls; and now and then she would have to lay the picture down and cry a little, silently, as she remembered where Charles had told her it would look best. Still, she sought to furnish the rooms as they had planned them in their mind; she made her surroundings, as nearly as she could, as they had pictured them together. One room she never went into; it was the room Charles had meant to have for the nursery. She had no child.

But she changed, as we all change, with the passing of the years. I first remember her as a woman middle-aged, sweet-faced, hardly like a widow, nor yet like an old maid. She was rather like a young girl in love, with her lover absent on a long journey. She lived more with the memory of her husband, she clung to him more than if she had had a child. She never married; you would have guessed that; but, after the professor's letter, she never quite seemed to realize that her husband was dead. Was he not coming back to her?

Never in all my knowledge of dear English women have I known a woman so much loved. In how many houses was she always the most welcome guest! How often we boys would go to her for sympathy! I know she was the confidante of all our love affairs. I cannot speak for girls; but I fancy she was much the same with them. Many of us owed our life's happiness to her. She would chide us gently in our pettiness and folly, and teach us, by her very presence and example, what thing it was that alone could keep life sweet. How well we all remember the little Surrey cottage, the little home fireside where the husband had never been! I think she grew to imagine his presence, even the presence of children: boys, curly-headed, like Charles, and sweet, blue-eyed daughters; and the fact that it was all imagining seemed but to make the place more holy. Charles still lived to her as she had believed him in the month that they were married; he lived through life with her as her young love had fancied he would be. She never thought of evil that might have occurred; of failing affection, of cares. Her happiness was in her mind alone; so all the earthly part was absent.

There were but two events in her life — that which was past and that which was to come. She had lived through his loss; now she lived on for his recovery. But, as I have said, she changed, as all things mortal change; all but the earth and the ice stream and the stars above it. She read much, and her mind grew deep and broad, none the less gentle with it all; she was wiser in the world; she knew the depths of human hope and sorrow. You remember her only as an old lady whom we loved. Only her heart did not change — I forgot that; her heart, and the memory of that last loving smile upon his face, as he bent down to look into her eyes, before he slipped and fell. She lived on, and waited for his body, as possibly his other self — who knows? — waited for hers. As she grew older she grew taller; her eyes were quieter, her hair a little straighter, darker than of yore; her face changed, only the expression remained the same. Mary Knollys!

Human lives rarely look more than a year, or five, ahead; Mary Knollys looked five and forty. Many of us wait, and grow weary in waiting, for those few years alone, and for some living friend. Mary Knollys waited five and forty years — for the dead. Still, after that first year, she never wore all black; only silvery grays, and white with a black ribbon or two. I have said she almost seemed to think her husband living. She would fancy his doing this and that with her; how he would joy in this good fortune, or share her sorrows — which were few, mercifully. His memory seemed to be a living thing to her, to go through life with her, hand in hand; it changed as she grew old; it altered itself to suit her changing thought; until the very memory of her memory seemed to make it sure that he had really been alive with her, really shared her happiness or sorrow, in the far-off days of her earliest widowhood. It hardly seemed that he had been gone already then — she remembered him so well. She could not think that he had never been with her in their little cottage. And now, at sixty, I know she thought of him as an old person, too, sitting by their fireside, late in life, mature, deep-souled, wise with the wisdom of years, going back with her, fondly, to recall the old, old happiness of their bridal journey, when they set off for the happy honeymoon abroad, and the long life now past stretched brightly out before them both. She never spoke of this, and you children never knew it; but it was always in her mind.

There was a plain stone in the little Surrey churchyard, now gray and moss-grown with the rains of forty years, on which you remember reading: "Charles Knollys — lost in Carinthia" — This was all she would have inscribed; he was but lost; no one *knew* that he was dead. Was he not yet to be found? There was no grassy mound beside it; the earth was smooth. Not even the date was there. But Mrs. Knollys never went to read it. She waited until he should come; until that last journey, repeating the travels of their wedding days, when she should go to Germany to bring him home.

So the woman's life went on in England, and the glacier in the Alps moved on slowly; and the woman waited for it to be gone.

IV

In the summer of 1882, the little Carinthian village of Heiligenblut was haunted by two persons. One was a young German scientist, with long hair and spectacles; and the other was a tall English lady, slightly bent, with a face wherein the finger of time had deeply written tender things. Her hair was white as silver, and she wore a long black veil. Their habits were strangely similar. Every morning, when the eastern light shone deepest into the ice cavern at the base of the great Pasterzen glacier, these two would walk thither; then both would sit for an hour or two and peer into its depths. Neither knew why the other was there. The woman would go back for an hour in the late afternoon; the man, never. He knew that the morning light was necessary for his search.

The man was the famous young Zimmermann, son of his father, the old Doctor, long since dead. But the Herr Doctor had written a famous tract, when late in life, refuting all Splüthners, past, present, and to come; and had charged his son, in his dying moments, as a most sacred trust, that he should repair to the base of the Pasterzen glacier in the year 1882, where he would find a leaden bullet, graven with his father's name, and the date A. U. C. 2590. All this would be vindication of his father's science. Splüthner, too, was a very old man, and Zimmermann the younger (for even he was no longer young) was fearful lest Splüthner should not live to witness his own refutation. The woman and the man never spoke to each other.

Alas, no one could have known Mrs. Knollys for the fair English girl who had been there in the young days of the century; not even the innkeeper, had he been there. But he, too, was long since dead. Mrs. Knollys was now bent and white-haired; she had forgotten, herself, how she had looked in those old days. Her life had been lived. She was now like a woman of another world; it seemed another world in which her fair hair had twined about her husband's fingers, and she and Charles had stood upon the evening mountain, and looked in one another's eyes. That was the world of her wedding days, but it seemed more like a world she had left when born on earth. And now he was coming back to her in this. Meantime the great Pasterzen glacier had moved on, marking only the centuries; the men upon its borders had seen no change; the same great waves lifted their snowy heads upon its surface; the same crevasse still was where he had fallen. At night, the moonbeams, falling, still shivered off its glassy face; its pale presence filled the night, and immortality lay brooding in its hollow.

Friends were with Mrs. Knollys, but she left them at the

inn. One old guide remembered her, and asked to bear her company. He went with her in the morning, and sat a few yards from her, waiting. In the afternoon she went alone. He would not have credited you, had you told him that the glacier moved. He thought it but an Englishwoman's fancy, but he waited with her. Himself had never forgotten that old day. And Mrs. Knollys sat there silently, searching the clear depths of the ice, that she might find her husband.

One night she saw a ghost. The latest beam of the sun, falling on a mountain opposite, had shone back into the ice cavern; and seemingly deep within, in the grave azure light, she fancied she saw a face turned toward her. She even thought she saw Charles's yellow hair, and the selfsame smile his lips had worn when he bent down to her before he fell. It could be but a fancy. She went home, and was silent with her friends about what had happened. In the moonlight she went back, and again the next morning before dawn. She told no one of her going; but the old guide met her at the door, and walked silently behind her. She had slept, the glacier ever present in her dreams.

The sun had not yet risen when she came; and she sat a long time in the cavern, listening to the murmur of the river, flowing under the glacier at her feet. Slowly the dawn began, and again she seemed to see the shimmer of a face — such a face as one sees in the coals of a dying fire. Then the full sun came over the eastern mountain, and the guide heard a woman's cry. There before her was Charles Knollys! The face seemed hardly pale; and there was the same faint smile — a smile like her memory of it, five and forty years gone by. Safe in the clear ice, still, unharmed, there lay — O God! not her Charles; not the Charles of her own thought, who had lived through life with her and shared her sixty years; not the old man she had borne thither in her mind — but a boy, a boy of one and twenty lying asleep, a ghost from another world coming to confront her from the distant past, immortal in the immortality of the glacier. There was his quaint coat, of the fashion of half a century before; his blue eyes open; his young, clear brow; all the form of the past she had forgotten; and she his bride stood there to welcome him, with her wrinkles, her bent figure, and thin white hairs. She was living, he was dead; and she was two and forty years older than he.

Then at last the long-kept tears came to her, and she bent her white head in the snow. The old man came up with his pick, silently, and began working in the ice. The woman lay weeping, and the boy with his still, faint smile, lay looking at them, through the clear ice-veil, from his open eyes.

I believe that the professor found his bullet; I know not. I believe that the scientific world rang with his name and the thesis that he published on the glacier's motion, and the changeless temperature his father's lost thermometer had shown. All this you may read. I know no more.

But I know that in the English churchyard there are now two graves, and a single stone to Charles Knollys and Mary, his wife; and the boy of one and twenty sleeps there with his bride of sixty-three; his young frame

with her old one, his yellow hair beside her white. And
I do not know that there is not some place, not here,
where they are still together, and he is twenty-one and
she is still eighteen. I do not know this; but I know
that all the pamphlets of the German doctor cannot tell
me it is false.

Meantime the great Pasterzen glacier moves on, and
the rocks with it; and the mountain flings his shadow of
the planets in its face.

NOTE. — There is at the center of this story a
striking idea, at once novel and fascinating. But
the mere ingenuity of the closely linked incidents
is subordinated to the interest in the chief figure,
in the pure pathos of her long waiting and in the
final meeting of the young husband who is dead
with the elderly wife who is alive. What might
have been sensational or even gruesome in less
tender hands is here treated with simple dignity
and unparaded poetry. To be noted also is the
skill with which the glacier itself is ever insisted
on; it is with the glacier that the story opens and
it is with the glacier that the story closes.

XX. THE NECKLACE

By Guy de Maupassant (1850-1893)

Maupassant was a born story-teller; and he was severely trained by that rigid realist Flaubert, who taught him the art of construction, the principles of description, and the value of concentration and unity. He is one of the great masters of the short-story. He deals more with the deeds of his characters than with their sentiments; but we are made to understand their emotions by the stern narration of their acts. In terseness, in tenseness, in compactness, Maupassant is unrivaled. Pathos and even compassion are to be seen in his stories only, as it were, by accident. He began to publish only when he was thirty, when he was master of his method; and this specimen of his skill was published in the early eighties. The present translation is by the editor.

THE NECKLACE

She was one of those pretty and charming girls, born by a blunder of destiny in a family of employees. She had no dowry, no expectations, no means of being known, understood, loved, married by a man rich and distin-

THE NECKLACE

guished; and she let them make a match for her with a little clerk in the Department of Education.

She was simple since she could not be adorned; but she was unhappy as though kept out of her own class; for women have no caste and no descent, their beauty, their grace, and their charm serving them instead of birth and fortune. Their native keenness, their instinctive elegance, their flexibility of mind, are their only hierarchy; and these make the daughters of the people the equals of the most lofty dames.

She suffered intensely, feeling herself born for every delicacy and every luxury. She suffered from the poverty of her dwelling, from the worn walls, the abraded chairs, the ugliness of the stuffs. All these things, which another woman of her caste would not even have noticed, tortured her and made her indignant. The sight of the little girl from Brittany who did her humble housework awoke in her desolated regrets and distracted dreams. She let her mind dwell on the quiet vestibules, hung with Oriental tapestries, lighted by tall lamps of bronze, and on the two tall footmen in knee breeches who dozed in the large armchairs, made drowsy by the heat of the furnace. She let her mind dwell on the large parlors, decked with old silk, with their delicate furniture, supporting precious bric-a-brac, and on the coquettish little rooms, perfumed, prepared for the five o'clock chat with the most intimate friends, men well known and sought after, whose attentions all women envied and desired.

When she sat down to dine, before a tablecloth three days old, in front of her husband, who lifted the cover of the tureen, declaring with an air of satisfaction, "Ah, the good *pot-au-feu*. I don't know anything better than that," she was thinking of delicate repasts, with glittering silver, with tapestries peopling the walls with ancient figures and with strange birds in a fairy-like forest; she was thinking of exquisite dishes, served in marvelous platters, of compliment whispered and heard with a sphinx-like smile, while she was eating the rosy flesh of a trout or the wings of a quail.

She had no dresses, no jewelry, nothing. And she loved nothing else; she felt herself made for that only. She would so much have liked to please, to be envied, to be seductive and sought after.

She had a rich friend, a comrade of her convent days, whom she did not want to go and see any more, so much did she suffer as she came away. And she wept all day long, from chagrin, from regret, from despair, and from distress.

But one evening her husband came in with a proud air, holding in his hand a large envelope.

"There," said he, "there's something for you."

She quickly tore the paper and took out of it a printed card which bore these words: —

"The Minister of Education and Mme. Georges Rampouneau beg M. and Mme. Loisel to do them the honor to pass the evening with them at the palace of the Ministry, on Monday, January 18."

Instead of being delighted, as her husband hoped, she threw the invitation on the table with annoyance, murmuring —

"What do you want me to do with that?"

THE NECKLACE

"But, my dear, I thought you would be pleased. You never go out, and here's a chance, a fine one. I had the hardest work to get it. Everybody is after them; they are greatly sought for and not many are given to the clerks. You will see there all the official world."

She looked at him with an irritated eye and she declared with impatience: —

"What do you want me to put on my back to go there?"

He had not thought of that; he hesitated: —

"But the dress in which you go to the theater. That looks very well to me —"

He shut up, astonished and distracted at seeing that his wife was weeping. Two big tears were descending slowly from the corners of the eyes to the corners of the mouth. He stuttered: —

"What's the matter? What's the matter?"

But by a violent effort she had conquered her trouble, and she replied in a calm voice as she wiped her damp cheeks: —

"Nothing. Only I have no clothes, and in consequence I cannot go to this party. Give your card to some colleague whose wife has a better outfit than I."

He was disconsolate. He began again: —

"See here, Mathilde, how much would this cost, a proper dress, which would do on other occasions; something very simple?"

She reflected a few seconds, going over her calculations, and thinking also of the sum which she might ask without meeting an immediate refusal and a frightened exclamation from the frugal clerk.

"At last, she answered hesitatingly: —

"I don't know exactly, but it seems to me that with four hundred francs I might do it."

He grew a little pale, for he was reserving just that sum to buy a gun and treat himself to a little shooting, the next summer, on the plain of Nanterre, with some friends who used to shoot larks there on Sundays.

But he said: —

"All right. I will give you four hundred francs. But take care to have a pretty dress."

The day of the party drew near, and Mme. Loisel seemed sad, restless, anxious. Yet her dress was ready. One evening her husband said to her: —

"What's the matter? Come, now, you have been quite queer these last three days."

And she answered: —

"It annoys me not to have a jewel, not a single stone, to put on. I shall look like distress. I would almost rather not go to this party."

He answered: —

"You will wear some natural flowers. They are very stylish this time of the year. For ten francs you will have two or three magnificent roses."

But she was not convinced.

"No; there's nothing more humiliating than to look poor among a lot of rich women."

But her husband cried: —

"What a goose you are! Go find your friend, Mme. Forester, and ask her to lend you some jewelry. You know her well enough to do that."

She gave a cry of joy:—

"That's true. I had not thought of it."

The next day she went to her friend's and told her about her distress.

Mme. Forester went to her mirrored wardrobe, took out a large casket, brought it, opened it, and said to Mme. Loisel:—

"Choose, my dear."

She saw at first bracelets, then a necklace of pearls, then a Venetian cross of gold set with precious stones of an admirable workmanship. She tried on the ornaments before the glass, hesitated, and could not decide to take them off and to give them up. She kept on asking:—

"You haven't anything else?"

"Yes, yes. Look. I do not know what will happen to please you."

All at once she discovered, in a box of black satin, a superb necklace of diamonds, and her heart began to beat with boundless desire. Her hands trembled in taking it up. She fastened it round her throat, on her high dress, and remained in ecstasy before herself.

Then, she asked, hesitating, full of anxiety:—

"Can you lend me this, only this?"

"Yes, yes, certainly."

She sprang to her friend's neck, kissed her with ardor, and then escaped with her treasure.

The day of the party arrived. Mme. Loisel was a success. She was the prettiest of them all, elegant, gracious, smiling, and mad with joy. All the men were looking at her, inquiring her name, asking to be introduced. All the attaches of the Cabinet wanted to dance with her. The Minister took notice of her.

She danced with delight, with passion, intoxicated with pleasure, thinking of nothing, in the triumph of her beauty, in the glory of her success, in a sort of cloud of happiness made up of all these tributes, of all the admirations, of all these awakened desires, of this victory so complete and so sweet to a woman's heart.

She went away about four in the morning. Since midnight — her husband has been dozing in a little anteroom with three other men whose wives were having a good time.

He threw over her shoulders the wraps he had brought to go home in, modest garments of every-day life, the poverty of which was out of keeping with the elegance of the ball dress. She felt this, and wanted to fly so as not to be noticed by the other women, who were wrapping themselves up in rich furs.

Loisel kept her back —

"Wait a minute; you will catch cold outside; I'll call a cab."

But she did not listen to him, and went downstairs rapidly. When they were in the street, they could not find a carriage, and they set out in search of one, hailing the drivers whom they saw passing in the distance.

They went down toward the Seine, disgusted, shivering. Finally, they found on the Quai one of those old night-hawk cabs which one sees in Paris only after night has fallen, as though they are ashamed of their misery in the daytime.

It brought them to their door, rue des Martyrs; and they went up their own stairs sadly. For her it was

THE NECKLACE

finished. And he was thinking that he would have to be at the Ministry at ten o'clock.

She took off the wraps with which she had covered her shoulders, before the mirror, so as to see herself once more in her glory. But suddenly she gave a cry. She no longer had the necklace around her throat!

Her husband, half undressed already, asked —

"What is the matter with you?"

She turned to him, terror-stricken: —

"I — I — I have not Mme. Forester's diamond necklace!"

He jumped up, frightened —

"What? How? It is not possible!"

And they searched in the folds of the dress, in the folds of the wrap, in the pockets, everywhere. They did not find it.

He asked: —

"Are you sure you still had it when you left the ball?"

"Yes, I touched it in the vestibule of the Ministry."

"But if you had lost it in the street, we should have heard it fall. It must be in the cab."

"Yes. That is probable. Did you take the number?"

"No. And you — you did not even look at it?"

"No."

They gazed at each other, crushed. At last Loisel dressed himself again.

"I'm going," he said, "back the whole distance we came on foot, to see if I cannot find it."

And he went out. She stayed there, in her ball dress, without strength to go to bed, overwhelmed, on a chair, without a fire, without a thought.

Her husband came back about seven o'clock. He had found nothing.

Then he went to police headquarters, to the newspapers to offer a reward, to the cab company; he did everything, in fact, that a trace of hope could urge him to.

She waited all day, in the same dazed state in face of this horrible disaster.

Loisel came back in the evening, with his face worn and white; he had discovered nothing.

"You must write to your friend," he said, "that you have broken the clasp of her necklace and that you are having it repaired. That will give us time to turn around."

She wrote as he dictated.

At the end of a week they had lost all hope. And Loisel, aged by five years, declared: —

"We must see how we can replace those jewels."

The next day they took the case which had held them to the jeweler whose name was in the cover. He consulted his books.

"It was not I, madam, who sold this necklace. I only supplied the case."

Then they went from jeweler to jeweler, looking for a necklace like the other, consulting their memory, — sick both of them with grief and anxiety.

In a shop in the Palais Royal, they found a diamond necklace that seemed to them absolutely like the one they were seeking. It was priced forty thousand francs. They could have it for thirty-six.

They begged the jeweler not to sell it for three days.

And they made a bargain that he should take it back for thirty-four thousand, if the first was found before the end of February.

Loisel possessed eighteen thousand francs which his father had left him. He had to borrow the remainder.

He borrowed, asking a thousand francs from one, five hundred from another, five here, three louis there. He gave promissory notes, made ruinous agreements, dealt with usurers, with all kinds of lenders. He compromised the end of his life, risked his signature without even knowing whether it could be honored; and, frightened by all the anguish of the future, by the black misery which was about to settle down on him, by the perspective of all sorts of physical deprivations and of all sorts of moral tortures, he went to buy the new diamond necklace, laying down on the jeweler's counter thirty-six thousand francs.

When Mme. Loisel took back the necklace to Mme. Forester, the latter said, with an irritated air: —

"You ought to have brought it back sooner, for I might have needed it."

She did not open the case, which her friend had been fearing. If she had noticed the substitution, what would she have thought? What would she have said? Might she not have been taken for a thief?

Mme. Loisel learned the horrible life of the needy. She made the best of it, moreover, frankly, heroically. The frightful debt must be paid. She would pay it. They dismissed the servant; they changed their rooms; they took an attic under the roof.

She learned the rough work of the household, the odious

labors of the kitchen. She washed the dishes, wearing out her pink nails on the greasy pots and the bottoms of the pans. She washed the dirty linen, the shirts and the towels, which she dried on a rope; she carried down the garbage to the street every morning, and she carried up the water, pausing for breath on every floor. And, dressed like a woman of the people, she went to the fruiterer, the grocer, the butcher, a basket on her arm, bargaining, insulted, fighting for her wretched money, sou by sou.

Every month they had to pay notes, to renew others to gain time.

The husband worked in the evening keeping up the books of a shopkeeper, and at night often he did copying at five sous the page.

And this life lasted ten years.

At the end of ten years they had paid everything back, everything, with the rates of usury and all the accumulation of heaped-up interest.

Mme. Loisel seemed aged now. She had become the robust woman, hard and rough, of a poor household. Badly combed, with her skirts awry and her hands red, her voice was loud, and she washed the floor with splashing water.

But sometimes, when her husband was at the office, she sat down by the window and she thought of that evening long ago, of that ball, where she had been so beautiful and so admired.

What would have happened if she had not lost that necklace? Who knows? Who knows? How singular life is, how changeable! What a little thing it takes to save you or to lose you.

THE NECKLACE

Then, one Sunday, as she was taking a turn in the Champs Elysées, as a recreation after the labors of the week, she perceived suddenly a woman walking with a child. It was Mme. Forester, still young, still beautiful, still seductive.

Mme. Loisel felt moved. Should she speak to her? Yes, certainly. And now that she had paid up, she would tell her all. Why not?

She drew near.

"Good morning, Jeanne."

The other did not recognize her, astonished to be hailed thus familiarly by this woman of the people. She hesitated —

"But — madam — I don't know — are you not making a mistake?"

"No. I am Mathilde Loisel."

Her friend gave a cry —

"Oh! — My poor Mathilde, how you are changed."

"Yes, I have had hard days since I saw you, and many troubles, — and that because of you."

"Of me? — How so?"

"You remember that diamond necklace that you lent me to go to the ball at the Ministry?"

"Yes. And then?"

"Well, I lost it."

"How can that be? — since you brought it back to me?"

"I brought you back another just like it. And now for ten years we have been paying for it. You will understand that it was not easy for us, who had nothing. At last, it is done, and I am mighty glad."

Mme. Forester had guessed.

"You say that you bought a diamond necklace to replace mine?"

"Yes. You did not notice it, even, did you? They were exactly alike?"

And she smiled with proud and naïve joy.

Mme. Forester, much moved, took her by both hands: —

"Oh, my poor Mathilde. But mine were false. At most they were worth five hundred francs!"

NOTE. — Masterly as this narrative is, it is chilly and almost cruel. The suffering it sets forth seems to have been almost needless, — due as it is to the accident of misunderstanding. But the craftsmanship is marvelous; and so is the skill with which the surprise is withheld to the end.

XXI. MARKHEIM

By Robert Louis Stevenson (1850–1894)

Stevenson was one of the earliest of British writers to perceive the artistic possibilities of the true short-story as it had been formulated by Poe and as it had been practiced in America and in France. He wrote long romantic fictions and he essayed the novel of adventure; but he was most indisputably within his powers in the compact short-story. His most successful work of fiction, "The Strange Case of Dr. Jekyll and Mr. Hyde," is a novelette, but it has the swiftness and the compactness of the short-story. And he was no happy-go-lucky story-teller; he held a theory of the art closely akin to Poe's, although he had a wider outlook on life than his American predecessor, a keener relish for humanity, and a far richer sense of morality. In "Markheim," which was written in 1884, he combines the inventive ingenuity of Poe with the ethical insight of Hawthorne.

MARKHEIM

"Yes," said the dealer, "our windfalls are of various kinds. Some customers are ignorant, and then I touch a dividend on my superior knowledge. Some are dishonest," and here he held up the candle, so that the light fell strongly on his visitor, "and in that case," he continued, "I profit by my virtue."

Markheim had but just entered from the daylight streets, and his eyes had not yet grown familiar with the mingled shine and darkness in the shop. At these pointed words, and before the near presence of the flame, he blinked painfully and looked aside.

The dealer chuckled. "You come to me on Christmas Day," he resumed, "when you know that I am alone in my house, put up my shutters, and make a point of refusing business. Well, you will have to pay for that; you will have to pay for my loss of time, when I should be balancing my books; you will have to pay, besides, for a kind of manner that I remark in you to-day very strongly. I am the essence of discretion, and ask no awkward questions; but when a customer cannot look me in the eye, he has to pay for it." The dealer once more chuckled; and then, changing to his usual business voice, though still with a note of irony, "You can give, as usual, a clear account of how you came into the possession of the object?" he continued. "Still your uncle's cabinet? A remarkable collector, sir!"

And the little pale, round-shouldered dealer stood almost on tiptoe, looking over the top of his gold spectacles, and nodding his head with every mark of disbelief. Markheim returned his gaze with one of infinite pity, and a touch of horror.

"This time," said he, "you are in error. I have not come to sell, but to buy. I have no curios to dispose of; my uncle's cabinet is bare to the wainscot; even were it still intact, I have done well on the Stock Exchange, and should more likely add to it than otherwise, and my errand to-day is simplicity itself. I seek a Christmas present for a lady," he continued, waxing more fluent as he struck into the speech he had prepared; "and certainly I owe you every excuse for thus disturbing you upon so small a matter. But the thing was neglected yesterday; I must produce my little compliment at dinner; and, as you very well know, a rich marriage is not a thing to be neglected."

There followed a pause, during which the dealer seemed to weigh this statement incredulously. The ticking of many clocks among the curious lumber of the shop, and the faint rushing of the cabs in a near thoroughfare, filled up the interval of silence.

"Well, sir," said the dealer, "be it so. You are an old customer after all; and if, as you say, you have the chance of a good marriage, far be it from me to be an obstacle. Here is a nice thing for a lady, now," he went on, "this hand glass — fifteenth century, warranted; comes from a good collection, too; but I reserve the name, in the interests of my customer, who was just like yourself, my dear sir, the nephew and sole heir of a remarkable collector."

The dealer, while he thus ran on in his dry and biting voice, had stooped to take the object from its place; and, as he had done so, a shock had passed through Markheim, a start both of hand and foot, a sudden leap of many tumultuous passions to the face. It passed as swiftly as it came, and left no trace beyond a certain trembling of the hand that now received the glass.

"A glass," he said hoarsely, and then paused, and repeated it more clearly. "A glass? For Christmas? Surely not?"

"And why not?" cried the dealer. "Why not a glass?"

Markheim was looking upon him with an indefinable expression. "You ask me why not?" he said. "Why, look here — look in it — look at yourself! Do you like to see it? No! nor I — nor any man."

The little man had jumped back when Markheim had so suddenly confronted him with the mirror; but now, perceiving there was nothing worse on hand, he chuckled. "Your future lady, sir, must be pretty hard favored," said he.

"I ask you," said Markheim, "for a Christmas present, and you give me this — this damned reminder of years and sins and follies — this hand-conscience! Did you mean it? Had you a thought in your mind? Tell me. It will be better for you if you do. Come, tell me about yourself. I hazard a guess now, that you are in secret a very charitable man?"

The dealer looked closely at his companion. It was very odd, Markheim did not appear to be laughing; there was something in his face like an eager sparkle of hope, but nothing of mirth.

"What are you driving at?" the dealer asked.

"Not charitable?" returned the other, gloomily. "Not charitable; not pious; not scrupulous; unloving, unbeloved; a hand to get money, a safe to keep it. Is that all? Dear God, man, is that all?"

"I will tell you what it is," began the dealer, with

MARKHEIM

some sharpness, and then broke off again into a chuckle. "But I see this is a love match of yours, and you have been drinking the lady's health."

"Ah!" cried Markheim, with a strange curiosity. "Ah, have you been in love? Tell me about that."

"I!" cried the dealer. "I in love! I never had the time, nor have I the time to-day for all this nonsense. Will you take the glass?"

"Where is the hurry?" returned Markheim. "It is very pleasant to stand here talking; and life is so short and insecure that I would not hurry away from any pleasure — no, not even from so mild a one as this. We should rather cling, cling to what little we can get, like a man at a cliff's edge. Every second is a cliff, if you think upon it — a cliff a mile high — high enough, if we fall, to dash us out of every feature of humanity. Hence it is best to talk pleasantly. Let us talk of each other; why should we wear this mask? Let us be confidential. Who knows, we might become friends?"

"I have just one word to say to you," said the dealer. "Either make your purchase, or walk out of my shop."

"True, true," said Markheim. "Enough fooling. To business. Show me something else."

The dealer stooped once more, this time to replace the glass upon the shelf, his thin blond hair falling over his eyes as he did so. Markheim moved a little nearer, with one hand in the pocket of his greatcoat; he drew himself up and filled his lungs; at the same time many different emotions were depicted together on his face — terror, horror, and resolve, fascination, and a physical repulsion; and through a haggard lift of his upper lip, his teeth looked out.

"This, perhaps, may suit," observed the dealer; and then, as he began to re-arise, Markheim bounded from behind upon his victim. The long, skewer-like dagger flashed and fell. The dealer struggled like a hen, striking his temple on the shelf, and then tumbled on the floor in a heap.

Time had some score of small voices in that shop, some stately and slow as was becoming to their great age, others garrulous and hurried. All these told out the seconds in an intricate chorus of tickings. Then the passage of a lad's feet, heavily running on the pavement, broke in upon these smaller voices and startled Markheim into the consciousness of his surroundings. He looked about him awfully. The candle stood on the counter, its flame solemnly wagging in a draught; and by that inconsiderable movement, the whole room was filled with noiseless bustle and kept heaving like a sea: the tall shadows nodding, the gross blots of darkness swelling and dwindling as with respiration, the faces of the portraits and the china gods changing and wavering like images in water. The inner door stood ajar, and peered into that leaguer of shadows with a long slit of daylight like a pointing finger.

From these fear-stricken rovings, Markheim's eyes returned to the body of his victim, where it lay both humped and sprawling, incredibly small and strangely meaner than in life. In these poor, miserly clothes, in that ungainly attitude, the dealer lay like so much sawdust. Markheim had feared to see it, and, lo! it was nothing.

And yet, as he gazed, this bundle of old clothes and pool of blood began to find eloquent voices. There it must lie; there was none to work the cunning hinges or direct the miracle of locomotion — there it must lie till it was found. Found! aye, and then? Then would this dead flesh lift up a cry that would ring over England, and fill the world with the echoes of pursuit. Aye, dead or not, this was still the enemy. "Time was that when the brains were out," he thought; and the first word struck into his mind. Time, now that the deed was accomplished — time, which had closed for the victim, had become instant and momentous for the slayer.

The thought was yet in his mind, when, first one and then another, with every variety of pace and voice — one deep as the bell from a cathedral turret, another ringing on its treble notes the prelude of a waltz — the clocks began to strike the hour of three in the afternoon.

The sudden outbreak of so many tongues in that dumb chamber staggered him. He began to bestir himself, going to and fro with the candle, beleaguered by moving shadows, and startled to the soul by chance reflections. In many rich mirrors, some of home designs, some from Venice or Amsterdam, he saw his face repeated and repeated, as it were an army of spies; his own eyes met and detected him; and the sound of his own steps, lightly as they fell, vexed the surrounding quiet. And still as he continued to fill his pockets, his mind accused him, with a sickening iteration, of the thousand faults of his design. He should have chosen a more quiet hour; he should have prepared an alibi; he should not have used a knife; he should have been more cautious, and only bound and gagged the dealer, and not killed him; he should have been more bold, and killed the servant also; he should have done all things otherwise; poignant regrets, weary, incessant toiling of the mind to change what was unchangeable, to plan what was now useless, to be the architect of the irrevocable past. Meanwhile, and behind all this activity, brute terrors, like the scurrying of rats in a deserted attic, filled the more remote chambers of his brain with riot; the hand of the constable would fall heavy on his shoulder, and his nerves would jerk like a hooked fish; or he beheld, in galloping defile, the dock, the prison, the gallows, and the black coffin.

Terror of the people in the street sat down before his mind like a besieging army. It was impossible, he thought, but that some rumor of the struggle must have reached their ears and set on edge their curiosity; and now, in all the neighboring houses, he divined them sitting motionless and with uplifted ear — solitary people, condemned to spend Christmas dwelling alone on memories of the past, and now startlingly recalled from that tender exercise; happy family parties, struck into silence round the table, the mother still with raised finger: every degree and age and humor, but all, by their own hearths, prying and hearkening and weaving the rope that was to hang him. Sometimes it seemed to him he could not move too softly; the clink of the tall Bohemian goblets rang out loudly like a bell; and alarmed by the bigness of the ticking, he was tempted to stop the clocks. And then, again, with a swift transition of his terrors, the very silence of the place appeared a source of peril, and a thing to strike and freeze the passer-by; and he would step more boldly, and bustle aloud among the contents of the shop, and imitate, with elaborate bravado, the movements of a busy man at ease in his own house.

But he was now so pulled about by different alarms that, while one portion of his mind was still alert and cunning, another trembled on the brink of lunacy. One hallucination in particular took a strong hold on his credulity. The neighbor hearkening with white face beside his window, the passer-by arrested by a horrible surmise on the pavement — these could at worst suspect, they could not know; through the brick walls and shuttered windows only sounds could penetrate. But here, within the house, was he alone? He knew he was; he had watched the servant set forth sweethearting, in her poor best, "out for the day" written in every ribbon and smile. Yes, he was alone, of course; and yet, in the bulk of empty house about him, he could surely hear a stir of delicate footing — he was surely conscious, inexplicably conscious of some presence. Aye, surely; to every room and corner of the house his imagination followed it; and now it was a faceless thing, and yet had eyes to see with; and again it was a shadow of himself; and yet again behold the image of the dead dealer, reinspired with cunning and hatred.

At times, with a strong effort, he would glance at the open door which still seemed to repel his eyes. The house was tall, the skylight small and dirty, the day blind with fog; and the light that filtered down to the ground story was exceedingly faint, and showed dimly on the threshold of the shop. And yet, in that strip of doubtful brightness, did there not hang wavering a shadow?

Suddenly, from the street outside, a very jovial gentleman began to beat with a staff on the shop door, accompanying his blows with shouts and railleries in which the dealer was continually called upon by name. Markheim, smitten into ice, glanced at the dead man. But no! he lay quite still; he was fled away far beyond ear-shot of these blows and shoutings; he was sunk beneath seas of silence; and his name, which would once have caught his notice above the howling of a storm, had become an empty sound. And presently the jovial gentleman desisted from his knocking and departed.

Here was a broad hint to hurry what remained to be done, to get forth from this accusing neighborhood, to plunge into a bath of London multitudes, and to reach, on the other side of day, that haven of safety and apparent innocence — his bed. One visitor had come: at any moment another might follow and be more obstinate. To have done the deed, and yet not to reap the profit, would be too abhorrent a failure. The money, that was now Markheim's concern; and as a means to that, the keys.

He glanced over his shoulder at the open door, where the shadow was still lingering and shivering; and with no conscious repugnance of the mind, yet with a tremor of the belly, he drew near the body of his victim. The human character had quite departed. Like a suit halfstuffed with bran, the limbs lay scattered, the trunk doubled, on the floor; and yet the thing repelled him. Although so dingy and inconsiderable to the eye, he feared it might have more significance to the touch. He took the body by the shoulders, and turned it on its back. It was strangely light and supple, and the limbs, as if they had been broken, fell into the oddest postures. The face was robbed of all expression; but it was as pale as wax, and shockingly smeared with blood about one temple. That was, for Markheim, the one displeasing circumstance. It carried him back, upon the instant, to a certain fair day in a fishers' village: a gray day, a piping wind, a crowd upon the street, the blare of brasses, the booming of drums, the nasal voice of a ballad singer; and a boy going to and fro, buried over head in the crowd and divided between interest and fear, until, coming out upon the chief place of concourse, he beheld a booth and a great screen with pictures, dismally designed, garishly colored: Brownrigg with her apprentice; the Mannings with their murdered guest; Weare in the death grip of Thurtell; and a score besides of famous crimes. The thing was as clear as an illusion; he was once again that little boy; he was looking once again, and with the same sense of physical revolt, at these vile pictures; he was still stunned by the thumping of the drums. A bar of that day's music returned upon his memory; and at that, for the first time, a qualm came over him, a breath of nausea, a sudden weakness of the joints, which he must instantly resist and conquer.

He judged it more prudent to confront than to flee from these considerations; looking the more hardily in the dead face, bending his mind to realize the nature and greatness of his crime. So little a while ago that face had moved with every change of sentiment, that pale mouth had spoken, that body had been all on fire with governable energies; and now, and by his act, that piece of life had been arrested, as the horologist, with interjected finger, arrests the beating of the clock. So he reasoned in vain; he could rise to no more remorseful consciousness; the same heart which had shuddered before the painted effigies of crime, looked on its reality unmoved. At best, he felt a gleam of pity for one who had been endowed in vain with all those faculties that can make the world a garden of enchantment, one who had never lived and who was now dead. But of penitence, no, not a tremor.

With that, shaking himself clear of these considerations, he found the keys and advanced toward the open door of the shop. Outside, it had begun to rain smartly; and the sound of the shower upon the roof had banished silence. Like some dripping cavern, the chambers of the house were haunted by an incessant echoing, which filled the ear and mingled with the ticking of the clocks. And, as Markheim approached the door, he seemed to hear, in answer to his own cautious tread, the steps of another foot withdrawing up the stair. The shadow still palpitated loosely on the threshold. He threw a ton's weight of resolve upon his muscles, and drew back the door.

The faint, foggy daylight glimmered dimly on the bare floor and stairs; on the bright suit of armor posted, halbert in hand, upon the landing; and on the dark wood carvings and framed pictures that hung against the yellow panels of the wainscot. So loud was the beating of the rain through all the house that, in Markheim's ears, it began to be distinguished into many different sounds.

Footsteps and sighs, the tread of regiments marching in the distance, the chink of money in the counting, and the creaking of doors held stealthily ajar, appeared to mingle with the patter of the drops upon the cupola and the gushing of the water in the pipes. The sense that he was not alone grew upon him to the verge of madness. On every side he was haunted and begirt by presences. He heard them moving in the upper chambers; from the shop, he heard the dead man getting to his legs; and as he began with a great effort to mount the stairs, feet fled quietly before him and followed stealthily behind. If he were but deaf, he thought, how tranquilly he would possess his soul! And then again, and hearkening with ever fresh attention, he blessed himself for that unresting sense which held the outposts and stood a trusty sentinel upon his life. His head turned continually on his neck; his eyes, which seemed starting from their orbits, scouted on every side, and on every side were half rewarded as with the tail of something nameless vanishing. The four-and-twenty steps to the first floor were four-and-twenty agonies.

On that first story the doors stood ajar, three of them like three ambushes, shaking his nerves like the throats of cannon. He could never again, he felt, be sufficiently immured and fortified from men's observing eyes; he longed to be home, girt in by walls, buried among bedclothes, and invisible to all but God. And at that thought he wondered a little, recollecting tales of other murderers and the fear they were said to entertain of heavenly avengers. It was not so, at least, with him. He feared the laws of nature, lest, in their callous and immutable procedure, they should preserve some damning evidence of his crime. He feared tenfold more, with a slavish, superstitious terror, some scission in the continuity of man's experience, some willful illegality of nature. He played a game of skill, depending on the rules, calculating consequence from cause; and what if nature, as the defeated tyrant overthrew the chessboard, should break the mold of their succession? The like had befallen Napoleon (so writers said) when the winter changed the time of its appearance. The like might befall Markheim: the solid walls might become transparent and reveal his doings like those of bees in a glass hive; the stout planks might yield under his foot like quicksands and detain him in their clutch; aye, and there were soberer accidents that might destroy him: if, for instance, the house should fall and imprison him beside the body of his victim; or the house next door should fly on fire, and the firemen invade him from all sides. These things he feared; and, in a sense, these things might be called the hands of God reached forth against sin. But about God himself he was at ease; his act was doubtless exceptional, but so were his excuses, which God knew; it was there, and not among men, that he felt sure of justice.

When he got safe into the drawing-room, and shut the door behind him, he was aware of a respite from alarms. The room was quite dismantled, uncarpeted besides, and strewn with packing cases and incongruous furniture; several great pier glasses, in which he beheld himself at various angles, like an actor on a stage; many pictures, framed and unframed, standing, with their faces to the wall; a fine Sheraton sideboard, a cabinet of marquetry, and a great old bed, with tapestry hangings. The windows opened to the floor; but by great good fortune the lower part of the shutters had been closed, and this concealed him from the neighbors. Here, then, Markheim drew in a packing case before the cabinet, and began to search among the keys. It was a long business, for there were many; and it was irksome, besides; for, after all, there might be nothing in the cabinet, and time was on the wing. But the closeness of the occupation sobered him. With the tail of his eye he saw the door — even glanced at it from time to time directly, like a besieged commander pleased to verify the good estate of his defenses. But in truth he was at peace. The rain falling in the street sounded natural and pleasant. Presently, on the other side, the notes of a piano were wakened to the music of a hymn, and the voices of many children took up the air and words. How stately, how comfortable was the melody! How fresh the youthful voices! Markheim gave ear to it smilingly, as he sorted out the keys; and his mind was thronged with answerable ideas and images; church-going children and the pealing of the high organ; children afield, bathers by the brookside, ramblers on the brambly common, kite-flyers in the windy and cloud-navigated sky; and then, at another cadence of the hymn, back again to church, and the somnolence of summer Sundays, and the high, genteel voice of the parson (which he smiled a little to recall), and the painted Jacobean tombs, and the dim lettering of the Ten Commandments in the chancel.

And as he sat thus, at once busy and absent, he was startled to his feet. A flash of ice, a flash of fire, a bursting gush of blood, went over him, and then he stood transfixed and thrilling. A step mounted the stair slowly and steadily, and presently a hand was laid upon the knob, and the lock clicked, and the door opened.

Fear held Markheim in a vise. What to expect he knew not, whether the dead man walking, or the official ministers of human justice, or some chance witness blindly stumbling in to consign him to the gallows. But when a face was thrust into the aperture, glanced round the room, looked at him, nodded and smiled as if in friendly recognition, and then withdrew again, and the door closed behind it, his fear broke loose from his control in a hoarse cry. At the sound of this the visitant returned.

"Did you call me?" he asked pleasantly, and with that he entered the room and closed the door behind him.

Markheim stood and gazed at him with all his eyes. Perhaps there was a film upon his sight, but the outlines of the newcomer seemed to change and waver like those of the idols in the wavering candlelight of the shop: and at times he thought he knew him; and at times he thought he bore a likeness to himself; and always, like a lump of living terror, there lay in his bosom the conviction that this thing was not of the earth and not of God.

And yet the creature had a strange air of the commonplace, as he stood looking on Markheim with a smile; and when he added: "You are looking for the money, I believe?" it was in the tones of every-day politeness.

Markheim made no answer.

"I should warn you," resumed the other, "that the maid has left her sweetheart earlier than usual and will soon be here. If Mr. Markheim be found in this house, I need not describe to him the consequences."

"You know me?" cried the murderer.

The visitor smiled. "You have long been a favorite of mine," he said; "and I have long observed and often sought to help you."

"What are you?" cried Markheim: "the devil?"

"What I may be," returned the other, "cannot affect the service I propose to render you."

"It can," cried Markheim; "it does! Be helped by you? No, never; not by you! You do not know me yet; thank God, you do not know me!"

"I know you," replied the visitant, with a sort of kind severity or rather firmness. "I know you to the soul."

"Know me!" cried Markheim. "Who can do so? My life is but a travesty and slander on myself. I have lived to belie my nature. All men do; all men are better than this disguise that grows about and stifles them. You see each dragged away by life, like one whom bravos have seized and muffled in a cloak. If they had their own control — if you could see their faces, they would be altogether different, they would shine out for heroes and saints! I am worse than most; myself is more overlaid; my excuse is known to me and God. But, had I the time, I could disclose myself."

"To me?" inquired the visitant.

"To you before all," returned the murderer. "I supposed you were intelligent. I thought — since you exist — you would prove a reader of the heart. And yet you would propose to judge me by my acts! Think of it; my acts! I was born and I have lived in a land of giants; giants have dragged me by the wrists since I was born out of my mother — the giants of circumstance.

And you would judge me by my acts! But can you not look within? Can you not understand that evil is hateful to me? Can you not see within me the clear writing of conscience, never blurred by any willful sophistry, although too often disregarded? Can you not read me for a thing that surely must be common as humanity — the unwilling sinner?"

"All this is very feelingly expressed," was the reply, "but it regards me not. These points of consistency are beyond my province, and I care not in the least by what compulsion you may have been dragged away, so as you are but carried in the right direction. But time flies; the servant delays, looking in the faces of the crowd and at the pictures on the hoardings, but still she keeps moving nearer; and remember, it is as if the gallows itself were striding toward you through the Christmas streets! Shall I help you — I, who know all? Shall I tell you where to find the money?"

"For what price?" asked Markheim.

"I offer you the service for a Christmas gift," returned the other.

Markheim could not refrain from smiling with a kind of bitter triumph. "No," said he, "I will take nothing at your hands; if I were dying of thirst, and it was your hand that put the pitcher to my lips, I should find the courage to refuse. It may be credulous, but I will do nothing to commit myself to evil."

"I have no objection to a death-bed repentance," observed the visitant.

"Because you disbelieve their efficacy!" Markheim cried.

"I do not say so," returned the other; "but I look on these things from a different side, and when the life is done my interest falls. The man has lived to serve me, to spread black looks under color of religion, or to sow tares in the wheat field, as you do, in a course of weak compliance with desire. Now that he draws so near to his deliverance, he can add but one act of service — to repent, to die smiling, and thus to build up in confidence and hope the more timorous of my surviving followers. I am not so hard a master. Try me. Accept my help. Please yourself in life as you have done hitherto; please yourself more amply, spread your elbows at the board; and when the night begins to fall and the curtains to be drawn, I tell you, for your greater comfort, that you will find it even easy to compound your quarrel with your conscience, and to make a truckling peace with God. I came but now from such a death-bed, and the room was full of sincere mourners, listening to the man's last words; and when I looked into that face, which had been set as a flint against mercy, I found it smiling with hope."

"And do you, then, suppose me such a creature?" asked Markheim. "Do you think I have no more generous aspirations than to sin, and sin, and sin, and, at last, sneak into heaven? My heart rises at the thought. Is this, then, your experience of mankind? or is it because you find me with red hands that you presume such baseness? and is this crime of murder indeed so impious as to dry up the very springs of good?"

"Murder is to me no special category," replied the other. "All sins are murder, even as all life is war. I behold your race, like starving mariners on a raft, plucking crusts out of the hands of famine and feeding on each other's lives. I follow sins beyond the moment of their acting; I find in all that the last consequence is death; and to my eyes, the pretty maid who thwarts her mother with such taking graces on a question of a ball, drips no less visibly with human gore than such a murderer as yourself. Do I say that I follow sins? I follow virtues also; they differ not by the thickness of a nail, they are both scythes for the reaping angel of Death. Evil, for which I live, consists not in action but in character. The bad man is dear to me; not the bad act, whose fruits, if we could follow them far enough down the hurtling cataract of the ages, might yet be found more blessed than those of the rarest virtues. And it is not because you have killed a dealer, but because you are Markheim, that I offered to forward your escape."

"I will lay my heart open to you," answered Markheim. "This crime on which you find me is my last. On my way to it I have learned many lessons; itself is a lesson, a momentous lesson. Hitherto I have been driven with revolt to what I would not; I was a bondslave to poverty, driven and scourged. There are robust virtues that can stand in these temptations; mine was not so: I had a thirst of pleasure. But to-day, and out of this deed, I pluck both warning and riches — both the power and a fresh resolve to be myself. I become in all things a free actor in the world; I begin to see myself all changed, these hands the agents of good, this heart at peace. Something comes over me out of the past; something of what I have dreamed on Sabbath evenings to the sound of the church organ, of what I forecast when I shed tears over noble books, or talked, an innocent child, with my mother. There lies my life; I have wandered a few years, but now I see once more my city of destination."

"You are to use this money on the Stock Exchange, I think?" remarked the visitor; "and there, if I mistake not, you have already lost some thousands?"

"Ah," said Markheim, "but this time I have a sure thing."

"This time, again, you will lose," replied the visitor, quietly.

"Ah, but I keep back the half!" cried Markheim.

"That also you will lose," said the other.

The sweat started upon Markheim's brow. "Well, then, what matter?" he exclaimed. "Say it be lost, say I am plunged again in poverty, shall one part of me, and that the worse, continue until the end to override the better? Evil and good run strong in me, hailing me both ways. I do not love the one thing, I love all. I can conceive great deeds, renunciations, martyrdoms; and though I be fallen to such a crime as murder, pity is no stranger to my thoughts. I pity the poor; who knows their trials better than myself? I pity and help them; I prize love, I love honest laughter; there is no good thing nor true thing on earth but I love it from my heart. And are my vices only to direct my life, and my virtues to lie without effect, like some passive lumber of the mind? Not so; good, also, is a spring of acts."

But the visitant raised his finger. "For six-and-thirty years that you have been in this world," said he, "through many changes of fortune and varieties of humor, I have watched you steadily fall. Fifteen years ago you would have started at a theft. Three years back you would have blenched at the name of murder. Is there any crime, is there any cruelty or meanness, from which you still recoil? — five years from now I shall detect you in the fact! Downward, downward lies your way; nor can anything but death avail to stop you."

"It is true," Markheim said huskily, "I have in some degree complied with evil. But it is so with all: the very saints, in the mere exercise of living, grow less dainty, and take on the tone of their surroundings."

"I will propound to you one simple question," said the other; "and as you answer, I shall read to you your moral horoscope. You have grown in many things more lax; possibly you do right to be so; and at any account, it is the same with all men. But granting that, are you in any one particular, however trifling, more difficult to please with your own conduct, or do you go in all things with a looser rein?"

"In any one?" repeated Markheim, with an anguish of consideration. "No," he added, with despair, "in none! I have gone down in all."

"Then," said the visitor, "content yourself with what you are, for you will never change; and the words of your part on this stage are irrevocably written down."

Markheim stood for a long while silent, and indeed it was the visitor who first broke the silence. "That being so," he said, "shall I show you the money?"

"And grace?" cried Markheim.

"Have you not tried it?" returned the other. "Two or three years ago, did I not see you on the platform of revival meetings, and was not your voice the loudest in the hymn?"

"It is true," said Markheim; "and I see clearly what remains for me by way of duty. I thank you for these lessons from my soul; my eyes are opened, and I behold myself at last for what I am."

At this moment, the sharp note of the door bell rang through the house; and the visitant, as though this were some concerted signal for which he had been waiting, changed at once in his demeanor.

"The maid!" he cried. "She has returned, as I forewarned you, and there is now before you one more difficult passage. Her master, you must say, is ill; you must let her in, with an assured but rather serious countenance — no smiles, no overacting, and I promise you success! Once the girl within, and the door closed, the same dexterity that has already rid you of the dealer will relieve you of this last danger in your path. Thenceforward you have the whole evening — the whole night, if needful — to ransack the treasures of the house and to make good your safety. This is help that comes to you with the mask of danger. Up!" he cried: "up, friend; your life hangs trembling in the scales: up, and act!"

Markheim steadily regarded his counselor. "If I be condemned to evil acts," he said, "there is still one door of freedom open — I can cease from action. If my life be an ill thing, I can lay it down. Though I be, as you say truly, at the beck of every small temptation, I can yet, by one decisive gesture, place myself beyond the reach of all. My love of good is damned to barrenness; it may, and let it be! But I have still my hatred of evil;

and from that, to your galling disappointment, you shall see that I can draw both energy and courage."

The features of the visitor began to undergo a wonderful and lovely change: they brightened and softened with a tender triumph; and, even as they brightened, faded and dislimned. But Markheim did not pause to watch or understand the transformation. He opened the door and went downstairs very slowly, thinking to himself. His past went soberly before him; he beheld it as it was, ugly and strenuous like a dream, random as chance-medley — a scene of defeat. Life, as he thus reviewed it, tempted him no longer; but on the farther side he perceived a quiet haven for his bark. He paused in the passage, and looked into the shop, where the candle still burned by the dead body. It was strangely silent. Thoughts of the dealer swarmed into his mind, as he stood gazing. And then the bell once more broke out into impatient clamor.

He confronted the maid upon the threshold with something like a smile.

"You had better go for the police," said he: "I have killed your master."

NOTE. — This is truly one of the masterpieces of the short-story in its inexorable swiftness and in its perfect unity of tone. Every part adds to the effect of the whole; and the narrative moves irresistibly to its unexpected end, — an end which takes the reader suddenly by surprise and yet which is absolutely logical in its consistency with the character of the central figure.

XXII. THE MAN WHO WAS

By Rudyard Kipling (1865–)

Of all the recent writers of fiction in our language no one has written more admirable short-stories than Mr. Kipling. A journalist in his early manhood, he learned to tell a tale in the space of a column or two; and as he has grown in knowledge, in feeling, and in skill, he has continued to write short-stories of an extraordinary variety. He has given us mere anecdotes, sharp snapshots of society, character-studies, tragic fantasies, eerie tales of a haunting mystery. No one of his short-stories is more striking than "The Man Who Was," written in 1889, although certain of his later tales are simpler in style and more delicate in imagination.

THE MAN WHO WAS

Let it be clearly understood that the Russian is a delightful person till he tucks his shirt in. As an Oriental he is charming. It is only when he insists upon being treated as the most easterly of Western peoples, instead of the most westerly of Easterns, that he becomes a racial anomaly extremely difficult to handle. The host never knows which side of his nature is going to turn up next.

Dirkovitch was a Russian — a Russian of the Russians, as he said — who appeared to get his bread by serving the czar as an officer in a Cossack regiment, and corresponding for a Russian newspaper with a name that was never twice the same. He was a handsome young Oriental, with a taste for wandering through unexplored portions of the earth, and he arrived in India from nowhere in particular. At least no living man could ascertain whether it was by way of Balkh, Budukhshan, Chitral, Beloochistan, Nepaul, or anywhere else. The Indian government, being in an unusually affable mood, gave orders that he was to be civilly treated, and shown everything that was to be seen; so he drifted, talking bad English and worse French, from one city to another till he forgathered with her Majesty's White Hussars in the city of Peshawur, which stands at the mouth of that narrow sword-cut in the hills that men call the Khyber Pass. He was undoubtedly an officer, and he was decorated, after the manner of the Russians, with little enameled crosses, and he could talk, and (though this has nothing to do with his merits) he had been given up as a hopeless task or case by the Black Tyrones, who, individually and collectively, with hot whisky and honey, mulled brandy and mixed spirits of all kinds, had striven in all hospitality to make him drunk. And when the Black Tyrones, who are exclusively Irish, fail to disturb the peace of head of a foreigner, that foreigner is certain to be a superior man. This was the argument of the Black Tyrones, but they were ever an unruly and self-opinionated regiment, and they allowed junior subalterns of four years' service to choose their wines. The spirits were always purchased by the colonel and a committee of majors. And a regiment that would so behave may be respected but cannot be loved.

The White Hussars were as conscientious in choosing their wine as in charging the enemy. There was a brandy that had been purchased by a cultured colonel a few years after the battle of Waterloo. It has been maturing ever since, and it was a marvelous brandy at the purchasing. The memory of that liquor would cause men to weep as they lay dying in the teak forests of upper Burmah or the slime of the Irrawaddy. And there was a port which was notable; and there was a champagne of an obscure brand, which always came to mess without any labels, because the White Hussars wished none to know where the source of supply might be found. The officer on whose head the champagne choosing lay, was forbidden the use of tobacco for six weeks previous to sampling.

This particularity of detail is necessary to emphasize the fact that that champagne, that port, and above all, that brandy — the green and yellow and white liqueurs did not count — was placed at the absolute disposition of Dirkovitch, and he enjoyed himself hugely — even more than among the Black Tyrones.

But he remained distressingly European through it all. The White Hussars were — "My dear true friends," "Fellow-soldiers glorious," and "Brothers inseparable." He would unburden himself by the hour on the glorious future that awaited the combined arms of England and Russia when their hearts and their territories should run side by side, and the great mission of civilizing Asia should begin. That was unsatisfactory, because Asia is not going to be civilized after the methods of the West.

There is too much Asia, and she is too old. You cannot reform a lady of many lovers, and Asia has been insatiable in her flirtations aforetime. She will never attend Sunday school, or learn to vote save with swords for tickets.

Dirkovitch knew this as well as any one else, but it suited him to talk special-correspondently and to make himself as genial as he could. Now and then he volunteered a little, a very little, information about his own Sotnia of Cossacks, left apparently to look after themselves somewhere at the back of beyond. He had done rough work in Central Asia, and had seen rather more help-yourself fighting than most men of his years. But he was careful never to betray his superiority, and more than careful to praise on all occasions the appearance, drill, uniform, and organization of her Majesty's White Hussars. And, indeed, they were a regiment to be admired. When Mrs. Durgan, widow of the late Sir John Durgan, arrived in their station, and after a short time had been proposed to by every single man at mess, she put the public sentiment very neatly when she explained that they were all so nice that unless she could marry them all, including the colonel and some majors who were already married, she was not going to content herself with one of them. Wherefore she wedded a little man in a rifle regiment — being by nature contradictious — and the White Hussars were going to wear crape on their arms, but compromised by attending the wedding in full force, and lining the aisle with unutterable reproach. She had jilted them all — from Basset-Holmer, the senior captain, to Little Mildred, the last subaltern, and he could have given her four thousand a year and a title. He was a viscount, and on his arrival the mess had said he had better go into the Guards, because they were all sons of large grocers and small clothiers in the Hussars, but Mildred begged very hard to be allowed to stay, and behaved so prettily that he was forgiven, and became a man, which is much more important than being any sort of viscount.

The only persons who did not share the general regard for the White Hussars were a few thousand gentlemen of Jewish extraction who lived across the border, and answered to the name of Pathan. They had only met the regiment officially, and for something less than twenty minutes, but the interview, which was complicated with many casualties, had filled them with prejudice. They even called the White Hussars "children of the devil," and sons of persons whom it would be perfectly impossible to meet in decent society. Yet they were not above making their aversion fill their money belts. The regiment possessed carbines, beautiful Martini-Henri carbines, that would cob a bullet into an enemy's camp at one thousand yards, and were even handier than the long rifle. Therefore they were coveted all along the border, and since demand inevitably breeds supply, they were supplied at the risk of life and limb for exactly their weight in coined silver — seven and one half pounds of rupees, or sixteen pounds and a few shillings each, reckoning the rupee at par. They were stolen at night by snaky-haired thieves that crawled on their stomachs under the nose of the sentries; they disappeared mysteriously from armracks; and in the hot weather, when all the doors and windows were open, they vanished like puffs of their own smoke. The border people desired them first for their own family vendettas, and then for contingencies. But in the long cold nights of the Northern Indian winter they were stolen most extensively. The traffic of murder was liveliest among the hills at that season, and prices ruled high. The regimental guards were first doubled and then trebled. A trooper does not much care if he loses a weapon — government must make it good — but he deeply resents the loss of his sleep. The regiment grew very angry, and one night-thief who managed to limp away bears the visible marks of their anger upon him to this hour. That incident stopped the burglaries for a time, and the guards were reduced accordingly, and the regiment devoted itself to polo with unexpected results, for it beat by two goals to one that very terrible polo corps the Lushkar Light Horse, though the latter had four ponies apiece for a short hour's fight, as well as a native officer who played like a lambent flame across the ground.

Then they gave a dinner to celebrate the event. The Lushkar team came, and Dirkovitch came, in the fullest full uniform of Cossack officer, which is as full as a dressing-gown, and was introduced to the Lushkars, and opened his eyes as he regarded them. They were lighter men than the Hussars, and they carried themselves with the swing that is the peculiar right of the Punjab frontier force and all irregular horse. Like everything else in the service, it has to be learned; but, unlike many things, it is never forgotten, and remains on the body till death.

The great beam-roofed mess room of the White Hussars was a sight to be remembered. All the mess plate was on the long table — the same table that had served up the bodies of five dead officers in a forgotten fight long and long ago — the dingy, battered standards faced the door of entrance, clumps of winter roses lay between the silver candlesticks, the portraits of eminent officers deceased looked down on their successors from between the heads of sambhur, nilghai, maikhor, and, pride of all the mess, two grinning snow-leopards that had cost Basset-Holmer four months' leave that he might have spent in England instead of on the road to Thibet, and the daily risk of his life on ledge, snowslide, and glassy grass slope.

The servants, in spotless white muslin and the crest of their regiments on the brow of their turbans, waited behind their masters, who were clad in the scarlet and gold of the White Hussars and the cream and silver of the Lushkar Light Horse. Dirkovitch's dull green uniform was the only dark spot at the board, but his big onyx eyes made up for it. He was fraternizing effusively with the captain of the Lushkar team, who was wondering how many of Dirkovitch's Cossacks his own long, lathy down-countrymen could account for in a fair charge. But one does not speak of these things openly.

The talk rose higher and higher, and the regimental band played between the courses, as is the immemorial custom, till all tongues ceased for a moment with the removal of the dinner slips and the First Toast of Obligation, when the colonel, rising, said, "Mr. Vice, the Queen," and Little Mildred from the bottom of the table answered, "The Queen, God bless her!" and the big spurs clanked as the big men heaved themselves up and drank the Queen, upon whose pay they were falsely supposed to pay their mess bills. That sacrament of the mess never grows old, and never ceases to bring a lump

into the throat of the listener wherever he be, by land
or by sea. Dirkovitch rose with his "brothers glorious,"
but he could not understand. No one but an officer
can understand what the toast means; and the bulk have
more sentiment than comprehension. It all comes to
the same in the end, as the enemy said when he was
wriggling on a lance point. Immediately after the little
silence that follows on the ceremony there entered the
native officer who had played for the Lushkar team. He
could not of course eat with the alien, but he came in at
dessert, all six feet of him, with the blue-and-silver tur-
ban atop, and the big black top-boots below. The mess
rose joyously as he thrust forward the hilt of his saber,
in token of fealty, for the colonel of the White Hussars
to touch, and dropped into a vacant chair amid shouts
of "*Rung ho!* Hira Singh!" (which being translated
means "Go in and win!"). "Did I whack you over
the knee, old man?" "Ressaidar Sahib, what the devil
made you play that kicking pig of a pony in the last ten
minutes?" "Shabash, Ressaidar Sahib!" Then the
voice of the colonel, "The health of Ressaidar Hira
Singh!"

After the shouting had died away, Hira Singh rose to
reply, for he was the cadet of a royal house, the son of a
king's son, and knew what was due on these occasions.
Thus he spoke in the vernacular: —

"Colonel Sahib and officers of this regiment, much
honor have you done me. This will I remember. We
came down from afar to play you; but we were beaten."
("No fault of yours, Ressaidar Sahib. Played on our
own ground, y' know. Your ponies were cramped from

the railway. Don't apologize.") "Therefore perhaps we will come again if it be so ordained." ("Hear! Hear, hear, indeed! Bravo! Hsh!") "Then we will play you afresh" ("Happy to meet you"), "till there are left no feet upon our ponies. Thus far for sport." He dropped one hand on his sword hilt and his eye wandered to Dirkovitch lolling back in his chair. "But if by the will of God there arises any other game which is not the polo game, then be assured, Colonel Sahib and officers, that we shall play it out side by side, though *they*" — again his eye sought Dirkovitch — "though *they*, I say, have fifty ponies to our one horse." And with a deep-mouthed *Rung ho!* that rang like a musket butt on flagstones, he sat down amid shoutings.

Dirkovitch, who had devoted himself steadily to the brandy — the terrible brandy aforementioned — did not understand, nor did the expurgated translations offered to him at all convey the point. Decidedly the native officer's was the speech of the evening, and the clamor might have continued to the dawn had it not been broken by the noise of a shot without that sent every man feeling at his defenseless left side. It is notable that Dirkovitch "reached back," after the American fashion — a gesture that set the captain of the Lushkar team wondering how Cossack officers were armed at mess. Then there was a scuffle, and a yell of pain.

"Carbine stealing again!" said the adjutant, calmly sinking back in his chair. "This comes of reducing the guards. I hope the sentries have killed him."

The feet of armed men pounded on the veranda flags, and it sounded as though something was being dragged.

"Why don't they put him in the cells till the morning?" said the colonel, testily. "See if they've damaged him, sergeant."

The mess-sergeant fled out into the darkness, and returned with two troopers and a corporal, all very much perplexed.

"Caught a man stealin' carbines, sir," said the corporal. "Leastways 'e was crawling toward the barricks, sir, past the main-road sentries; an' the sentry 'e says, sir —"

The limp heap of rags upheld by the three men groaned. Never was seen so destitute and demoralized an Afghan. He was turbanless, shoeless, caked with dirt, and all but dead with rough handling. Hira Singh started slightly at the sound of the man's pain. Dirkovitch took another liqueur glass of brandy.

"*What* does the sentry say?" said the colonel.

"Sez he speaks English, sir," said the corporal.

"So you brought him into mess instead of handing him over to the sergeant! If he spoke all the tongues of the Pentecost you've no business —"

Again the bundle groaned and muttered. Little Mildred had risen from his place to inspect. He jumped back as though he had been shot.

"Perhaps it would be better, sir, to send the men away," said he to the colonel, for he was a much-privileged subaltern. He put his arms round the rag-bound horror as he spoke, and dropped him into a chair. It may not have been explained that the littleness of Mildred lay in his being six feet four, and big in proportion. The corporal, seeing that an officer was disposed to look after

THE MAN WHO WAS

the capture, and that the colonel's eye was beginning to blaze, promptly removed himself and his men. The mess was left alone with the carbine thief, who laid his head on the table and wept bitterly, hopelessly, and inconsolably, as little children weep.

Hira Singh leaped to his feet with a long-drawn vernacular oath. "Colonel Sahib," said he, "that man is no Afghan, for they weep '*Ai! Ai!*' Nor is he of Hindustan, for they weep '*Oh! Ho!*' He weeps after the fashion of the white men, who say '*Ow! Ow!*'"

"Now where the dickens did you get that knowledge, Hira Singh?" said the captain of the Lushkar team.

"Hear him!" said Hira Singh, simply, pointing at the crumpled figure that wept as though it would never cease.

"He said, 'My God!'" said Little Mildred. "I heard him say it."

The colonel and the mess room looked at the man in silence. It is a horrible thing to hear a man cry. A woman can sob from the top of her palate, or her lips, or anywhere else, but a man cries from his diaphragm, and it rends him to pieces. Also, the exhibition causes the throat of the on-looker to close at the top.

"Poor devil!" said the colonel, coughing tremendously.

"We ought to send him to hospital. He's been manhandled."

Now the adjutant loved his rifles. They were to him as his grandchildren — the men standing in the first place. He grunted rebelliously: "I can understand an Afghan stealing, because he's made that way. But I can't understand his crying. That makes it worse."

The brandy must have affected Dirkovitch, for he lay

back in his chair and stared at the ceiling. There was nothing special in the ceiling beyond a shadow as of a huge black coffin. Owing to some peculiarity in the construction of the mess room this shadow was always thrown when the candles were lighted. It never disturbed the digestion of the White Hussars. They were, in fact, rather proud of it.

"Is he going to cry all night?" said the colonel, "or are we supposed to sit up with Little Mildred's guest until he feels better?"

The man in the chair threw up his head and stared at the mess. Outside, the wheels of the first of those bidden to the festivities crunched the roadway.

"Oh, my God!" said the man in the chair, and every soul in the mess rose to his feet. Then the Lushkar captain did a deed for which he ought to have been given the Victoria Cross — distinguished gallantry in a fight against overwhelming curiosity. He picked up his team with his eyes as the hostess picks up the ladies at the opportune moment, and pausing only by the colonel's chair to say, "This isn't *our* affair, you know, sir," led the team into the veranda and the gardens. Hira Singh was the last, and he looked at Dirkovitch as he moved. But Dirkovitch had departed into a brandy paradise of his own. His lips moved without sound, and he was studying the coffin on the ceiling.

"White — white all over," said Basset-Holmer, the adjutant. "What a pernicious renegade he must be! I wonder where he came from?"

The colonel shook the man gently by the arm, and "Who are you?" said he.

There was no answer. The man stared round the mess room and smiled in the colonel's face. Little Mildred, who was always more of a woman than a man till "Boot and saddle" was sounded, repeated the question in a voice that would have drawn confidences from a geyser. The man only smiled. Dirkovitch, at the far end of the table, slid gently from his chair to the floor. No son of Adam, in this present imperfect world, can mix the Hussars' champagne with the Hussars' brandy by five and eight glasses of each without remembering the pit whence he has been digged and descending thither. The band began to play the tune with which the White Hussars, from the date of their formation, preface all their functions. They would sooner be disbanded than abandon that tune. It is a part of their system. The man straightened himself in his chair and drummed on the table with his fingers.

"I don't see why we should entertain lunatics," said the colonel; "call a guard and send him off to the cells. We'll look into the business in the morning. Give him a glass of wine first, though."

Little Mildred filled a sherry glass with the brandy and thrust it over to the man. He drank, and the tune rose louder, and he straightened himself yet more. Then he put out his long-taloned hands to a piece of plate opposite and fingered it lovingly. There was a mystery connected with that piece of plate in the shape of a spring, which converted what was a seven-branched candlestick, three springs each side and one in the middle, into a sort of wheel-spoke candelabrum. He found the spring, pressed it, and laughed weakly. He rose from his chair and inspected a picture on the wall, then moved on to another picture, the mess watching him without a word. When he came to the mantelpiece he shook his head and seemed distressed. A piece of plate representing a mounted hussar in full uniform caught his eye. He pointed to it, and then to the mantelpiece, with inquiry in his eyes.

"What is it — oh, what is it?" said Little Mildred. Then, as a mother might speak to a child, "That is a horse — yes, a horse."

Very slowly came the answer, in a thick, passionless guttural: "Yes, I — have seen. But — where is *the* horse?"

You could have heard the hearts of the mess beating as the men drew back to give the stranger full room in his wanderings. There was no question of calling the guard.

Again he spoke, very slowly, "Where is *our* horse?"

There is no saying what happened after that. There is but one horse in the White Hussars, and his portrait hangs outside the door of the mess room. He is the piebald drum-horse, the king of the regimental band, that served the regiment for seven-and-thirty years, and in the end was shot for old age. Half the mess tore the thing down from its place and thrust it into the man's hands. He placed it above the mantelpiece; it clattered on the ledge, as his poor hands dropped it, and he staggered toward the bottom of the table, falling into Mildred's chair. The band began to play the "River of Years" waltz, and the laughter from the gardens came into the tobacco-scented mess room. But nobody, even the youngest, was thinking of waltzes. They all spoke to one another something after this fashion: "The drum-horse hasn't hung over the mantelpiece since '67." "How does he know?" "Mildred, go and speak to him again." "Colonel, what are you going to do?" "Oh, dry up, and give the poor devil a chance to pull himself together!" "It isn't possible, anyhow. The man's a lunatic."

Little Mildred stood at the colonel's side talking into his ear. "Will you be good enough to take your seats, please, gentlemen?" he said, and the mess dropped into the chairs.

Only Dirkovitch's seat, next to Little Mildred's, was blank, and Little Mildred himself had found Hira Singh's place. The wide-eyed mess sergeant filled the glasses in dead silence. Once more the colonel rose, but his hand shook, and the port spilled on the table as he looked straight at the man in Little Mildred's chair and said, hoarsely, "Mr. Vice, the Queen." There was a little pause, but the man sprang to his feet and answered, without hesitation, "The Queen, God bless her!" and as he emptied the thin glass he snapped the shank between his fingers.

Long and long ago, when the Empress of India was a young woman, and there were no unclean ideals in the land, it was the custom in a few messes to drink the Queen's toast in broken glass, to the huge delight of the mess contractors. The custom is now dead, because there is nothing to break anything for, except now and again the word of a government, and that has been broken already.

"That settles it," said the colonel, with a gasp. "He's not a sergeant. What in the world is he?"

SHORT-STORY — 24

The entire mess echoed the word, and the volley of questions would have scared any man. Small wonder that the ragged, filthy invader could only smile and shake his head.

From under the table, calm and smiling urbanely, rose Dirkovitch, who had been roused from healthful slumber by feet upon his body. By the side of the man he rose, and the man shrieked and groveled at his feet. It was a horrible sight, coming so swiftly upon the pride and glory of the toast that had brought the strayed wits together.

Dirkovitch made no offer to raise him, but Little Mildred heaved him up in an instant. It is not good that a gentleman who can answer to the Queen's toast should lie at the feet of a subaltern of Cossacks.

The hasty action tore the wretch's upper clothing nearly to the waist, and his body was seamed with dry black scars. There is only one weapon in the world that cuts in parallel lines, and it is neither the cane nor the cat. Dirkovitch saw the marks, and the pupils of his eyes dilated — also, his face changed. He said something that sounded like "Shto ve takete"; and the man, fawning, answered, "Chetyre."

"What's that?" said everybody together.

"His number. That is number four, you know." Dirkovitch spoke very thickly.

"What has a Queen's officer to do with a qualified number?" said the colonel, and there rose an unpleasant growl round the table.

"How can I tell?" said the affable Oriental, with a sweet smile. "He is a — how you have it? — escape — runaway, from over there."

He nodded toward the darkness of the night.

"Speak to him, if he'll answer you, and speak to him gently," said Little Mildred, settling the man in a chair. It seemed most improper to all present that Dirkovitch should sip brandy as he talked in purring, spitting Russian to the creature who answered so feebly and with such evident dread. But since Dirkovitch appeared to understand, no man said a word. They breathed heavily, leaning forward, in the long gaps of the conversation. The next time that they have no engagements on hand the White Hussars intend to go to St. Petersburg and learn Russian.

"He does not know how many years ago," said Dirkovitch, facing the mess, "but he says it was very long ago, in a war. I think that there was an accident. He says he was of this glorious and distinguished regiment in the war."

"The rolls! The rolls! Holmer, get the rolls!" said Little Mildred, and the adjutant dashed off bareheaded to the orderly room where the rolls of the regiment were kept. He returned just in time to hear Dirkovitch conclude, "Therefore I am most sorry to say there was an accident, which would have been reparable if he had apologized to that our colonel, which he had insulted."

Another growl, which the colonel tried to beat down. The mess was in no mood to weigh insults to Russian colonels just then.

"He does not remember, but I think that there was an accident, and so he was not exchanged among the prisoners, but he was sent to another place — how do you say? — the country. *So,* he says, he came here.

He does not know how he came. Eh? He was at Chepany"—the man caught the word, nodded, and shivered—"at Zhigansk and Irkutsk. I cannot understand how he escaped. He says, too, that he was in the forests for many years, but how many years he has forgotten — that with many things. It was an accident; done because he did not apologize to that our colonel. Ah!"

Instead of echoing Dirkovitch's sigh of regret, it is sad to record that the White Hussars livelily exhibited unchristian delight and other emotions, hardly restrained by their sense of hospitality. Holmer flung the frayed and yellow regimental rolls on the table, and the men flung themselves atop of these.

"Steady! Fifty-six — fifty-five — fifty-four," said Holmer. "Here we are. 'Lieutenant Austin Limmason — *missing*.' That was before Sebastopol. What an infernal shame! Insulted one of their colonels, and was quietly shipped off. Thirty years of his life wiped out."

"But he never apologized. Said he'd see him —— first," chorused the mess.

"Poor devil! I suppose he never had the chance afterward. How did he come here?" said the colonel.

The dingy heap in the chair could give no answer.

"Do you know who you are?"

It laughed weakly.

"Do you know that you are Limmason — Lieutenant Limmason, of the White Hussars?"

Swift as a shot came the answer, in a slightly surprised tone, "Yes, I'm Limmason, of course." The light died out in his eyes, and he collapsed afresh, watching every motion of Dirkovitch with terror. A flight from Siberia may fix a few elementary facts in the mind, but it does not lead to continuity of thought. The man could not explain how, like a homing pigeon, he had found his way to his own old mess again. Of what he had suffered or seen he knew nothing. He cringed before Dirkovitch as instinctively as he had pressed the spring of the candlestick, sought the picture of the drum-horse, and answered to the Queen's toast. The rest was a blank that the dreaded Russian tongue could only in part remove. His head bowed on his breast, and he giggled and cowered alternately.

The devil that lived in the brandy prompted Dirkovitch at this extremely inopportune moment to make a speech. He rose, swaying slightly, gripped the table edge, while his eyes glowed like opals, and began:—

"Fellow-soldiers glorious — true friends and hospitables. It was an accident, and deplorable— most deplorable." Here he smiled sweetly all round the mess. "But you will think of this little, little thing. So little, is it not? The czar! Posh! I slap my fingers — I snap my fingers at him. Do I believe in him? No! But the Slav who has done nothing, *him* I believe. Seventy — how much? — millions that have done nothing — not one thing. Napoleon was an episode." He banged a hand on the table. "Hear you, old peoples, we have done nothing in the world — out here. All our work is to do: and it shall be done, old peoples. Get away!" He waved his hand imperiously, and pointed to the man. "You see him. He is not good to see. He was just one little — oh, so little — accident, that no one remembered. Now he is *That*. So will you be, brother-soldiers so brave — so will you be. But you will never come back. You will all go where he has gone, or " — he pointed to the great coffin shadow on the ceiling, and muttering, " Seventy millions — get away, you old people," fell asleep.

"Sweet, and to the point," said Little Mildred. " What's the use of getting wroth? Let's make the poor devil comfortable."

But that was a matter suddenly and swiftly taken from the loving hands of the White Hussars. The lieutenant had returned only to go away again three days later, when the wail of the " Dead March " and the tramp of the squadrons told the wondering station, that saw no gap in the table, an officer of the regiment had resigned his new-found commission.

And Dirkovitch — bland, supple, and always genial — went away too by a night train. Little Mildred and another saw him off, for he was the guest of the mess, and even had he smitten the colonel with the open hand the law of the mess allowed no relaxation of hospitality.

"Good-by, Dirkovitch, and a pleasant journey," said Little Mildred.

"*Au revoir*, my true friends," said the Russian.

" Indeed! But we thought you were going home?"

"Yes; but I will come again. My friends, is that road shut?" He pointed to where the north star burned over the Khyber Pass.

"By Jove! I forgot. Of course. Happy to meet you, old man, any time you like. Got everything you want, — cheroots, ice, bedding? That's all right. Well, *au revoir*, Dirkovitch."

"Um," said the other man, as the tail-lights of the train grew small. "Of — all — the — unmitigated — "

Little Mildred answered nothing, but watched the north star, and hummed a selection from a recent burlesque that had much delighted the White Hussars. It ran : —

> "I'm sorry for Mister Bluebeard,
>   I'm sorry to cause him pain;
> But a terrible spree there's sure to be
>   When he comes back again."

NOTE. — The opening paragraphs are almost journalistic in their easy commonplace; and they serve to provide us with the background of everyday existence, against which stands out the strange experience of the man who was. There is invention and ingenuity in the story, but they are not there for their own sake; they are the servants of the larger imagination, which brings before us the appealing figure of the man whose sufferings have been appalling.

XXIII. A SISTERLY SCHEME

By H. C. Bunner (1855-1896)

Bunner was a humorist who happened also to be a poet. His humor may be fanciful; he may imagine an impossible situation; he may deal with circumstances of a daring unexpectedness, but he is never forced or violent or exaggerated. He had a command of pathos also, but he never paraded it, allowing it rather to relieve and to soften. He was a student of the art of story-telling, relishing the ingenuity and the succinctness of Boccaccio. He fell captive to the craftsmanship of Maupassant. The various tales in his volume called "Short Sixes," published in 1890, of which the "Sisterly Scheme" is one, owe not a little to his interest in the consummate art of the Frenchman.

A SISTERLY SCHEME[1]

Away up in the very heart of Maine there is a mighty lake among the mountains. It is reached after a journey

[1] Printed by permission of *Puck*.

of many hours from the place where you "go in." That is the phrase of the country, and when you have once "gone in," you know why it is not correct to say that you have gone *through* the woods, or, simply, *to* your destination. You find that you have plunged into a new world — a world that has nothing in common with the world that you live in; a world of wild, solemn, desolate grandeur, a world of space and silence; a world that oppresses your soul — and charms you irresistibly. And after you have once "come out" of that world, there will be times, to the day of your death, when you will be homesick for it, and will long with a childlike longing to go back to it.

Up in this wild region you will find a fashionable summer hotel, with electric bells and seven-course dinners, and "guests" who dress three times a day. It is perched on a little flat point, shut off from the rest of the mainland by a huge rocky cliff. It is an impertinence in that majestic wilderness, and Leather-Stocking would doubtless have had a hankering to burn such an affront to Nature; but it is a good hotel, and people go to it and breathe the generous air of the great woods.

On the beach near this hotel, where the canoes were drawn up in line, there stood one summer morning a curly-haired, fair young man — not so very young, either — whose cheeks were uncomfortably red as he looked first at his own canoe, high and dry, loaded with rods and landing net and luncheon basket, and then at another canoe, fast disappearing down the lake wherein sat a young man and a young woman.

"Dropped again, Mr. Morpeth?"

The young man looked up and saw a saucy face laughing at him. A girl was sitting on the stringpiece of the dock. It was the face of a girl between childhood and womanhood. By the face and the figure, it was a woman grown. By the dress, you would have judged it a girl.

And you would have been confirmed in the latter opinion by the fact that the young person was doing something unpardonable for a young lady, but not inexcusable in the case of a youthful tomboy. She had taken off her canvas shoe, and was shaking some small stones out of it. There was a tiny hole in her black stocking, and a glimpse of her pink toe was visible. The girl was sunburnt, but the toe was prettily pink.

"Your sister," replied the young man with dignity, "was to have gone fishing with me; but she remembered at the last moment that she had a prior engagement with Mr. Brown."

"She hadn't," said the girl. "I heard them make it up last evening, after you went upstairs."

The young man clean forgot himself.

"She's the most heartless coquette in the world," he cried, and clinched his hands.

"She is all that," said the young person on the stringpiece of the dock, "and more too. And yet, I suppose, you want her all the same?"

"I'm afraid I do," said the young man miserably.

"Well," said the girl, putting her shoe on again, and beginning to tie it up, "I'll tell you what it is, Mr. Morpeth. You've been hanging around Pauline for a year, and you are the only one of the men she keeps on a string who hasn't snubbed me. Now, if you want me to, I'll give you a lift."

"A — a — *what?*"

"A lift. You're wasting your time. Pauline has no use for devotion. It's a drug in the market with her — has been for five seasons. There's only one way to get her worked up. Two fellows tried it, and they nearly got there; but they weren't game enough to stay to the bitter end. I think you're game, and I'll tell you. You've got to make her jealous."

"Make her jealous of me?"

"No," said his friend, with infinite scorn; "make her jealous of the other girl. *Oh!* but you men are stupid!"

The young man pondered a moment.

"Well, Flossy," he began, and then he became conscious of a sudden change in the atmosphere, and perceived that the young lady was regarding him with a look that might have chilled his soul.

"Miss Flossy — Miss Belton — " he hastily corrected himself. Winter promptly changed to summer in Miss Flossy Belton's expressive face.

"Your scheme," he went on, "is a good one. Only — it involves the discovery of another girl."

"Yes," assented Miss Flossy cheerfully.

"Well," said that young man, "doesn't it strike you that if I were to develop a sudden admiration for any one of these other young ladies whose charms I have hitherto neglected, it would come tardy off — lack artistic verisimilitude, so to speak?"

"Rather," was Miss Flossy's prompt and frank response; "especially as there isn't one of them fit to flirt with."

"Well, then, where am I to discover the girl?"

Miss Flossy untied and retied her shoe. Then she said, calmly:—

"What's the matter with —" a hardly perceptible hesitation — "*me?*"

"With *you?*" Mr. Morpeth was startled out of his manners.

"Yes!"

Mr. Morpeth simply stared.

"Perhaps," suggested Miss Flossy, "I'm not good-looking enough?"

"You are good-looking enough," replied Mr. Morpeth, recovering himself, "for *anything* —" and he threw a convincing emphasis into the last word as he took what was probably his first real inspection of his adored one's junior — "but — aren't you a trifle — young?"

"How old do you suppose I am?"

"I know. Your sister told me. You are sixteen."

"Sixteen!" repeated Miss Flossy, with an infinite and uncontrollable scorn, "yes, and I'm the kind of sixteen that stays sixteen till your elder sister's married. I was eighteen years old on the 3d of last December — unless they began to double on me before I was old enough to know the difference — it would be just like mamma to play it on me in some such way," she concluded, reflectively.

"Eighteen years old!" said the young man. "The deuce!" Do not think that he was an ill-bred young man. He was merely astonished, and he had much more astonishment ahead of him. He mused for a moment.

"Well," he said, "what's your plan of campaign? I am to — to discover you."

"Yes," said Miss Flossy calmly, "and to flirt with me like fun."

"And may I ask what attitude you are to take when you are — discovered?"

"Certainly," replied the imperturbable Flossy. "I am going to dangle you."

"To — to dangle me?"

"As a conquest, don't you know. Let you hang around and laugh at you."

"Oh, indeed?"

"There, don't be wounded in your masculine pride. You might as well face the situation. You don't think that Pauline's in love with you, do you?"

"No!" groaned the young man.

"But you've got lots of money. Mr. Brown has got lots more. You're eager. Brown is coy. That's the reason that Brown is in the boat and you are on the cold, cold shore, talking to Little Sister. Now if Little Sister jumps at you, why, she's simply taking Big Sister's leavings; it's all in the family, anyway, and there's no jealousy, and Pauline can devote her whole mind to Brown. There, *don't* look so limp. You men are simply childish. Now, after you've asked me to marry you — "

"Oh, I'm to ask you to marry me?"

"Certainly. You needn't look frightened, now. I won't accept you. But then you are to go around like a wet cat, and mope, and hang on worse than ever. Then

Big Sister will see that she can't afford to take that sort of thing from Little Sister, and then — there's your chance."

"Oh, there's my chance, is it?" said Mr. Morpeth. He seemed to have fallen into the habit of repetition.

"There's your *only* chance," said Miss Flossy, with decision.

Mr. Morpeth meditated. He looked at the lake, where there was no longer sign or sound of the canoe, and he looked at Miss Flossy, who sat calm, self-confident, and careless on the stringpiece of the dock.

"I don't know how feasible — " he began.

"It's feasible," said Miss Flossy, with decision. "Of course Pauline will write to mamma, and of course mamma will write and scold me. But she's got to stay in New York and nurse papa's gout; and the Miss Redingtons are all the chaperons we've got up here, and they don't amount to anything — so I don't care."

"But why," inquired the young man, and his tone suggested a complete abandonment to Miss Flossy's idea, "why should you take so much trouble for *me?*"

"Mr. Morpeth," said Miss Flossy solemnly, "I'm two years behind the time-table, and I've got to make a strike for liberty, or die. And besides," she added, "if you are *nice*, it needn't be such an *awful* trouble."

Mr. Morpeth laughed.

"I'll try to make it as little of a bore as possible," he said, extending his hand. The girl did not take it.

"Don't make any mistake," she cautioned him, searching his face with her eyes; "this isn't to be any little-girl affair. Little Sister doesn't want any kind, elegant, supercilious encouragement from Big Sister's young man.

It's got to be a *real* flirtation — devotion no end, and ten times as much as ever Pauline could get out of you — and you've got to keep your end 'way — 'way — 'way up!"

The young man smiled.

"I'll keep my end up," he said; "but are you certain that you can keep yours up?"

"Well, I think so," replied Miss Flossy. "Pauline will raise an awful row; but if she goes too far, I'll tell my age, *and hers, too.*"

Mr. Morpeth looked in Miss Flossy's calm face. Then he extended his hand once more.

"It's a bargain, so far as I'm concerned," he said.

This time a soft and small hand met his with a firm, friendly, honest pressure.

"And I'll refuse you," said Miss Flossy.

* * * * * * *

Within two weeks, Mr. Morpeth found himself entangled in a flirtation such as he had never dreamed of. Miss Flossy's scheme had succeeded only too brilliantly. The whole hotel was talking about the outrageous behavior of "that little Belton girl" and Mr. Morpeth, who certainly ought to know better.

Mr. Morpeth had carried out his instructions. Before the week was out, he found himself giving the most lifelike imitation of an infatuated lover that ever delighted the old gossips of a summer resort. And yet he had only done what Flossy told him to do.

He got his first lesson just about the time that Flossy, in the privacy of their apartments, informed her elder sister that if she, Flossy, found Mr. Morpeth's society agreeable, it was nobody's concern but her own, and that she was prepared to make some interesting additions to the census statistics if any one thought differently.

The lesson opened his eyes.

"Do you know," she said, "that it wouldn't be a bit of a bad idea to telegraph to New York for some real nice candy and humbly present it for my acceptance? I *might* take it — if the bonbonnière was pretty enough."

He telegraphed to New York, and received, in the course of four or five days, certain marvels of sweets in a miracle of an upholstered box. The next day he found her on the veranda, flinging the bonbons on the lawn for the children to scramble for.

"Awfully nice of you to send me these things," she said languidly, but loud enough for the men around her to hear, — she had men around her already: she had been discovered, — "but I never eat sweets, you know. Here, you little mite in the blue sash, don't you want this pretty box to put your doll's clothes in?"

And Maillard's finest bonbonnière went to a yellow-haired brat of three.

But this was the slightest and lightest of her caprices. She made him send for his dogcart and his horses, all the way from New York, only that he might drive her over the ridiculous little mile and a half of road that bounded the tiny peninsula. And she christened him "Muffets," a nickname presumably suggested by "Morpeth"; and she called him "Muffets" in the hearing of all the hotel people.

And did such conduct pass unchallenged? No. Pauline scolded, raged, raved. She wrote to mamma. Mamma

A SISTERLY SCHEME

wrote back and reproved Flossy. But mamma could not leave papa. His gout was worse. The Miss Redingtons must act. The Miss Redingtons merely wept, and nothing more. Pauline scolded; the flirtation went on; and the people at the big hotel enjoyed it immensely.

And there was more to come. Four weeks had passed. Mr. Morpeth was hardly on speaking terms with the elder Miss Belton; and with the younger Miss Belton he was on terms which the hotel gossips characterized as "simply scandalous." Brown glared at him when they met, and he glared at Brown. Brown was having a hard time. Miss Belton the elder was not pleasant of temper in those trying days.

"And now," said Miss Flossy to Mr. Morpeth, "it's time you proposed to me, Muffets."

They were sitting on the hotel veranda, in the evening darkness. No one was near them, except an old lady in a Shaker chair.

"There's Mrs. Melby. She's pretending to be asleep, but she isn't. She's just waiting for us. Now walk me up and down and ask me to marry you so that she can hear it. It'll be all over the hotel inside of half an hour. Pauline will just *rage*."

With this pleasant prospect before him, Mr. Morpeth marched Miss Flossy Belton up and down the long veranda. He had passed Mrs. Melby three times before he was able to say, in a choking, husky, uncertain voice: —

"Flossy — I — I — I *love* you!"

Flossy's voice was not choking nor uncertain. It rang out clear and silvery in a peal of laughter.

"Why, of course you do, Muffets, and I wish you

didn't. That's what makes you so stupid half the time."

"But —" said Mr. Morpeth vaguely; "but I —"

"But you're a silly boy," returned Miss Flossy; and she added in a swift aside: "*You haven't asked me to marry you!*"

"W-W-W-Will you be my wife?" stammered Mr. Morpeth.

"No!" said Miss Flossy, emphatically, "I will not. You are too utterly ridiculous. The idea of it! No, Muffets, you are charming in your present capacity; but you aren't to be considered seriously."

They strolled on into the gloom at the end of the great veranda.

"That's the first time," he said, with a feeling of having only the ghost of a breath left in his lungs, "that I ever asked a woman to marry me."

"I should think so," said Miss Flossy, "from the way you did it. And you were beautifully rejected, weren't you? Now — look at Mrs. Melby, will you? She's scudding off to spread the news."

And before Mr. Morpeth went to bed, he was aware of the fact that every man and woman in the hotel knew that he had "proposed" to Flossy Belton, and had been "beautifully rejected."

*   *   *   *   *   *   *

Two sulky men, one sulky woman, and one girl radiant with triumphant happiness started out in two canoes, reached certain fishing grounds known only to the elect, and began to cast for trout. They had indifferent luck.

Miss Belton and Mr. Brown caught a dozen trout; Miss Flossy Belton and Mr. Morpeth caught eighteen or nineteen, and the day was wearing to a close. Miss Flossy made the last cast of the day, just as her escort had taken the paddle. A big trout rose — just touched the fly — and disappeared.

"It's this wretched rod!" cried Miss Flossy; and she rapped it on the gunwale of the canoe so sharply that the beautiful split bamboo broke sharp off in the middle of the second joint. Then she tumbled it overboard, reel and all.

"I was tired of that rod, anyway, Muffets," she said; "row me home, now; I've got to dress for dinner."

Miss Flossy's elder sister, in the other boat, saw and heard this exhibition of tyranny; and she was so much moved that she stamped her small foot, and endangered the bottom of the canoe. She resolved that mamma should come back, whether papa had the gout or not.

Mr. Morpeth, wearing a grave expression, was paddling Miss Flossy toward the hotel. He had said nothing whatever, and it was a noticeable silence that Miss Flossy finally broke.

"You've done pretty much everything that I wanted you to do, Muffets," she said; "but you haven't saved my life yet, and I'm going to give you a chance."

It is not difficult to overturn a canoe. One twist of Flossie's supple body did it, and before he knew just what had happened, Morpeth was swimming toward the shore, holding up Flossy Belton with one arm, and fighting for life in the icy water of a Maine lake.

The people were running down, bearing blankets and

brandy, as he touched bottom in his last desperate struggle to keep the two of them above water. One yard further, and there would have been no strength left in him.

He struggled up on shore with her, and when he got breath enough, he burst out: —

"Why did you do it? It was wicked! It was cruel!"

"There!" she said, as she reclined composedly in his arms, "that will do, Muffets. I don't want to be scolded."

A delegation came along, bringing blankets and brandy, and took her from him.

* * * * * * *

At five o'clock of that afternoon, Mr. Morpeth presented himself at the door of the parlor attached to the apartments of the Belton sisters. Miss Belton, senior, was just coming out of the room. She received his inquiry after her sister's health with a white face and a quivering lip.

"I should think, Mr. Morpeth," she began, "that you had gone far enough in playing with the feelings of a m-m-mere child, and that — oh! I have no words to express my *contempt* for you!"

And in a most unladylike rage Miss Pauline Belton swept down the hotel corridor.

She had left the door open behind her. Morpeth heard a voice, weak, but cheery, addressing him from the far end of the parlor.

"You've got her!" it said. "She's crazy mad. She'll make up to you to-night — see if she don't."

Mr. Morpeth looked up and down the long corridor. It was empty. He pushed the door open, and entered. Flossy was lying on the sofa, pale, but bright-eyed.

"You can get her," she whispered, as he knelt down beside her.

"Flossy," he said, "don't you know that that is all ended? Don't you know that I love you and you only? Don't you know that I haven't thought about any one else since — since — oh, Flossy, don't you — is it possible that you don't understand?"

Flossy stretched out two weak arms, and put them around Mr. Morpeth's neck.

"Why have I had you in training all summer?" said she. "Did you think it was for Pauline?"

NOTE. — This is an intensely American story, — American in its background and in its characters, American in its ingenuity and in its humor. It reveals Bunner's mastery of surprise, for the end of the adventure is unexpected by the reader, and yet it is just what the reader ought to have expected, since it has been led up to carefully and cautiously.

APPENDIX

THE short-story differs essentially from all the longer forms of fiction because its brevity forces the writer to confine himself to a single one of the three elements which the author of a novel may combine at his pleasure. These three elements are the plot, the characters, and the setting. The novelist may pay equal attention to what happens, to the persons to whom these things happen, and to the places where they happen. But the limitations of space forbid this variety to the short-story writer; he has to make his choice among the three. If he centers his efforts on his plot, he has no time to elaborate either character or background; this is what Poe has done in the "Murders in the Rue Morgue." If he focuses the interest on a character, his plotting must be summary, and his setting can only be sketched in; this is what George W. Cable has preferred to do in "Posson Jone." If he concentrates the reader's attention on the environment, on the place where the event happens, on the atmosphere, so to speak, he must use character and incident only to intensify the impression of the place and the time;

this is what we find in Hamlin Garland's "Return of the Private." When once the writer has decided which of the three elements he intends to employ, he must abide by his decision.

In an admirable paper on the "Structure of the Short-story," by Clayton Hamilton (published in the *Reader*, February, 1906), we are told that "the aim of the short-story is to produce a single narrative effect with the greatest economy of means that is consistent with the utmost emphasis." Success is attained almost as much by what the author leaves out as by what he puts in. The examples in the present volume reveal that it was only very slowly that authors came to a full understanding of this principle. Even Boccaccio, a master of narrative, wastes time in the telling of his tale. Addison has more than one useless page in his story; and he also discounts the effect of what ought to be his most striking scene by letting out his secret in advance. Pushkin injures the forward movement of his story by shifting the point of view in the second half of the narrative. On the other hand, Lamb gains by making his story a monologue, and Dickens begins by striking exactly the right note with his opening words, — "Once there was a child." So Poe, intending the "Fall of the House of Usher" to be a study of a strange, weird place, begins with description, delaying until later the introduction of his shadowy characters. So Hawthorne, with admirable art, presents to us the family with whom the "Ambitious Guest" is to spend the night, before bringing forward that character. Maupassant, too, in the very first sentence of "The Necklace," centers our attention on the essential fact. Stimson begins and ends "Mrs. Knollys" with the glacier. Kipling, in the opening paragraph of the "Man who Was," states the thesis which the story is to illustrate. Bunner, in "A Sisterly Scheme," explains the summer hotel before he tells us about any of his characters, because it is only at an American summer hotel that this story is possible.

The teacher and the student will do well to consider carefully the analysis of the limitations of the short-story, — limitations that really create its possibilities, — contained in Chapter XII of Professor Bliss Perry's "Study of Prose Fiction." They will do well also to pay attention to the form in which the best writers have chosen to cast their stories, whether the telling is autobiographical or whether it is narrative in the third person, being told by the author, or whether it is in letters. Aldrich's "Marjorie Daw" consists of a series of letters and telegrams, with only a brief final passage of narrative. Another story, the "Documents in the Case," written by H. C. Bunner (in collaboration with the editor of this volume), is nothing but a string of letters, telegrams, newspaper paragraphs, advertisements, etc.; and the plot, the characters, the setting, are all necessarily subordinate to the method of telling. Stockton's "The Lady or the Tiger" is little more than a riddle, deriving its interest from the skill with which the author has forced us to ask ourselves an insoluble question.

Those students of the short-story who wish to see further specimens may be advised to read the other stories of the later masters of the form, examples of whose workmanship are included in this volume. For example, "Rip Van Winkle" is scarcely more characteristic of Irving than "The Legend of Sleepy Hollow" and "The Specter Bridegroom." "The Ambitious Guest" shows only one facet of Hawthorne's genius, displayed in "Rappaccini's Daughter" and "The Birthmark." And Poe is the author of a dozen masterpieces. "Tennessee's Partner," characteristic as it is, reveals only certain aspects of Bret Harte's gift as a story-teller; other aspects may be found in the other stories contained in the volume entitled "The Luck of Roaring Camp." The Far West is the scene also of the interesting adventures and character-sketches included in Owen Wister's "Red Men and White." The Middle West has been taken as the field for Hamlin Garland's "Main-Traveled Roads."

The several states of the South have not been neglected by American story-tellers. In his "Old Creole Days" George W. Cable has caught the evanescent charm of life in Louisiana before the Civil War; and "Jean-ah Poquelin" may be picked out as a study of character standing out sharply against the background. Joel Chandler Harris has studied the negro of Georgia with a like loving fidelity, especially in "Ananias" and in "Free Joe." Thomas Nelson Page has depicted the society of Virginia with a full appreciation of the contrasts between the white man and the black, particularly in "Marse Chan" and in "Meh Lady." In all these Southern stories the authors have striven to reproduce the speech of the uneducated negroes with phonetic fidelity to the uncouth dialect. They have been interested not only in the particular characters they were presenting, but also in the social conditions of the vanishing society in which these figures moved.

Life in the metropolis of the United States is the theme of many of H. C. Bunner's "Short Sixes," one of which, "The Tenor," may be selected as suggesting the shifting color of New York. The atmosphere of the city, its changing aspects, its infinite variety, moved the editor of this collection to the composition of his "Vignettes of Manhattan" and "Outlines in Local Color," in most of which character and incident are made subservient to the setting. A vivid impression of metropolitan life can be had also in the brisk "Van Bibber" tales of Richard Harding Davis. The Spanish-American colony in New York and the painter-folk have been put into fiction by Thomas A. Janvier.

But it is New England which was first discovered by the seekers after local color, and almost every aspect of life and character has been attempted by one or another of the native story-tellers. Harriet Beecher Stowe's "Sam Lawson's Fireside Stories" are almost too slight to be accepted as true short-stories; they are outline sketches of humorous character, but they preserve the full flavor of the soil. Mary E. Wilkins Freeman has studied the pale spinsterhood of her section and she has seized the underlying tragedy often concealed beneath placid commonplace. Her "New England Nun" and her "Revolt of Mother" may be singled out as specially noteworthy. There is a more delicate humor in the stories of Sarah Orne Jewett, a pleasanter playfulness, but no less veracity; and the stories contained in the volume called "The Country of the Pointed Firs" deserves careful study.

From New England also came Edward Everett Hale's ingenious inventions, of which "The Man without a Country" is deservedly the most famous. But "The Skeleton in the Closet" and "My Double and how he Undid me" have an equal ingenuity; and they are both excellent examples of the short-story in which plot is of more importance than either character or background. This may be said also about "A Struggle for Life" and "Madamoiselle Olympe Zabriskie," which T. B. Aldrich included in the volume with his most ingenious fantasy, "Marjorie Daw." And ingenuity, again combined with humor, is the chief characteristic of F. B. Perkins's "Devil-Puzzlers" and of his "Man-ufactory." Ingenuity once more, with a fantastic inventiveness, is to be found in F. R. Stockton's "Negative Gravity" and in his "Remarkable Wreck of the *Thomas Hyke*."

It was pointed out in the introduction that British authors have not cultivated the short-story form so abundantly as American authors. Yet James M. Barrie has emulated the New England writers in the skill with which he has caught the atmosphere of village life, especially in the series of sketches called "A Window in Thrums." R. L. Stevenson was influenced rather by Hawthorne and by Poe; his most brilliant feat is the series entitled "The New Arabian Nights," in which there is an exuberance of fanciful invention. But "Markheim" is not his only study in a more somber mood; and all his short-stories are inspired by a profound understanding of the possibilities and the limitations of the short-story form. A dozen masterly examples might be selected from the many volumes of Rudyard Kipling, — for example, "Without Benefit of Clergy," "The Man who would be King," "The Gate of a Hundred Sorrows," and "The Brushwood Boy." In "A Walking Delegate" and in "The Maltese Cat" he revived and rejuvenated the old beast-fable; and in "007" he applied the methods of the beast-fable to the steam horse, the modern locomotive.

The French have cultivated the short-story more diligently than the British, even if they have not been as prolific as the Americans. Mérimée's "Taking of the Redoubt" is perhaps not inferior in power to "Mateo Falcone"; and while "The Necklace" is possibly Maupassant's most noted effort, any one of the tales translated in "The Odd Number" may be recommended for analysis. Less vigorous and less varied are the short-stories of Ludovic Halévy and of François Coppée; but the student should not neglect the tales contained in the volumes entitled "Parisian Points of View" by the former, and "Ten Tales" by the latter. From Alphonse Daudet an even richer selection might be made, some of them studies of life in Paris, where he died, and some of them memories of Provence, where he was born. To be noted also are the Alsatian stories of Erckmann-Chatrian.

There is much to be gleaned in the other European literatures, although the strict principles of the form have been better understood by the French and by the Americans. In Italian there are the studies of Sicilian life, by Verga, the best known of which is "Cavelleria Rusticana." In German there are the " Black Forest Stories" of Auerbach and the more sentimental tales of Gustav Freytag. In Norwegian there are other studies from life — some of them as moving as "The Father" — by Björnson; and the significant stories of Alexander Kjelland, a selection of which can be found in the translated volume of "Tales of Two Countries." In Russian there are the rich and veracious narratives of Turgenieff, especially, "A Lear of the Steppe" and "Mumu," and there are the pathetic studies of peasant character by Tolstoi, perhaps a little less successful as a writer of short-stories than he is in his longer novels.

There are bibliographies of the recent books and articles dealing with the short-story in Professor Bliss Perry's "Study of Prose Fiction" (Houghton, Mifflin & Co.), and in my "Philosophy of the Short-story" (Houghton, Mifflin & Co.). For Professor Neilson's series of "Types of English Literature," Professor W. M. Hart is preparing a volume on the "Short-story, Medieval and Modern."